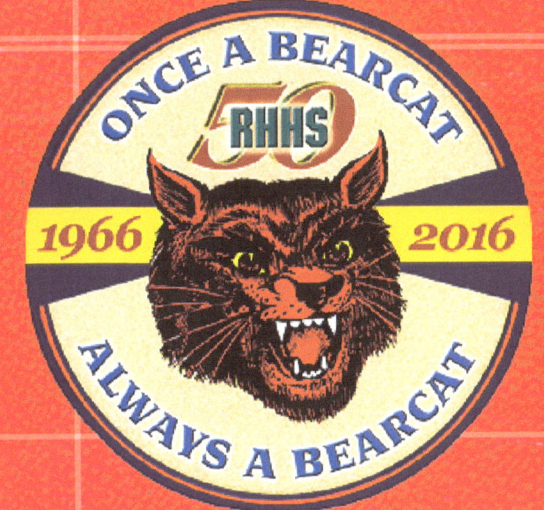

ONCE A BEARCAT
RHHS 50
1966 2016
ALWAYS A BEARCAT

REUNION PHOTOS
OFFICIAL PHOTOS
& CANDID SHOTS

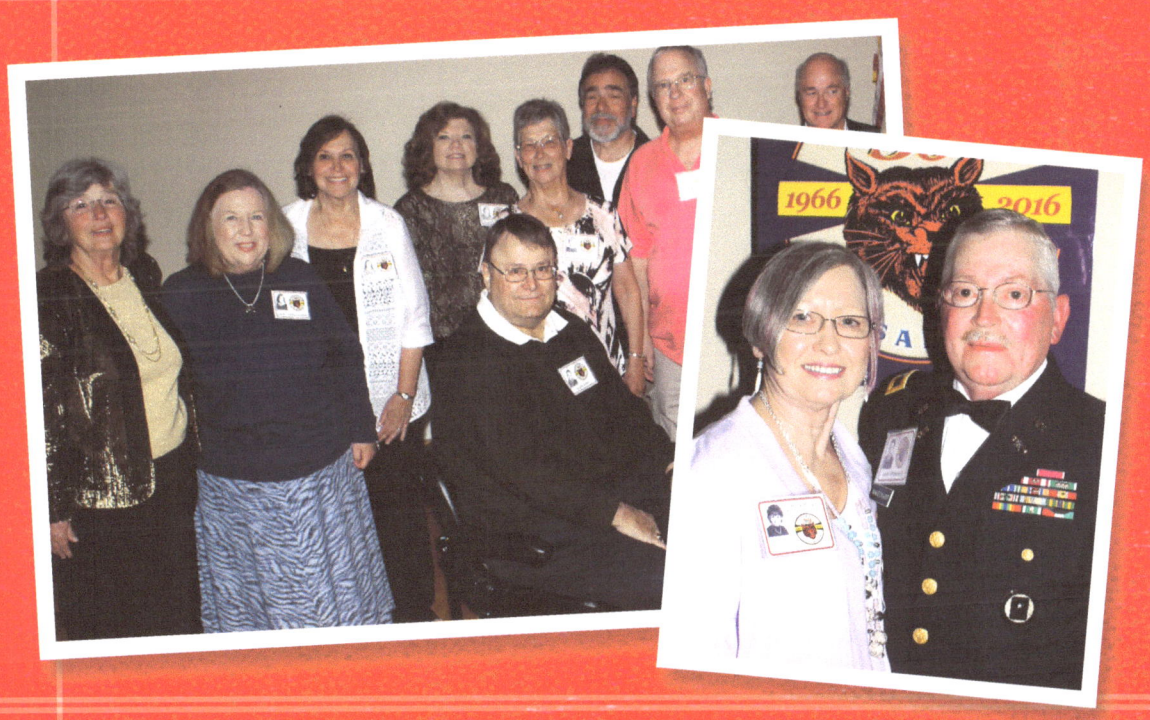

A Fort Canoga Press release, 2016

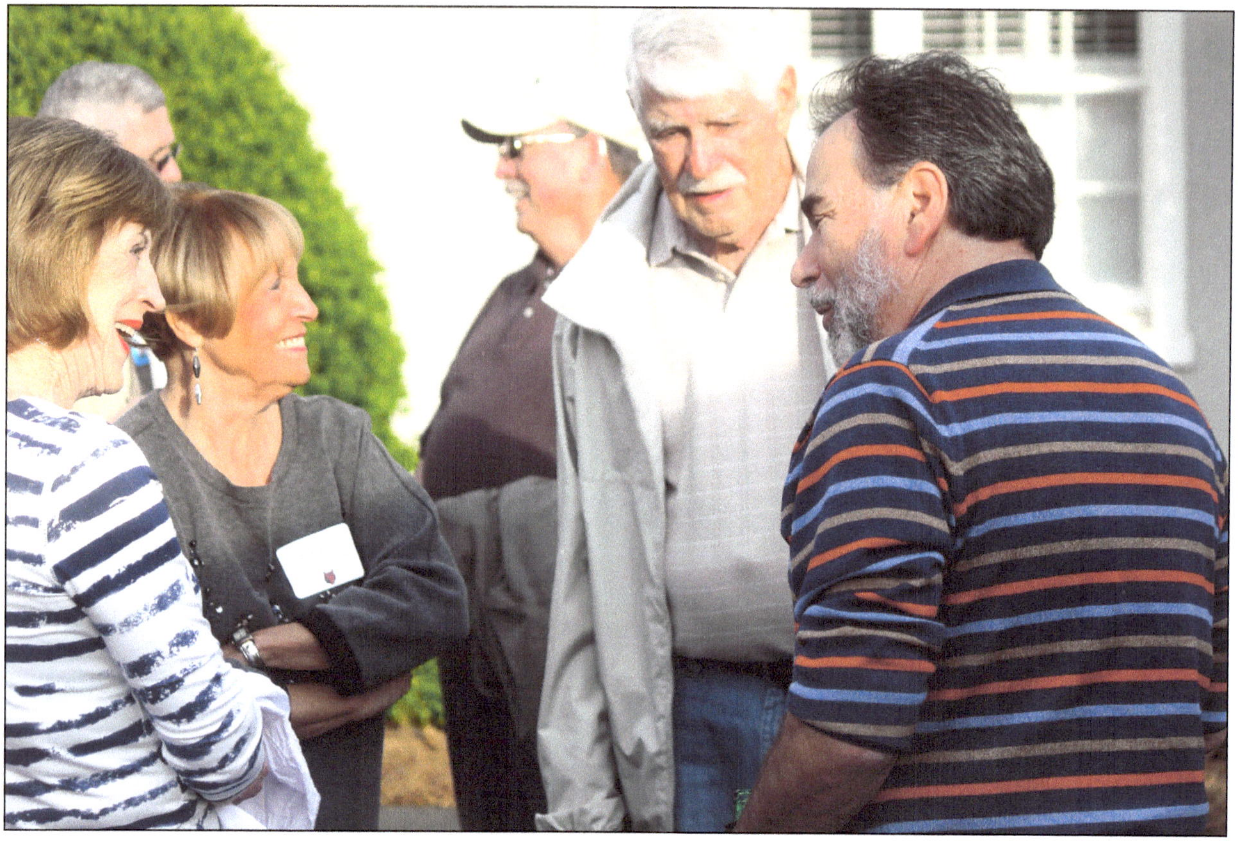

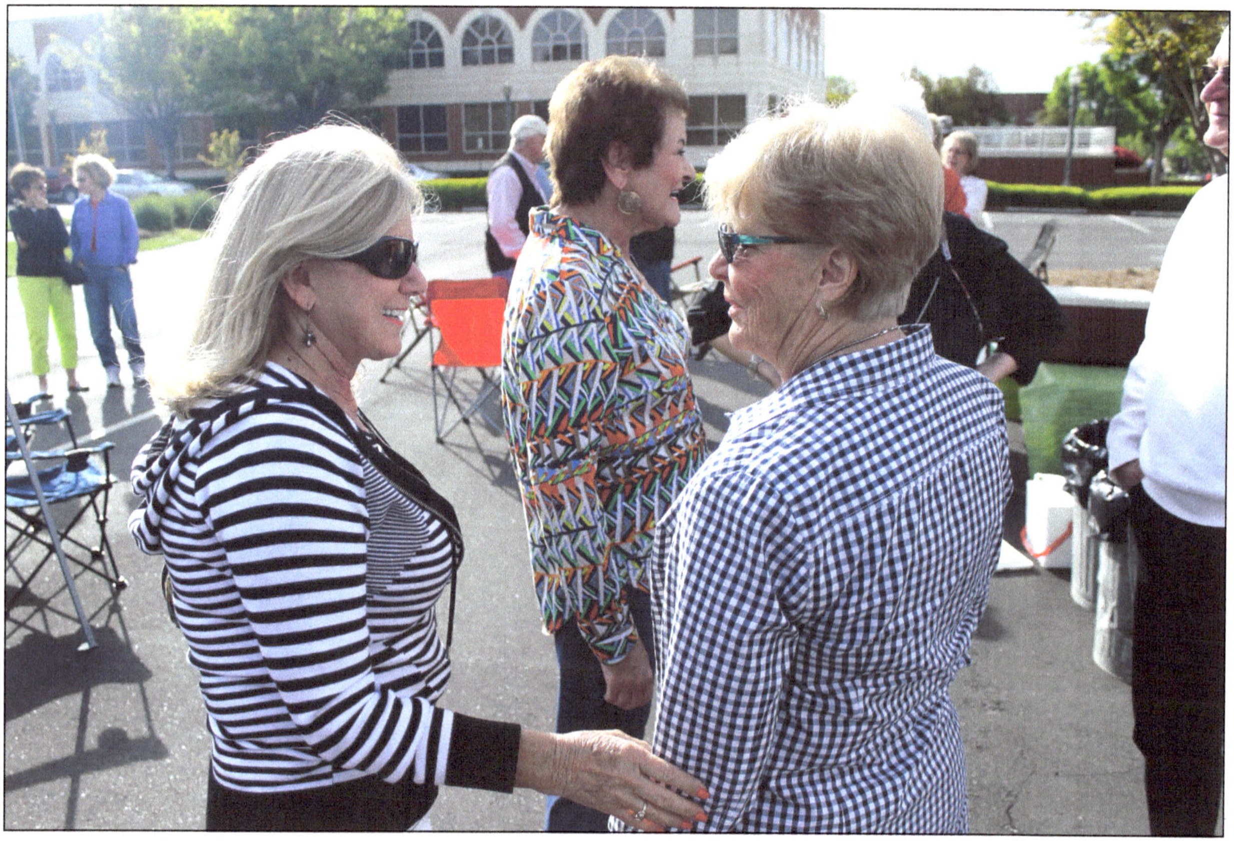

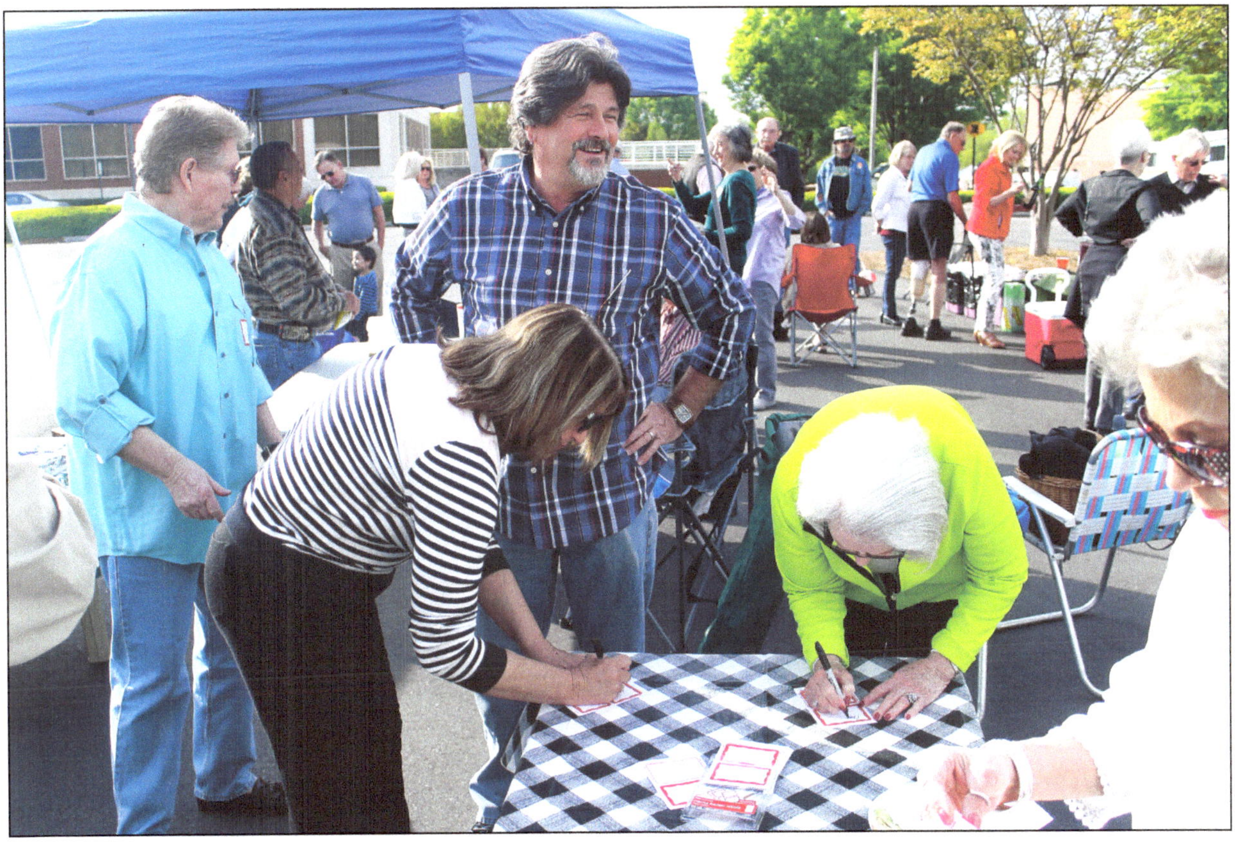

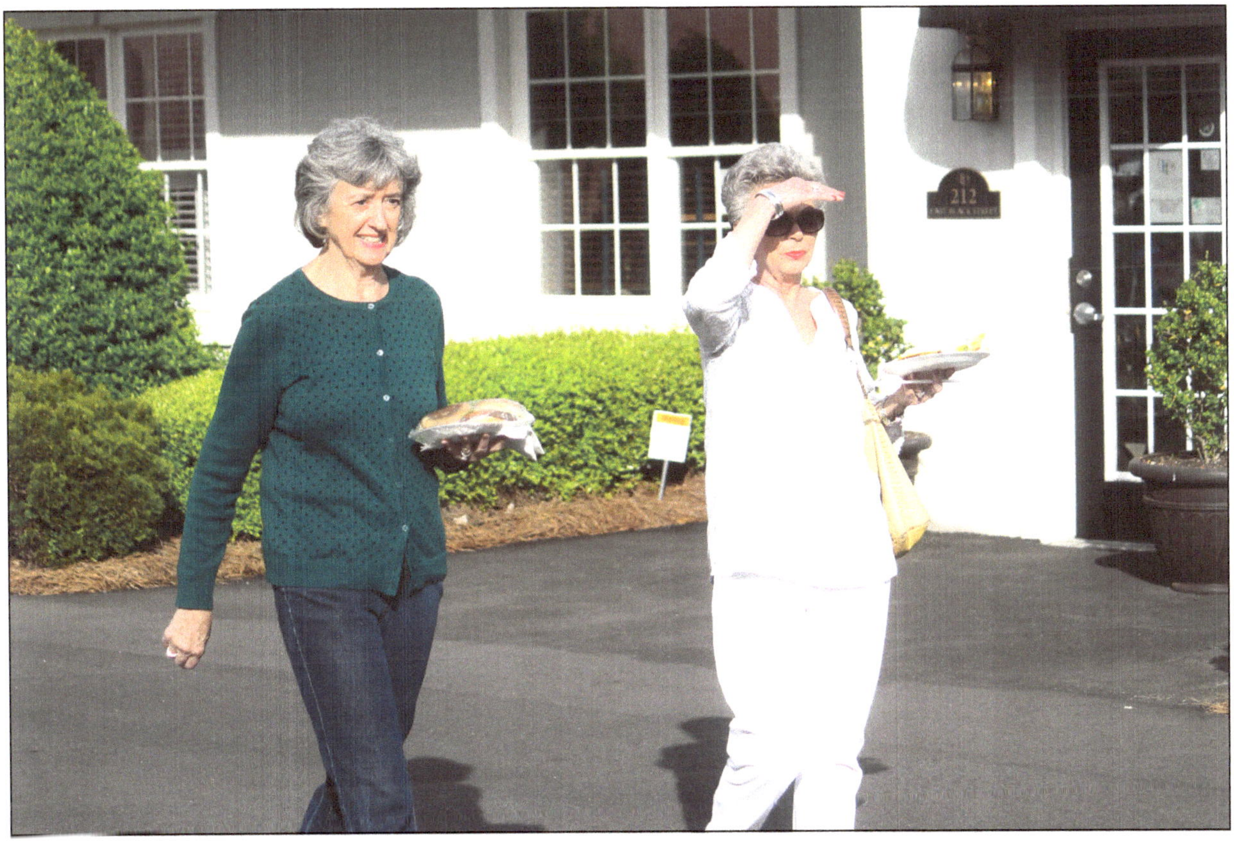
212

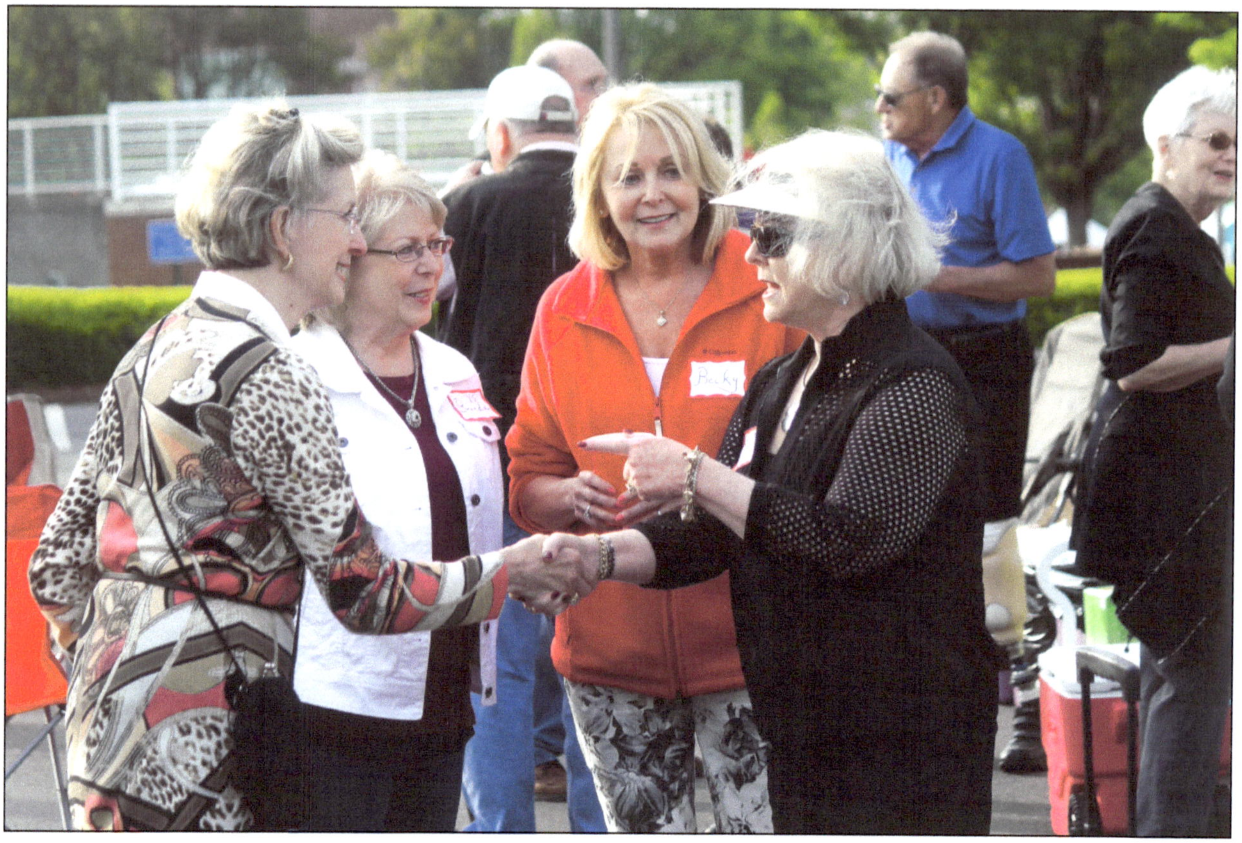

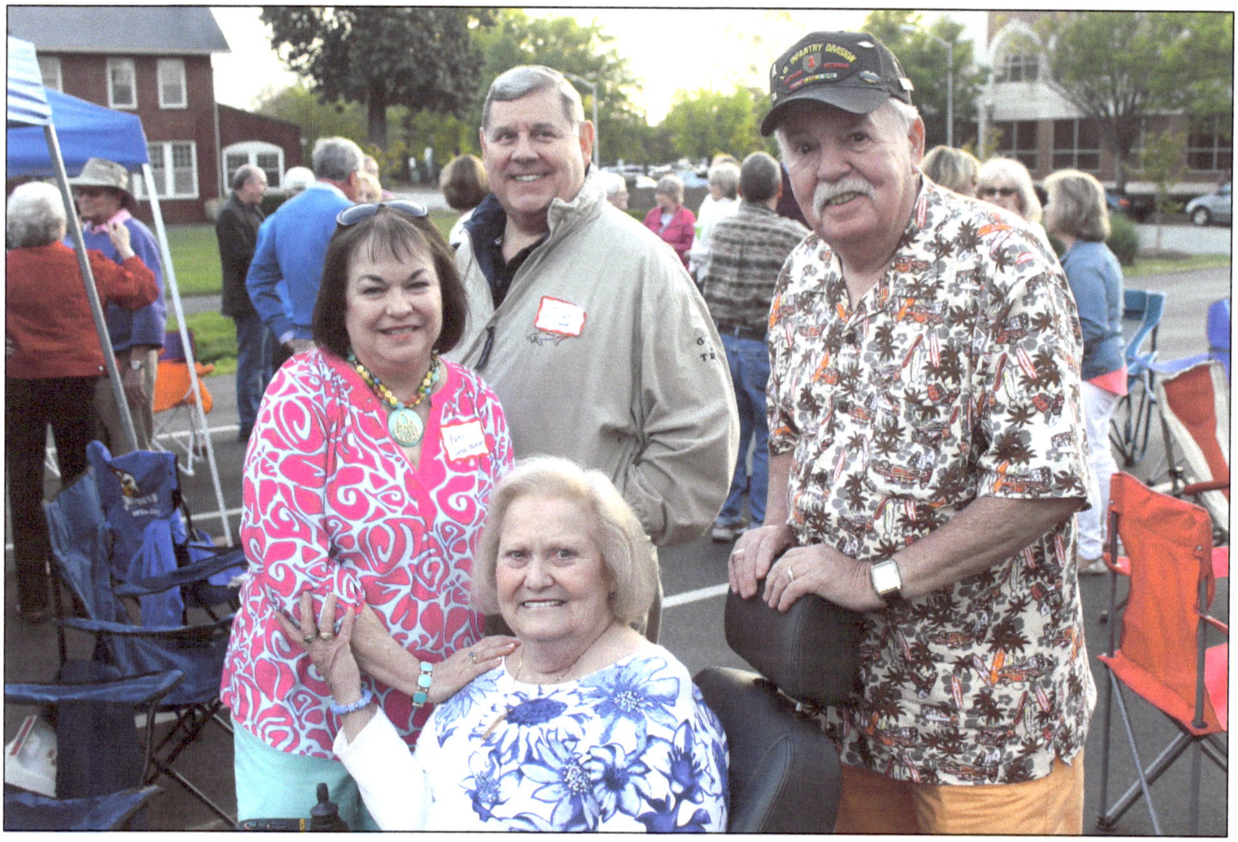

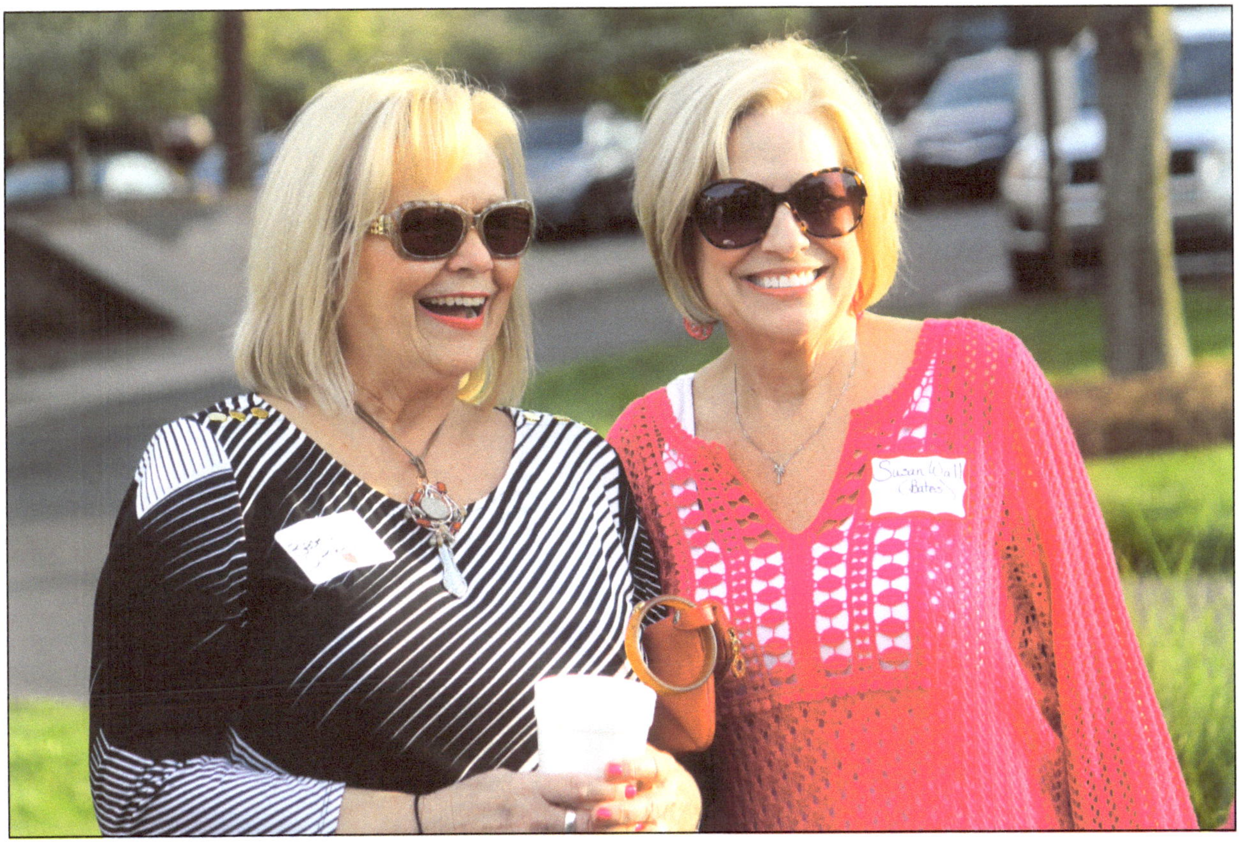

REUNION PHOTOS: OFFICIAL PHOTOS & CANDID SHOTS

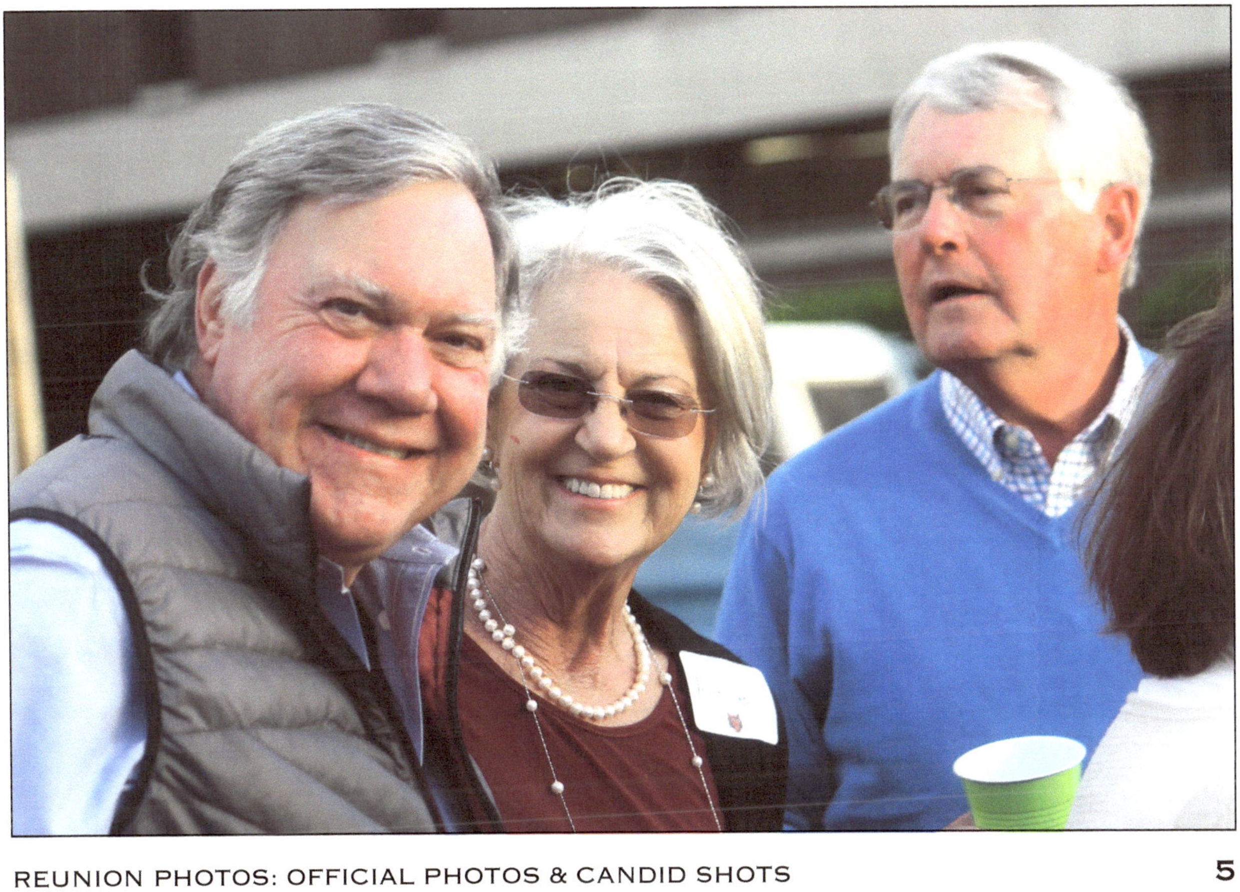

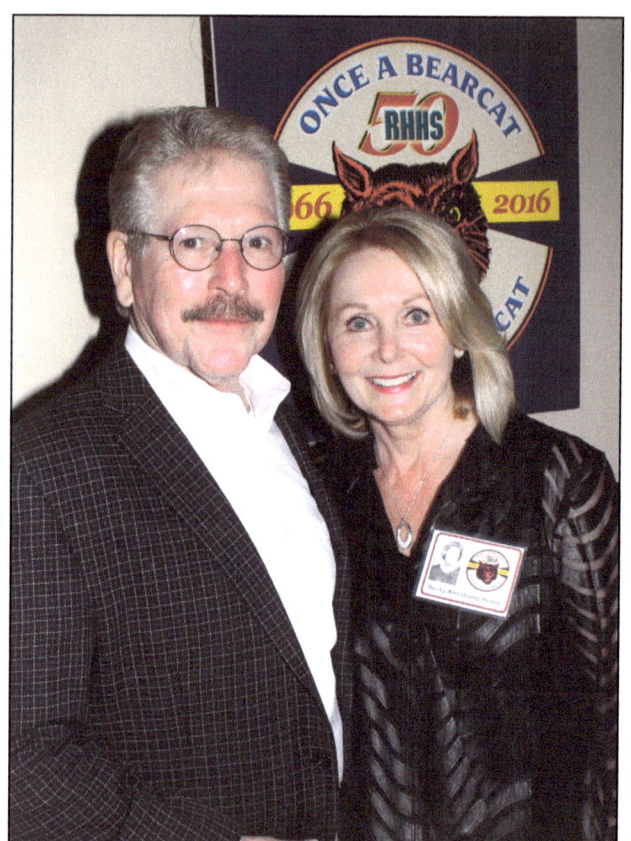

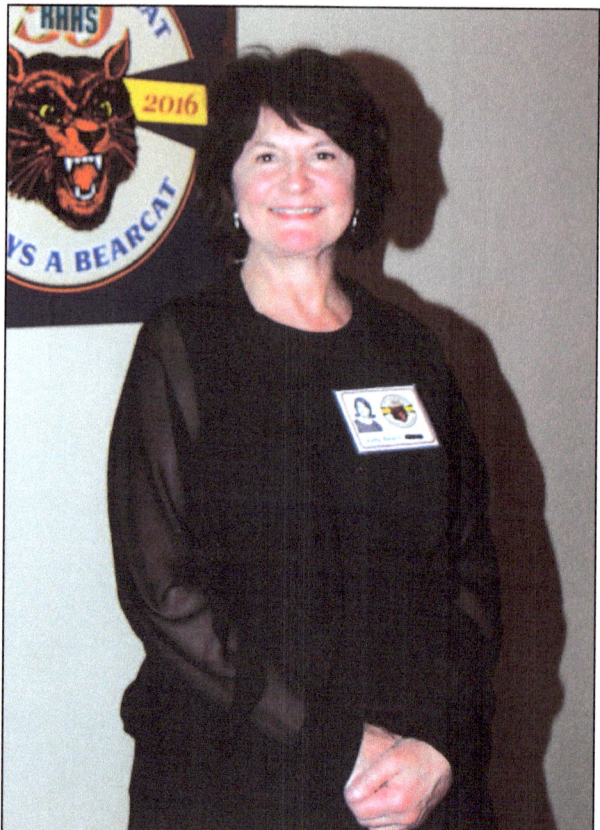

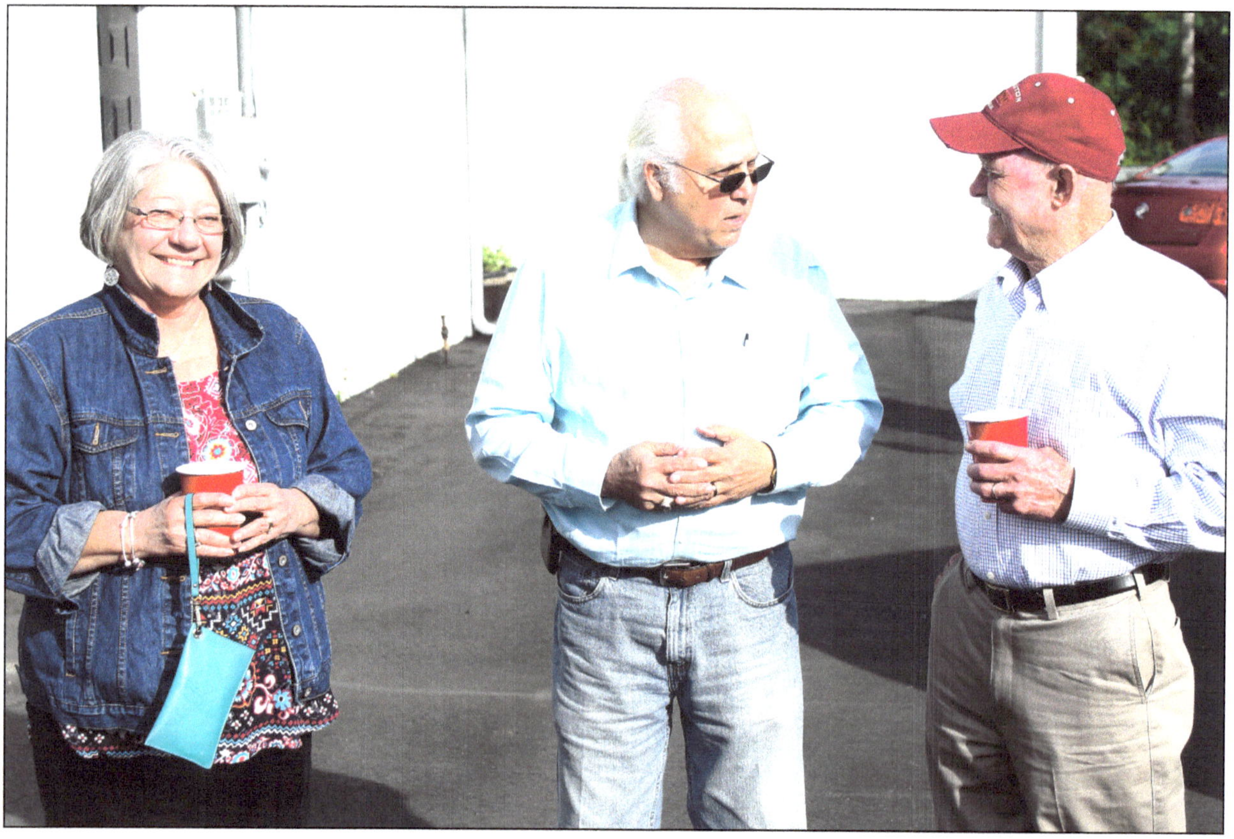

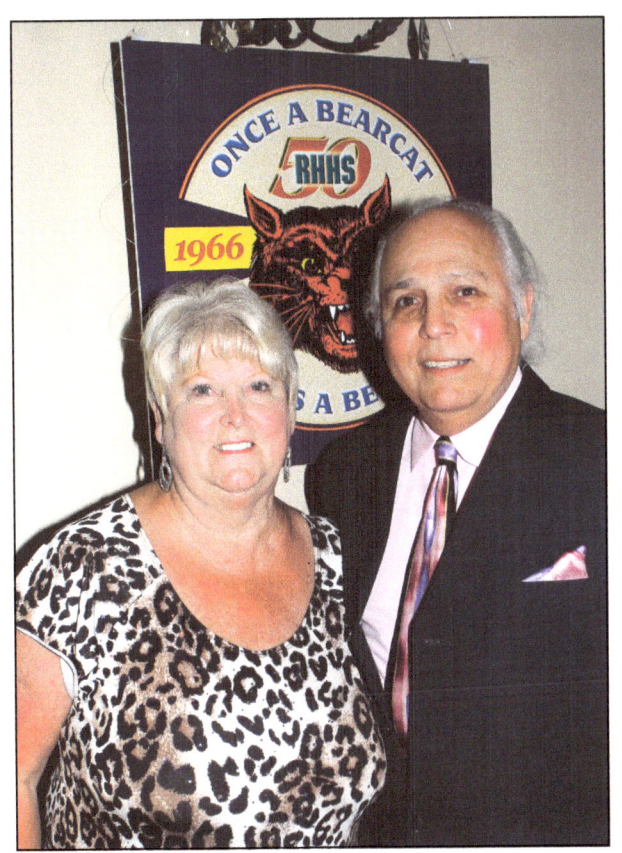

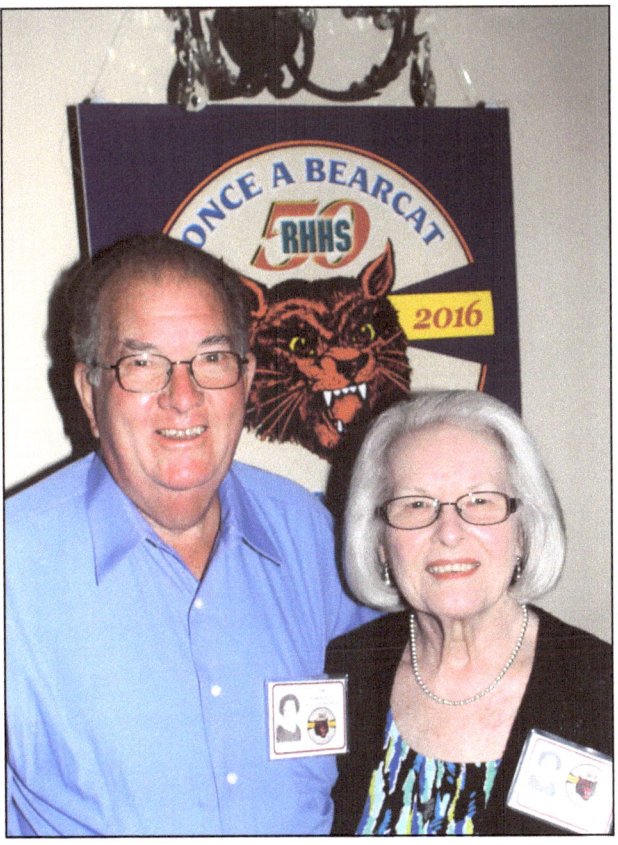

REUNION PHOTOS: OFFICIAL PHOTOS & CANDID SHOTS

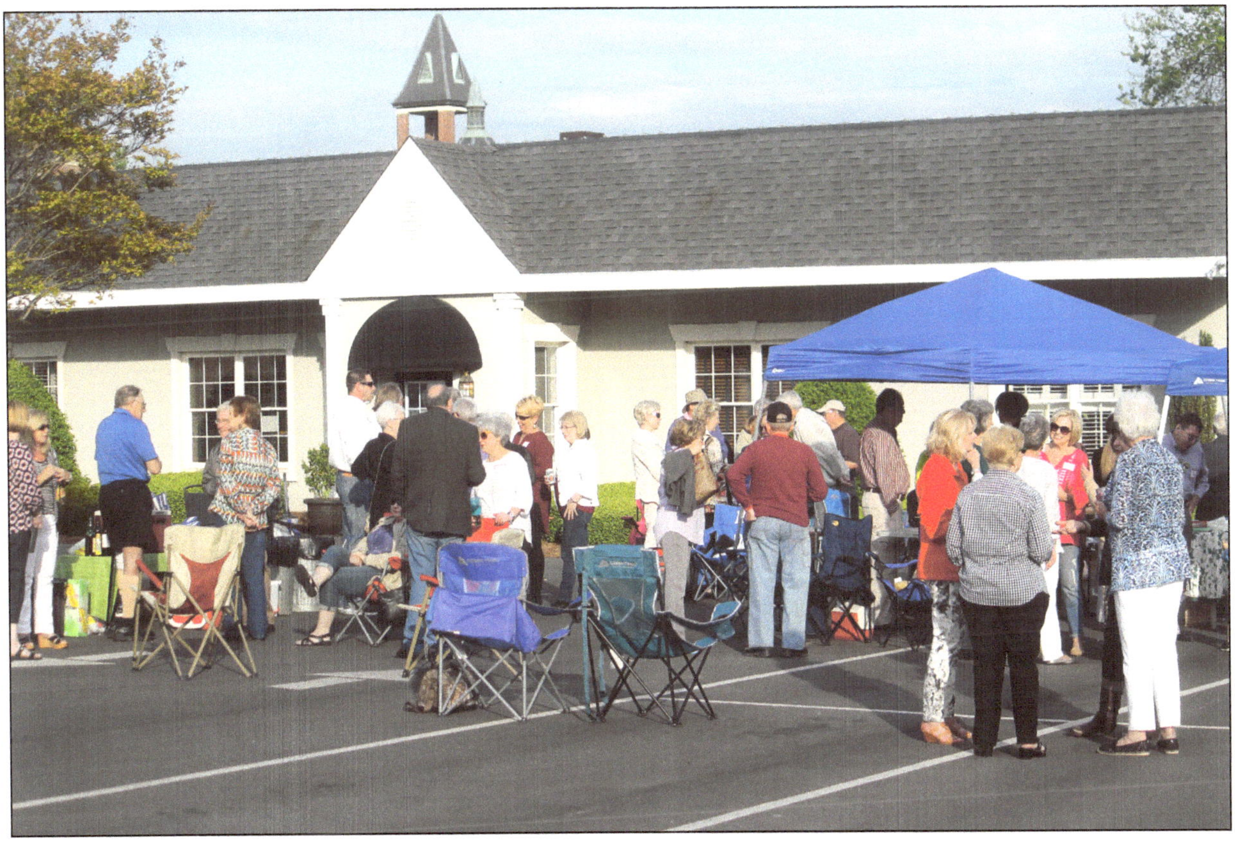

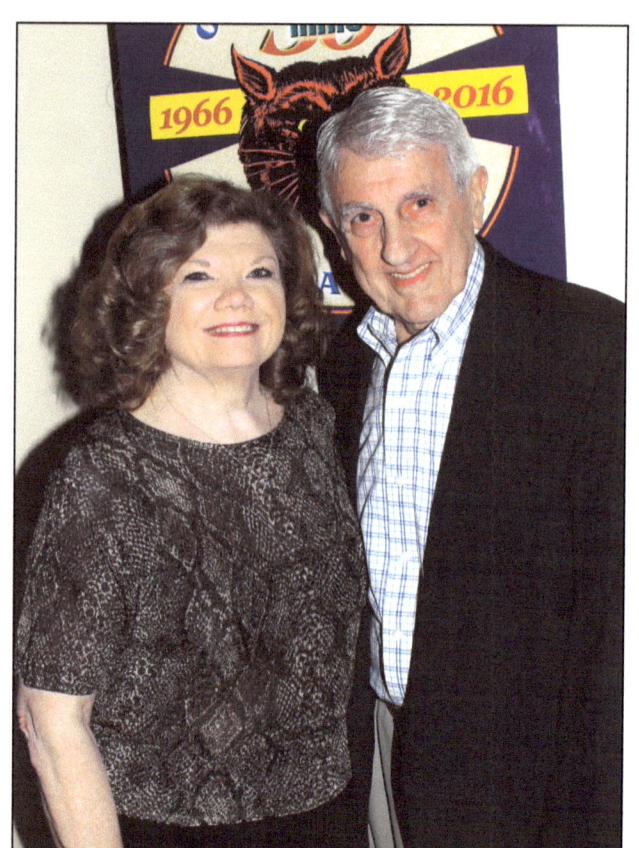

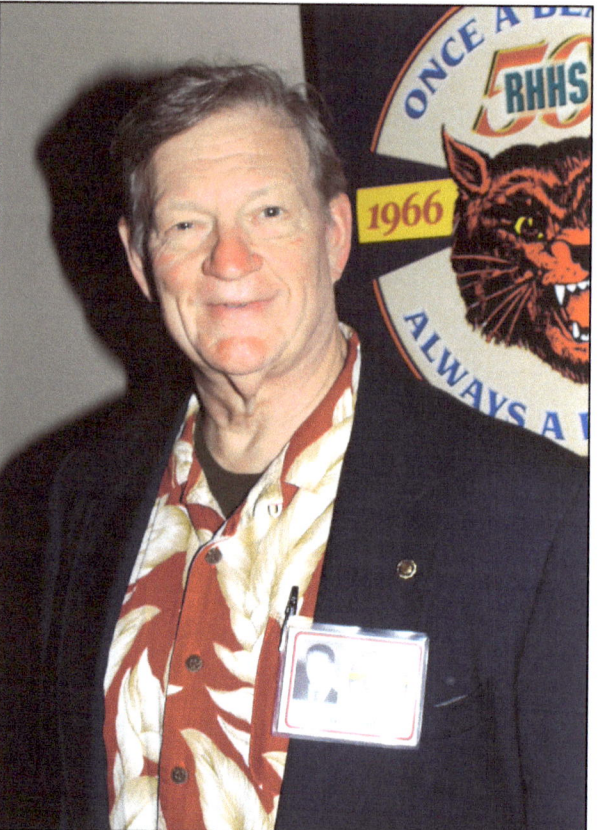

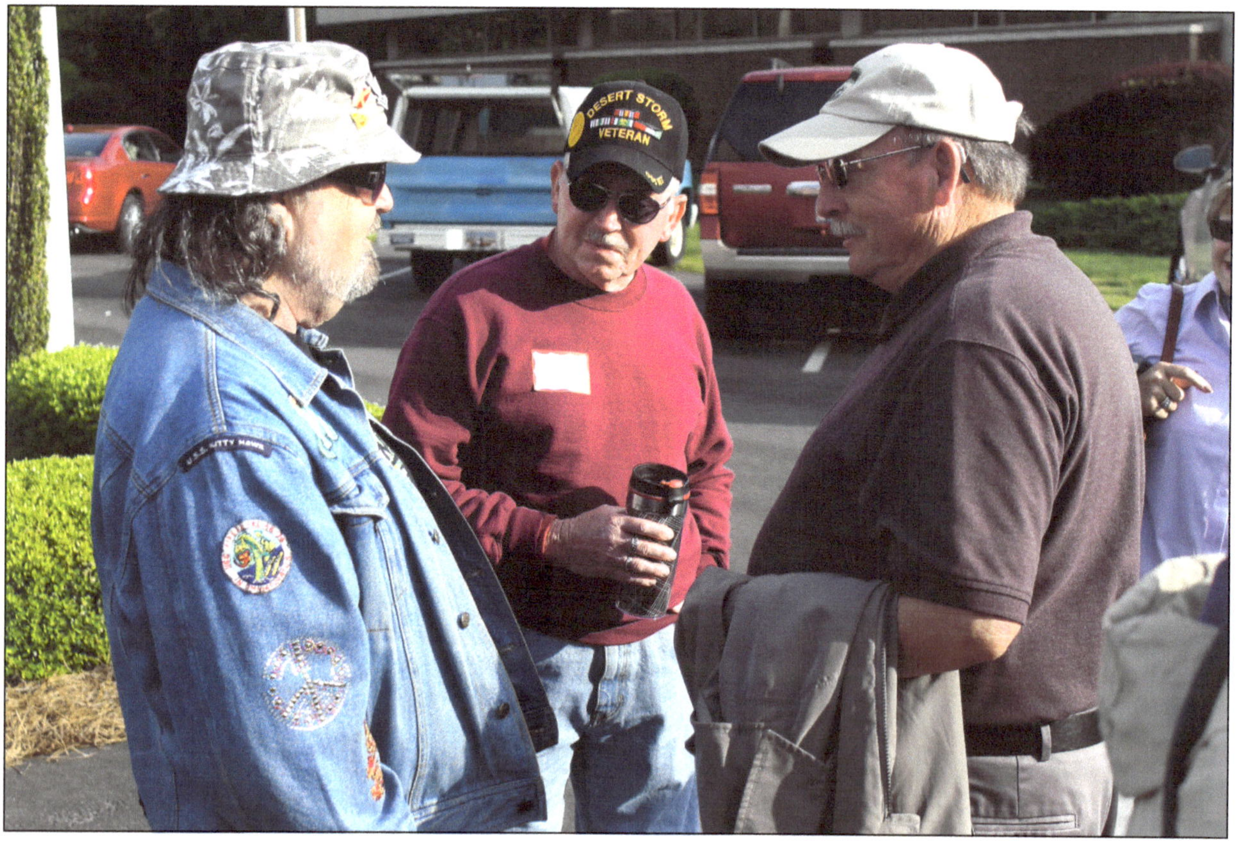

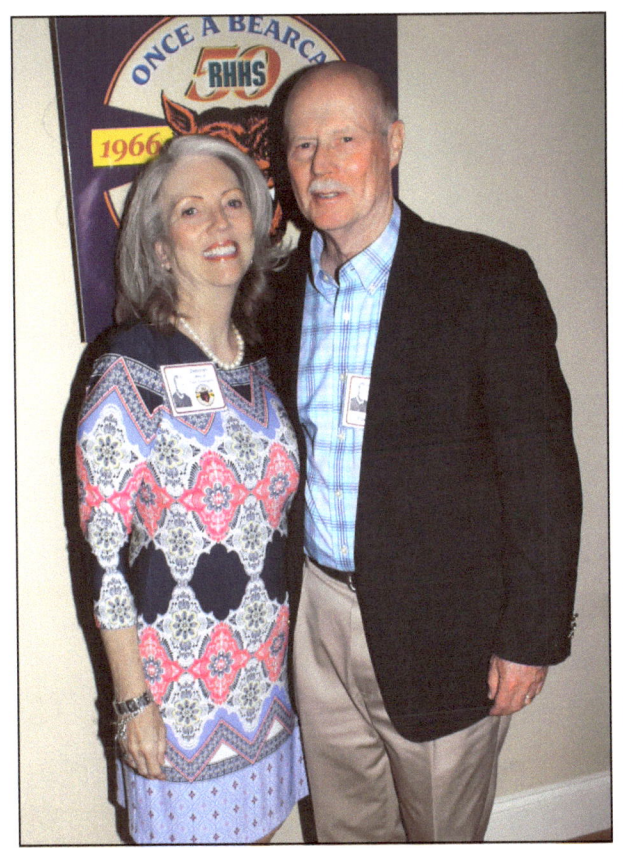

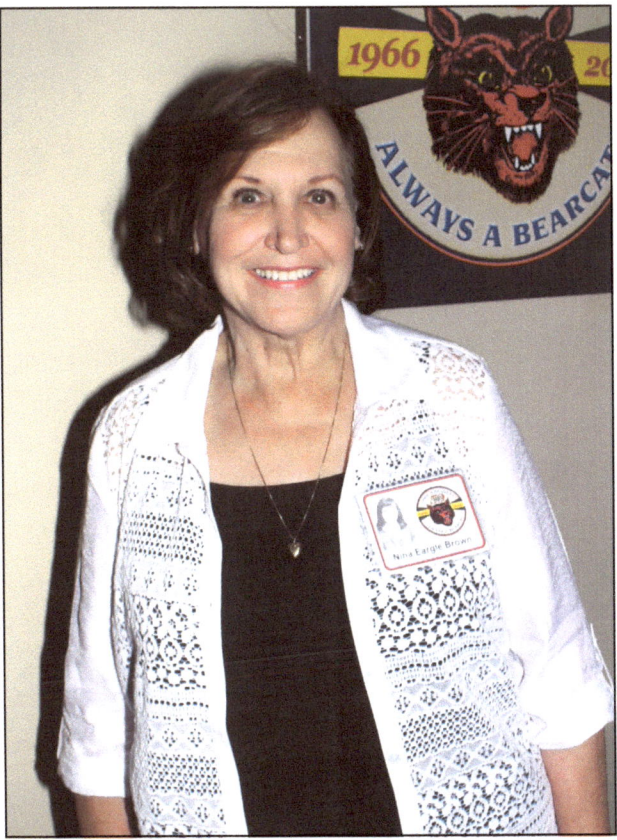

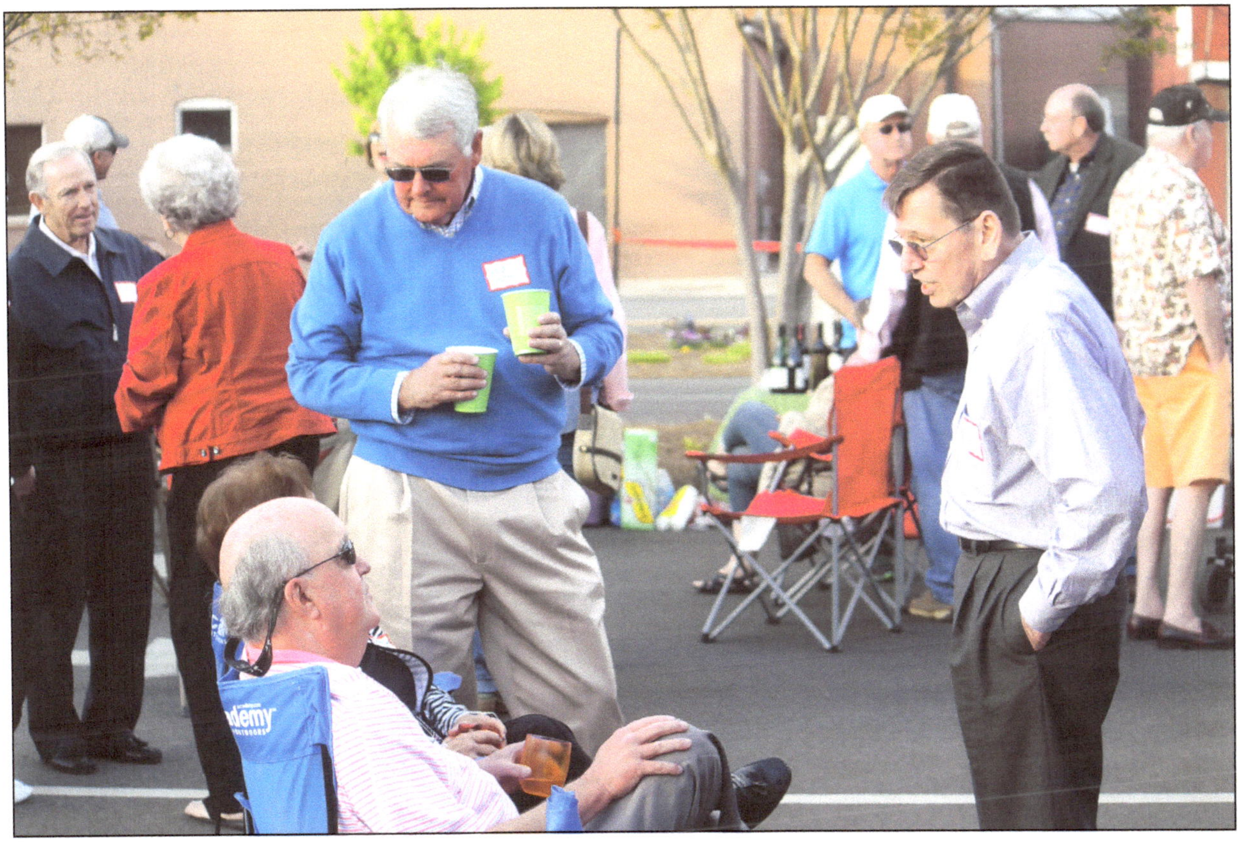

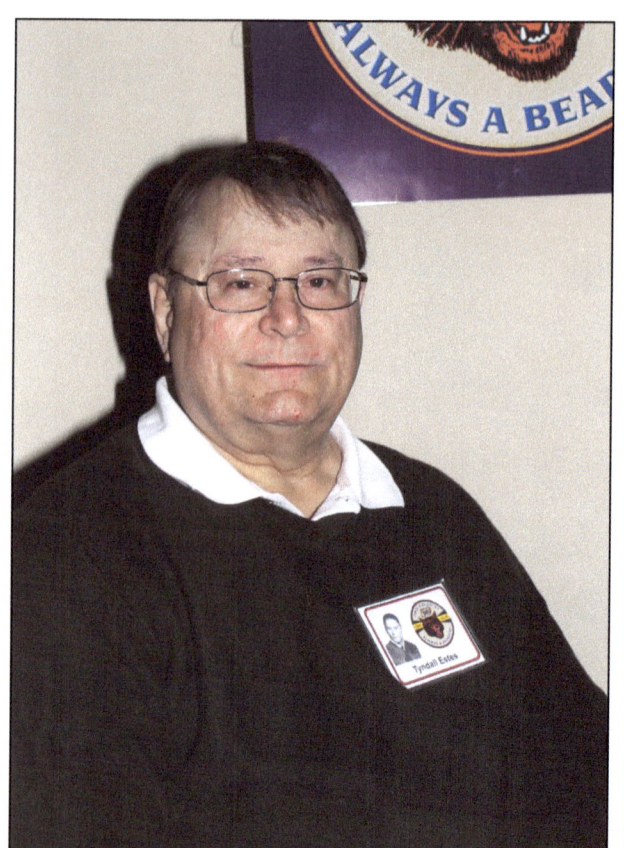

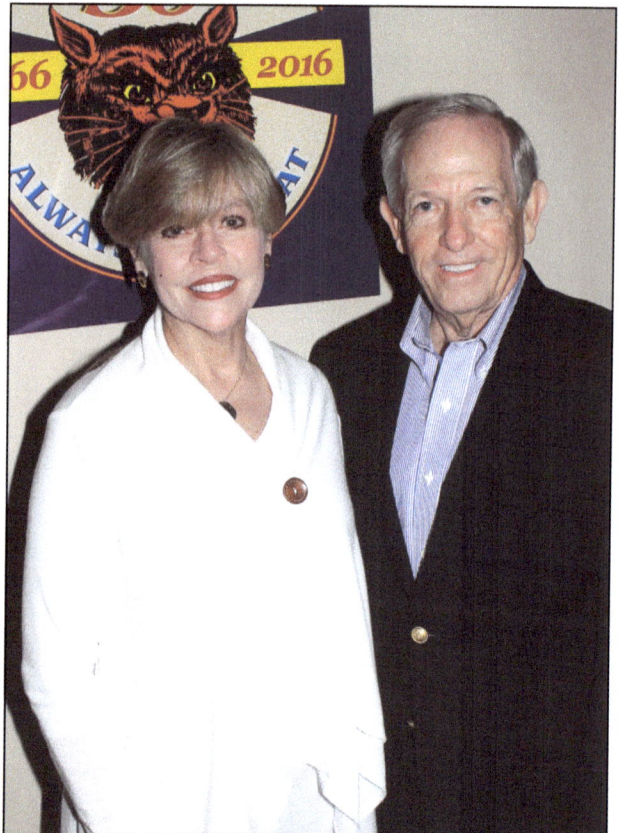

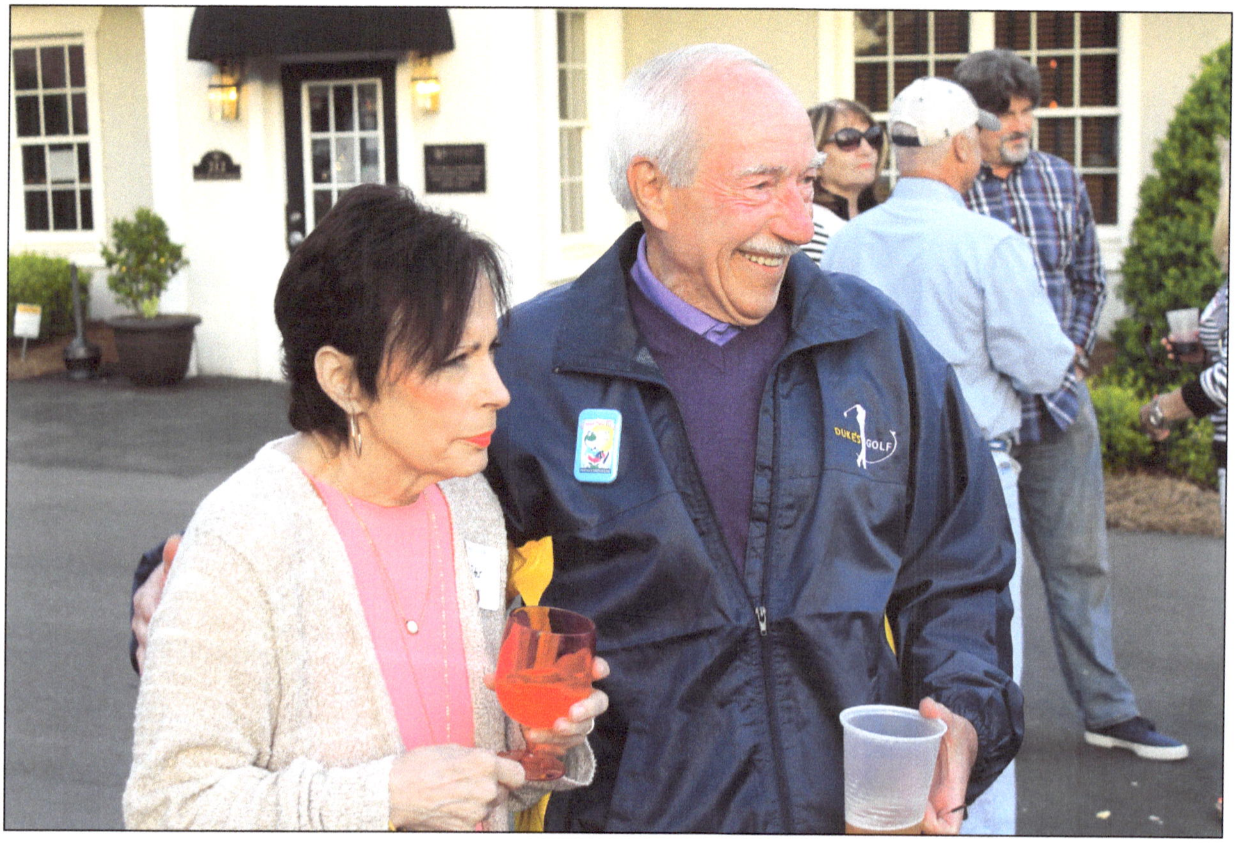

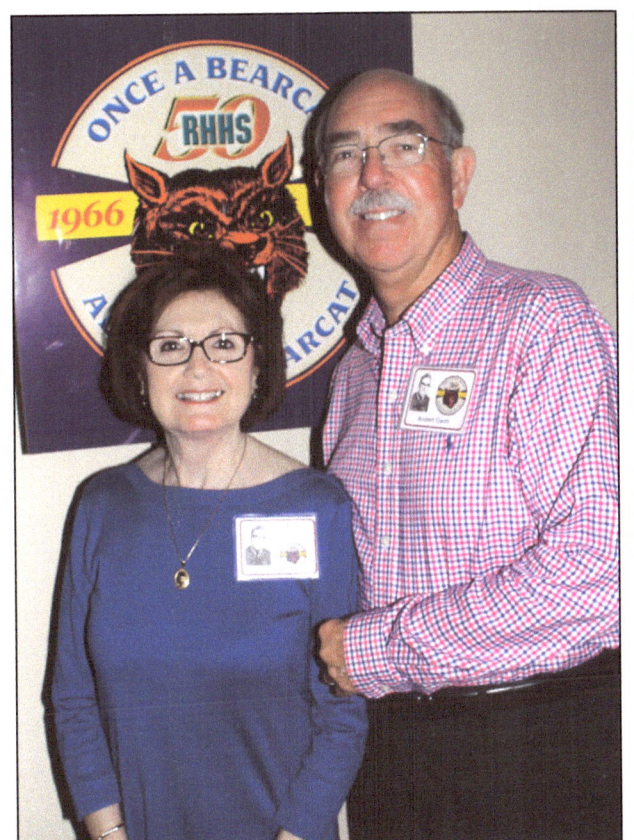

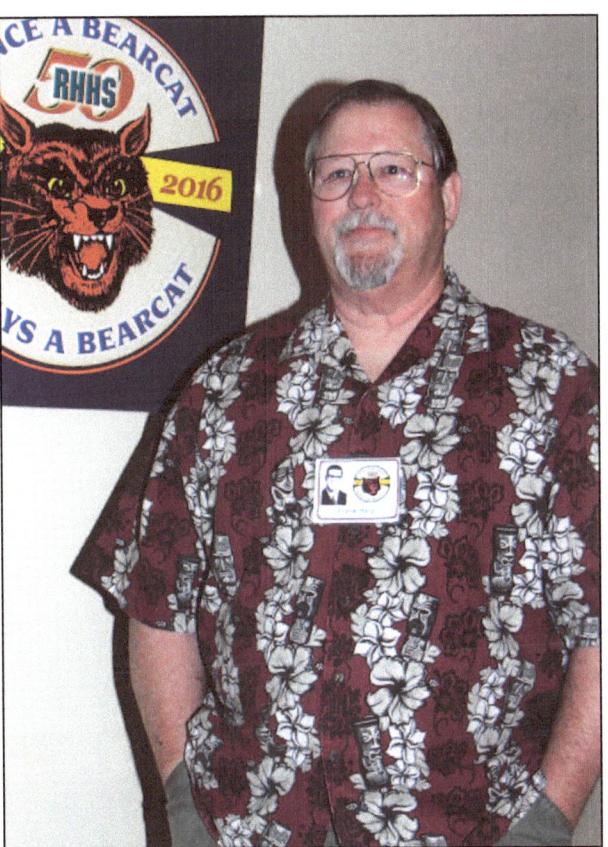

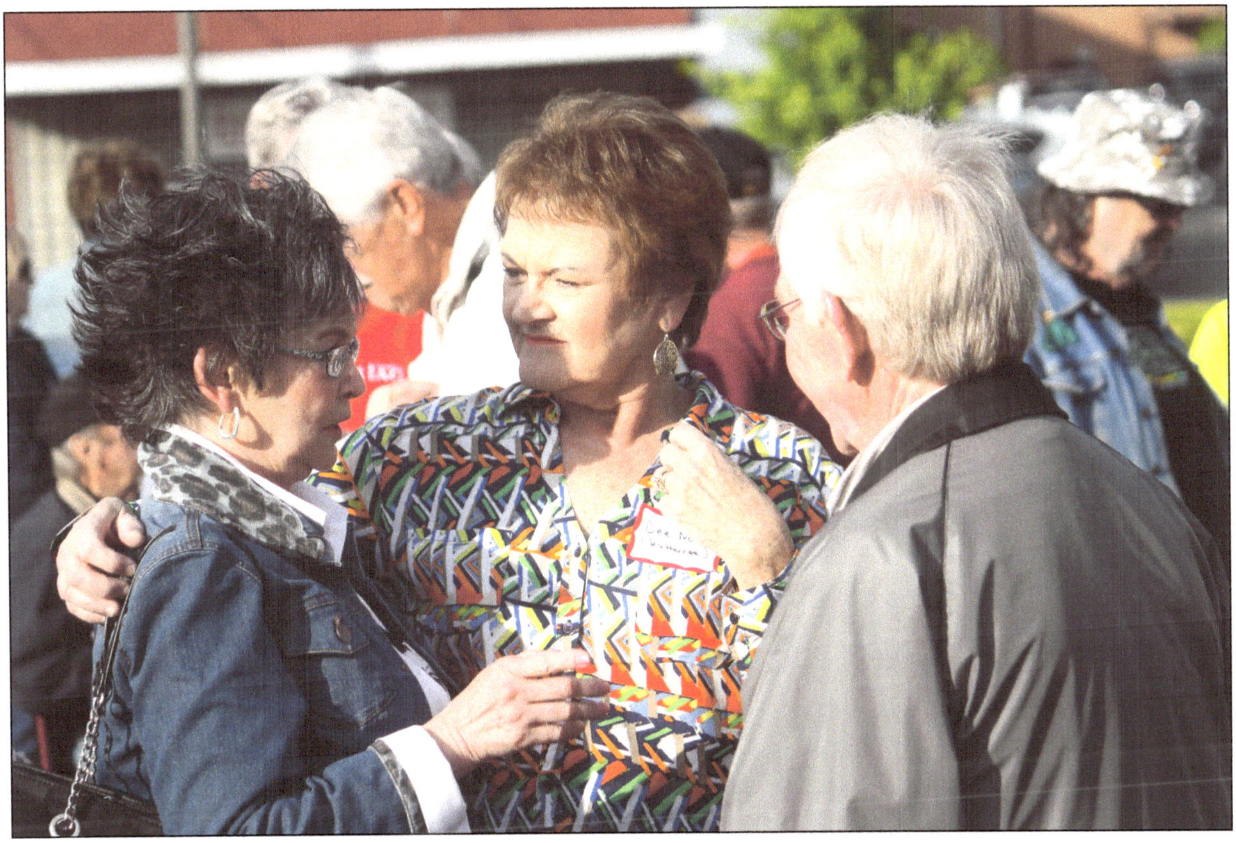

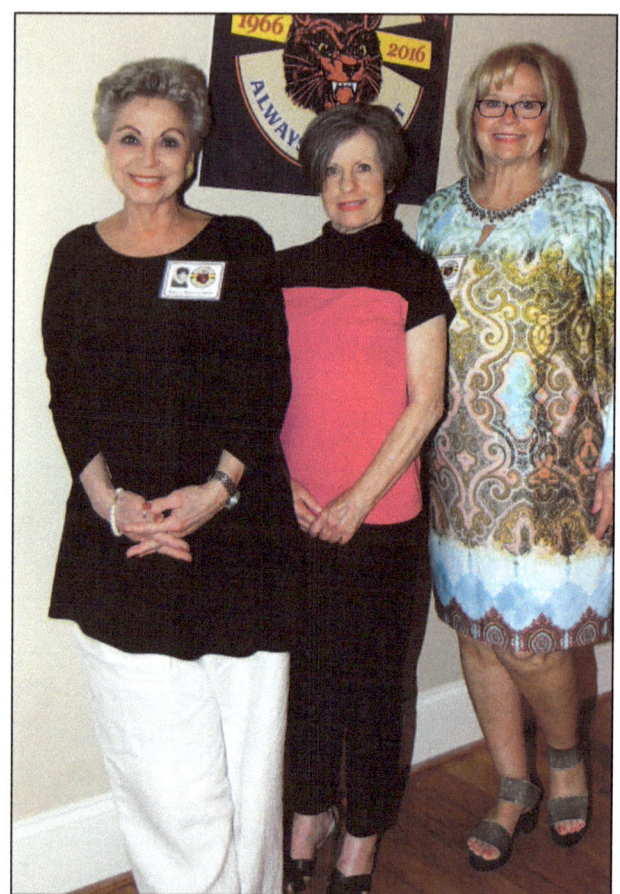

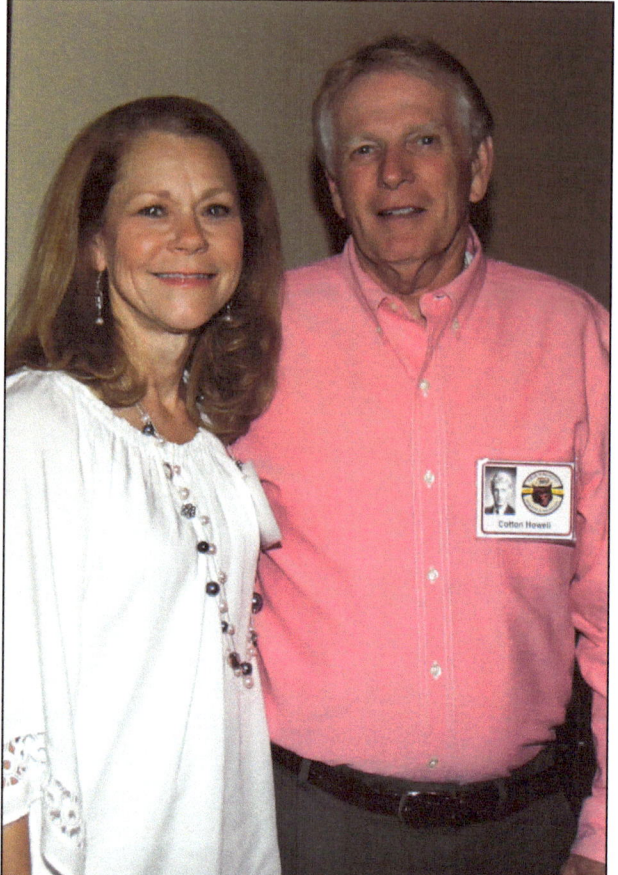

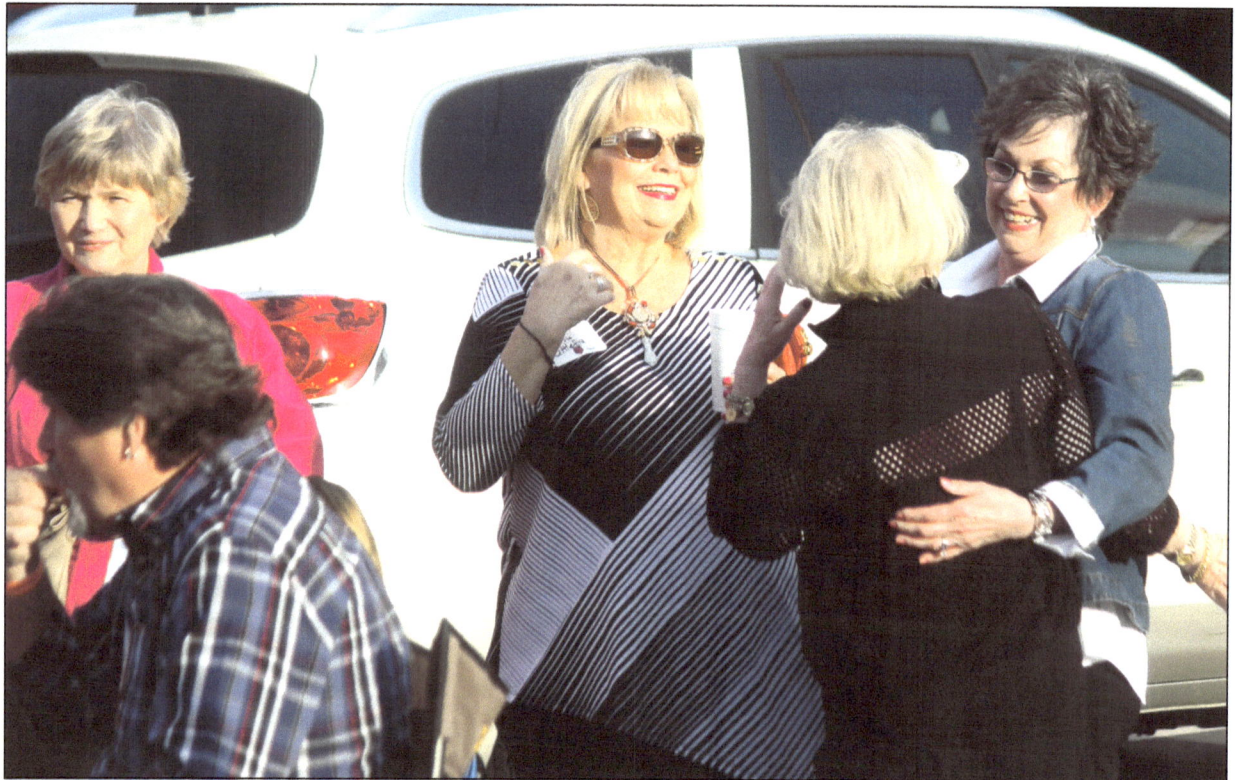

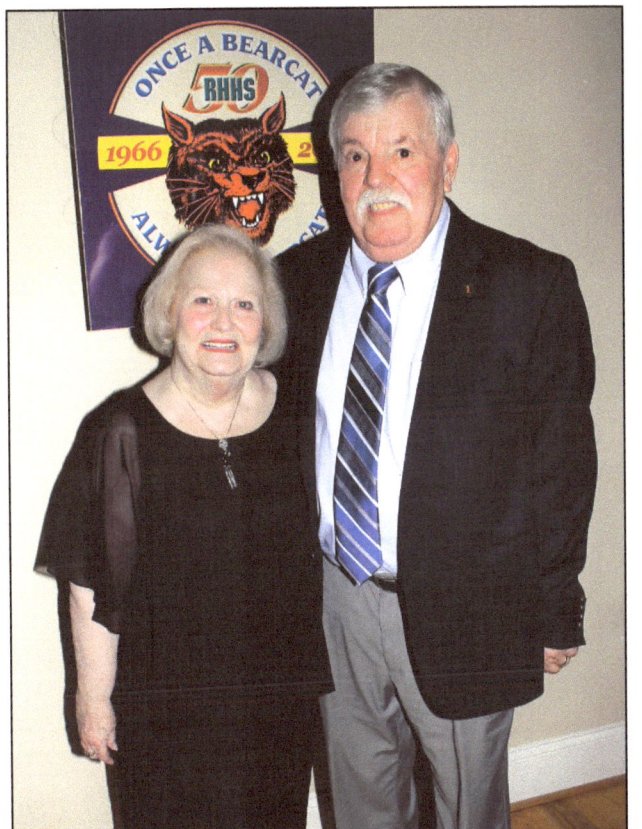

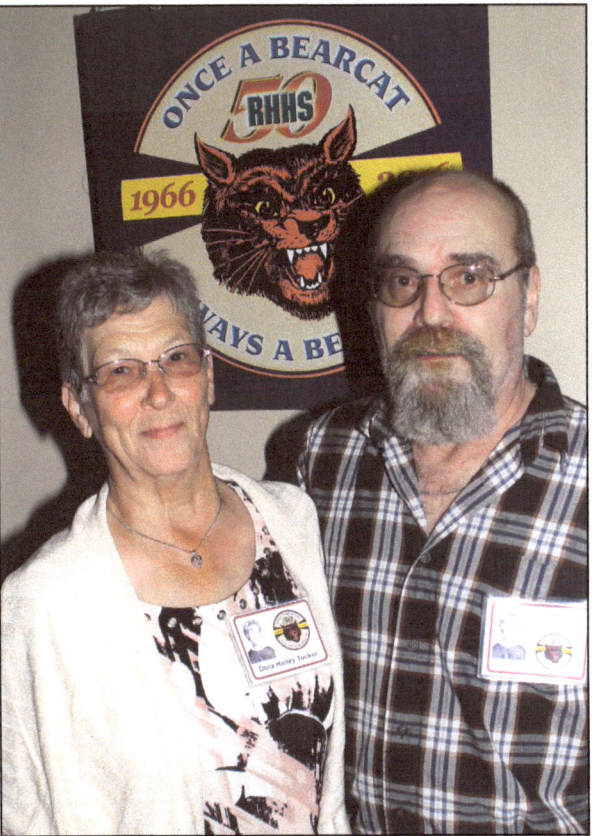

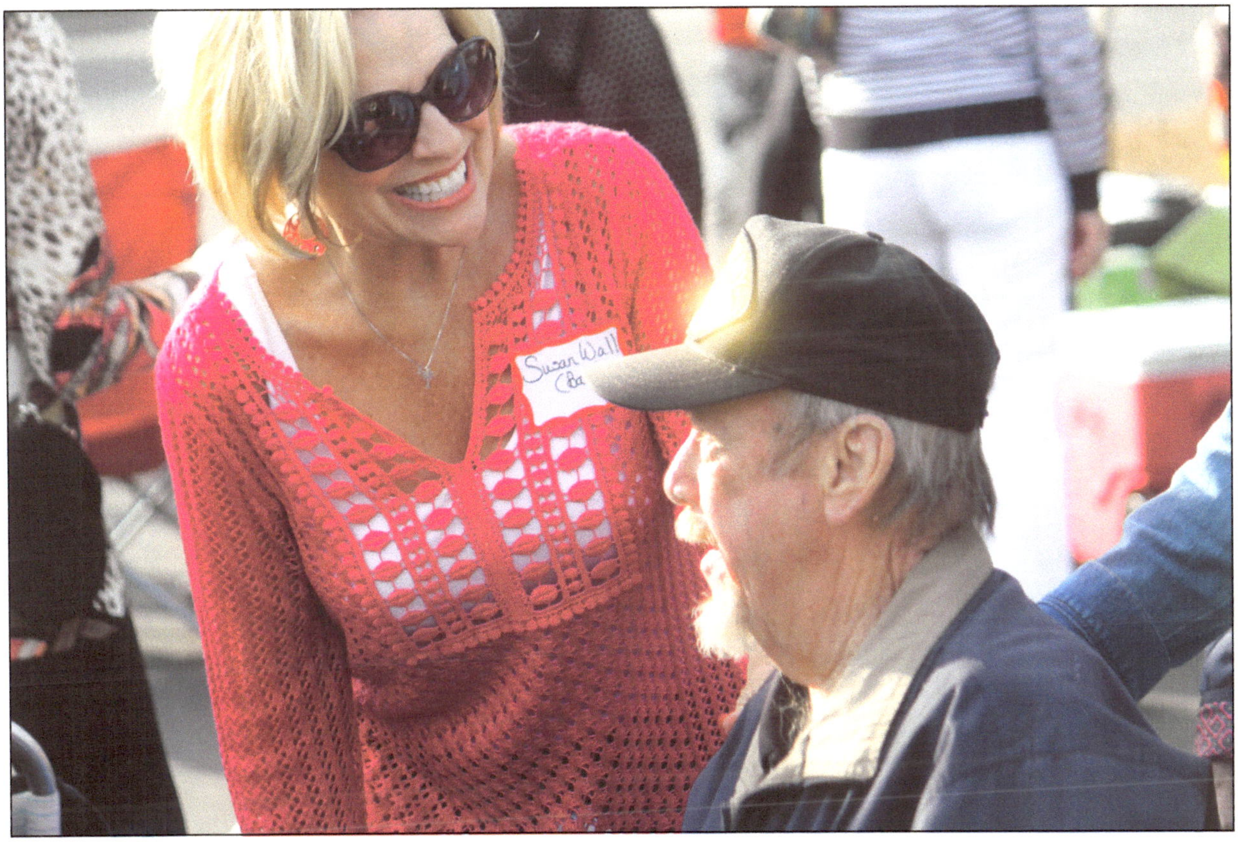

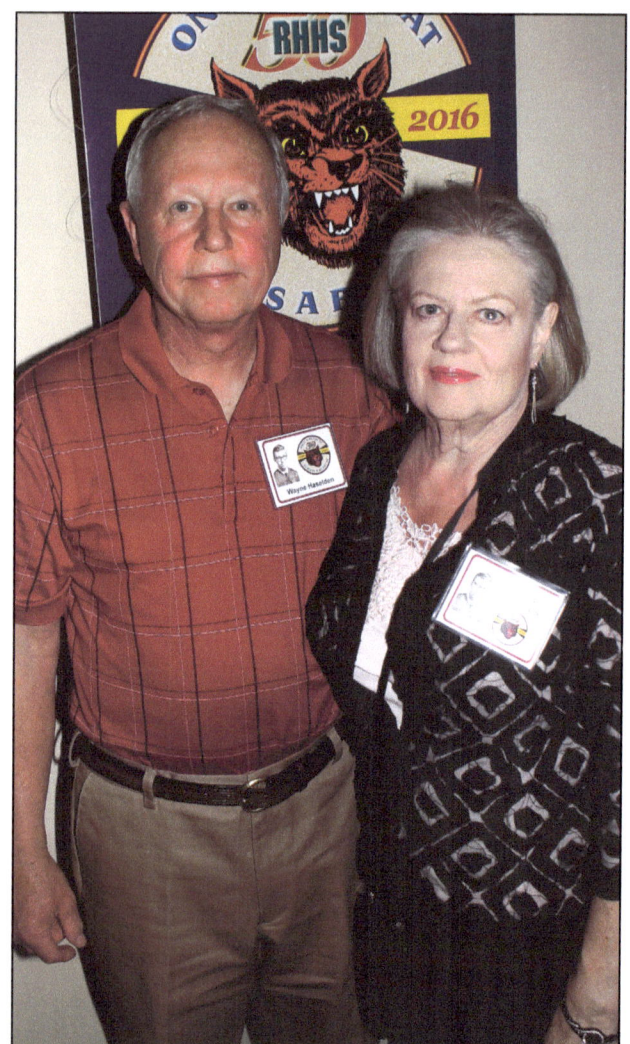

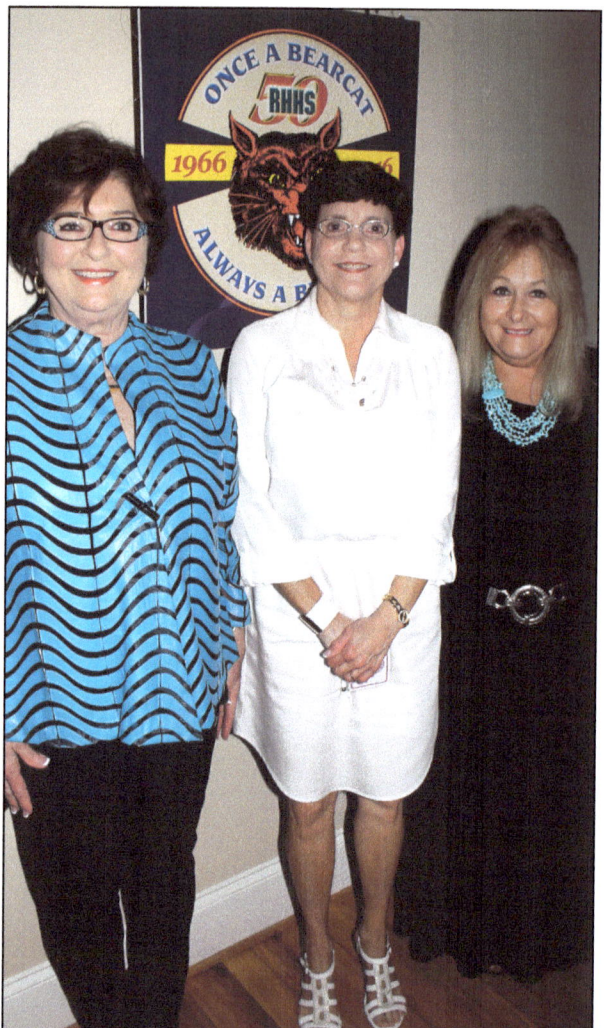

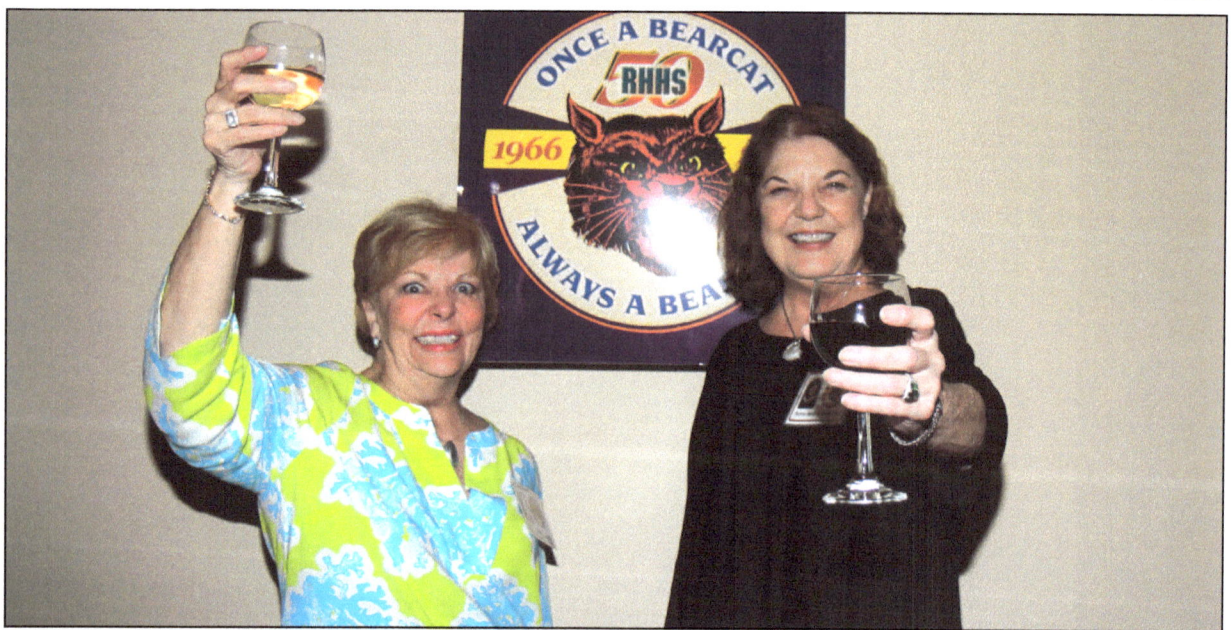

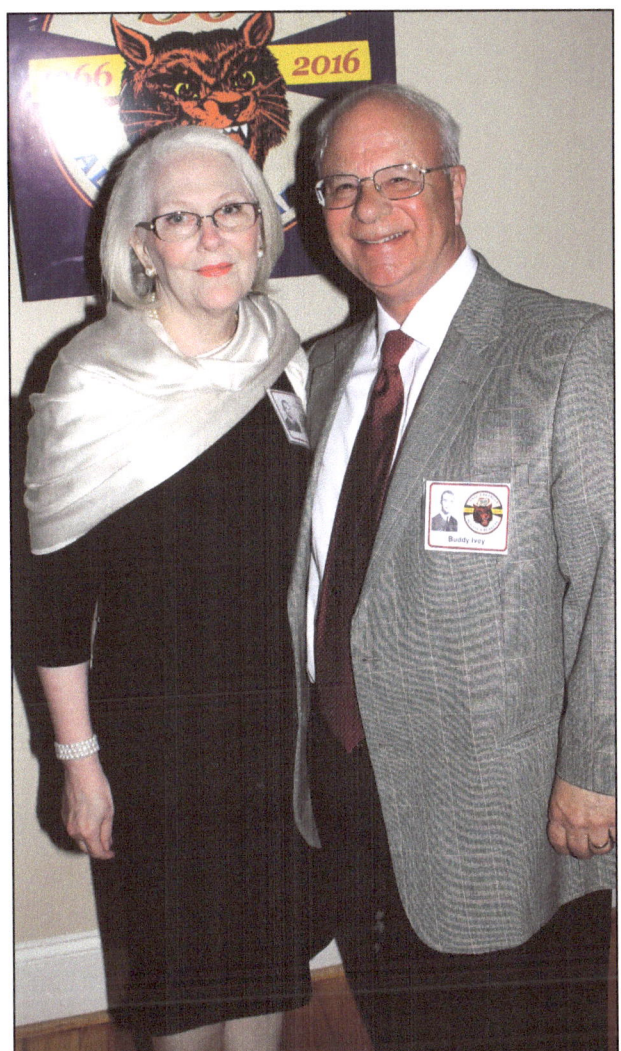

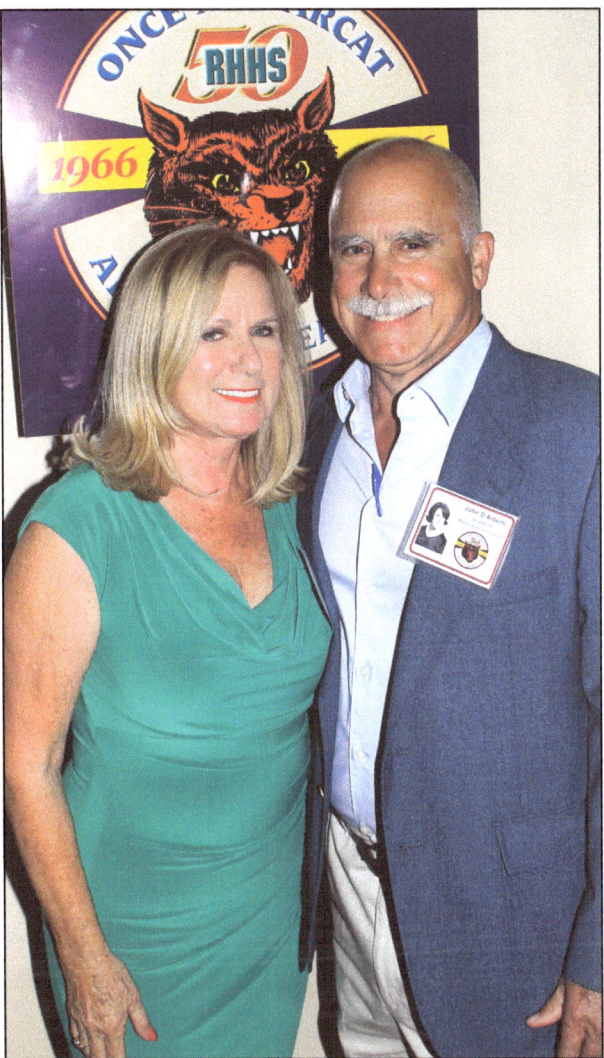

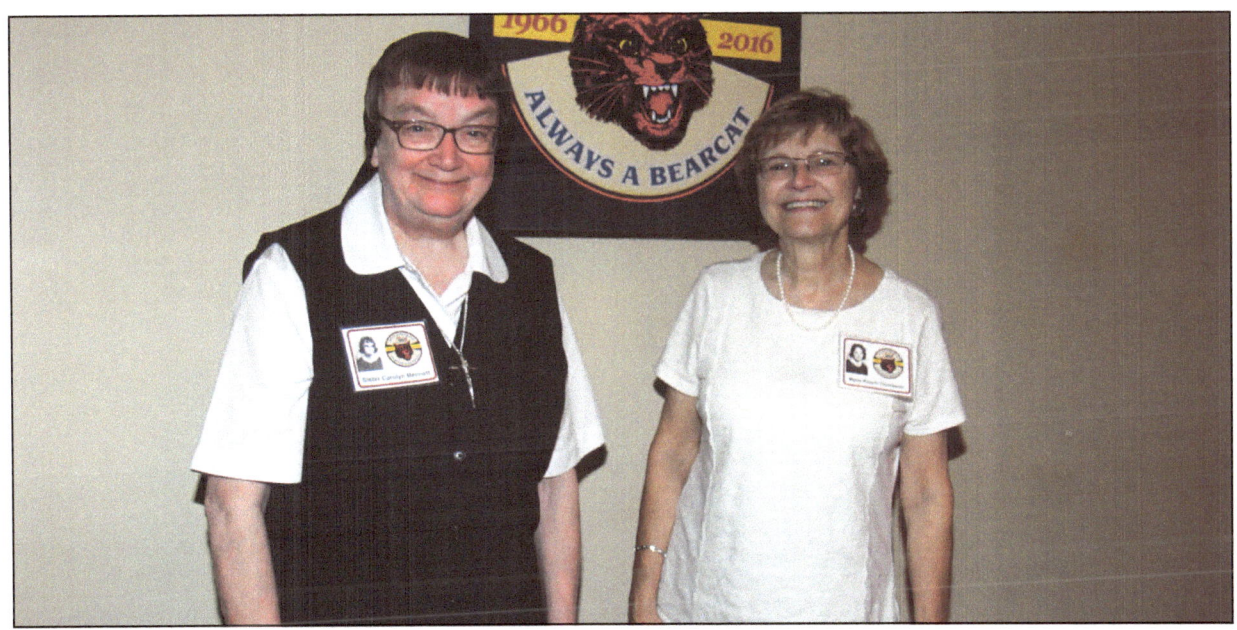

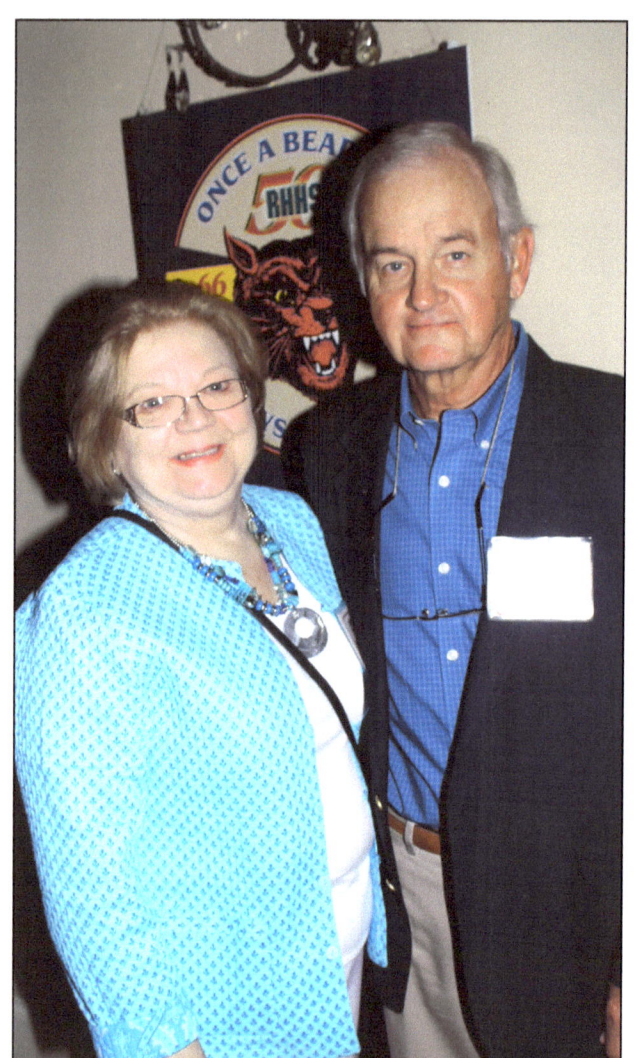

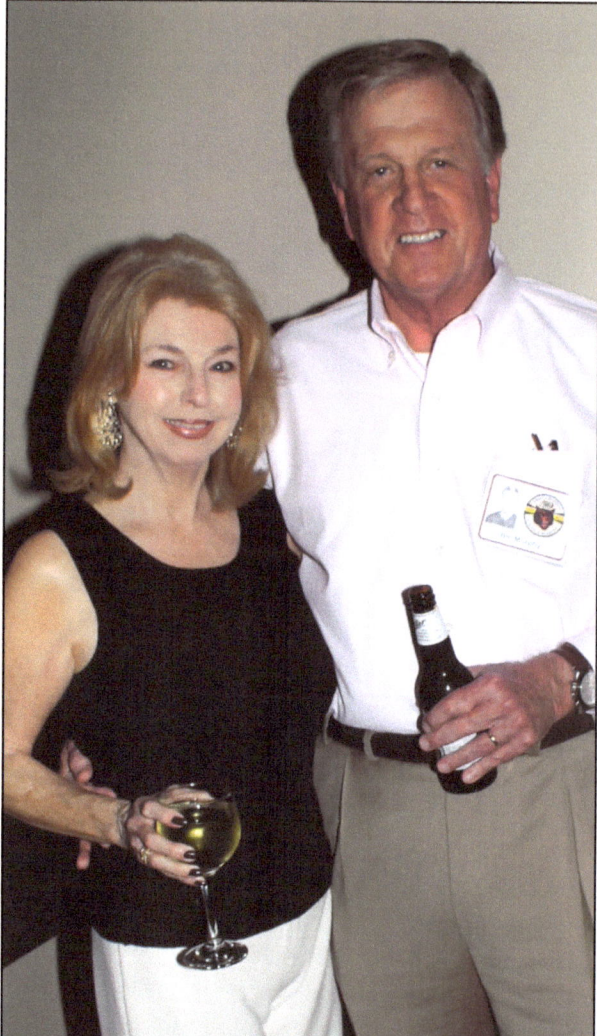

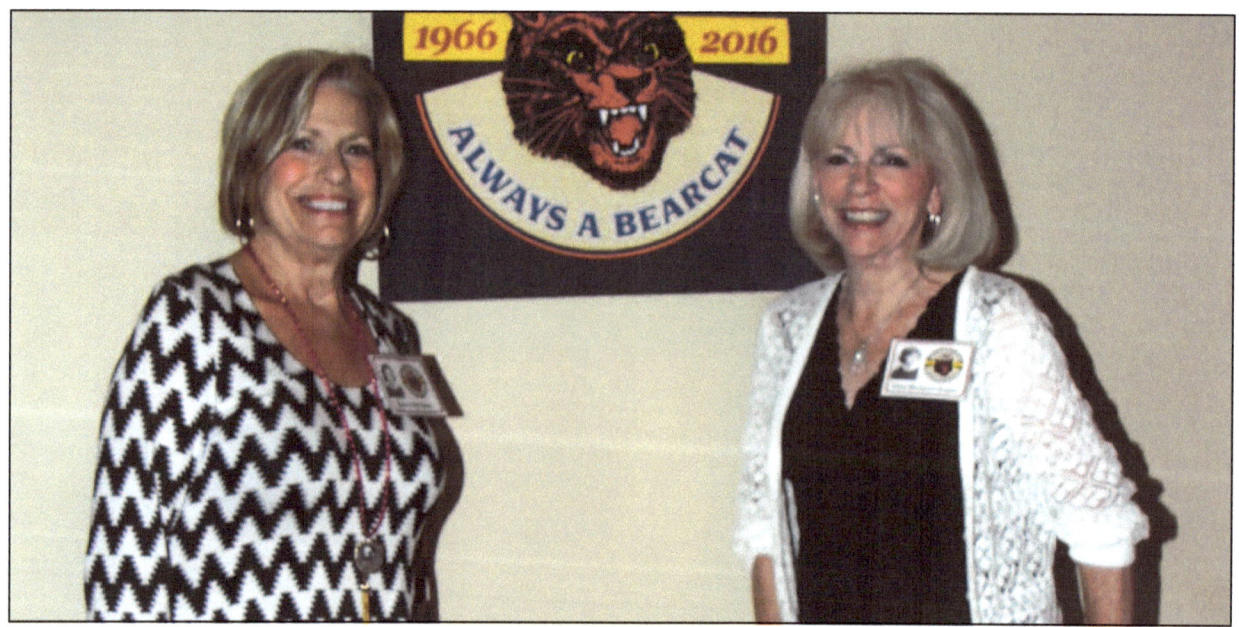

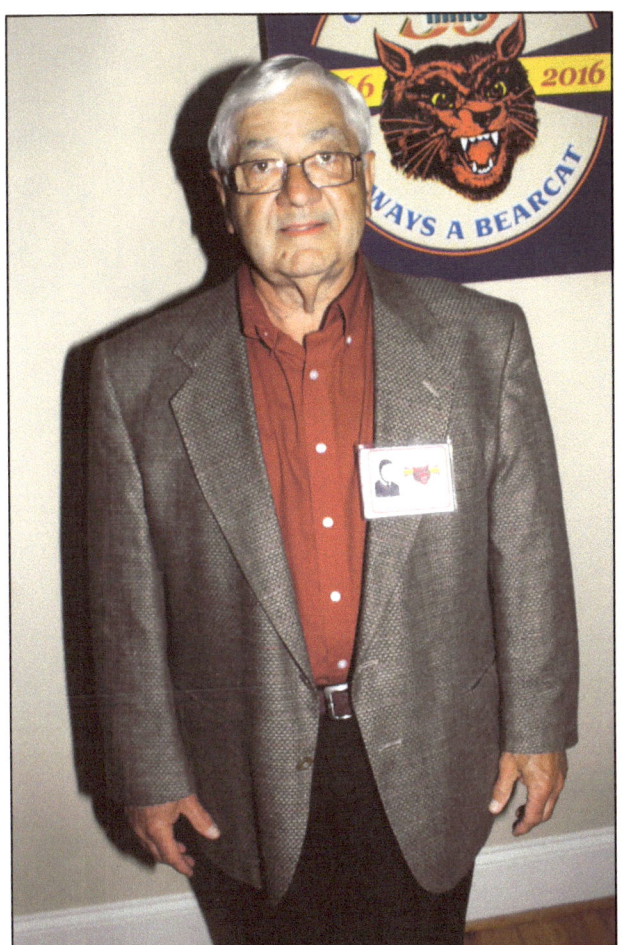
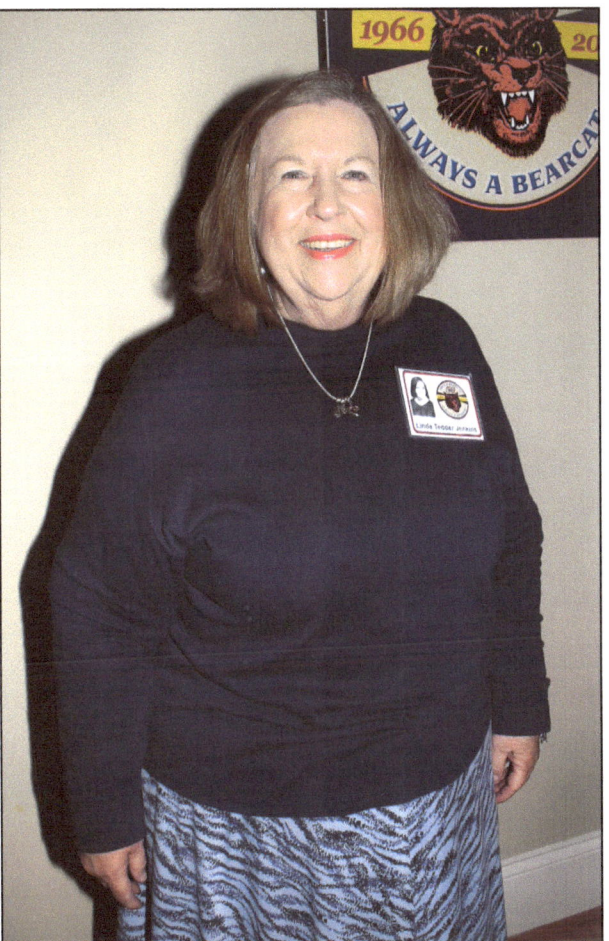
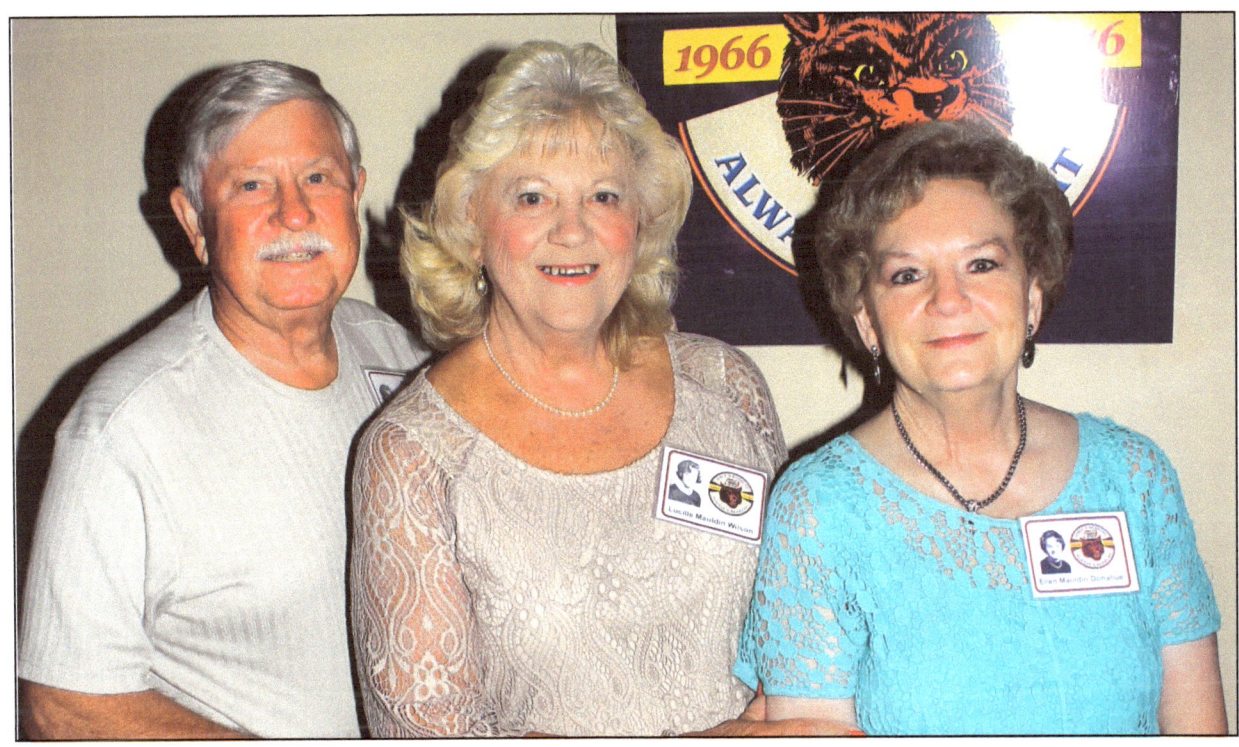

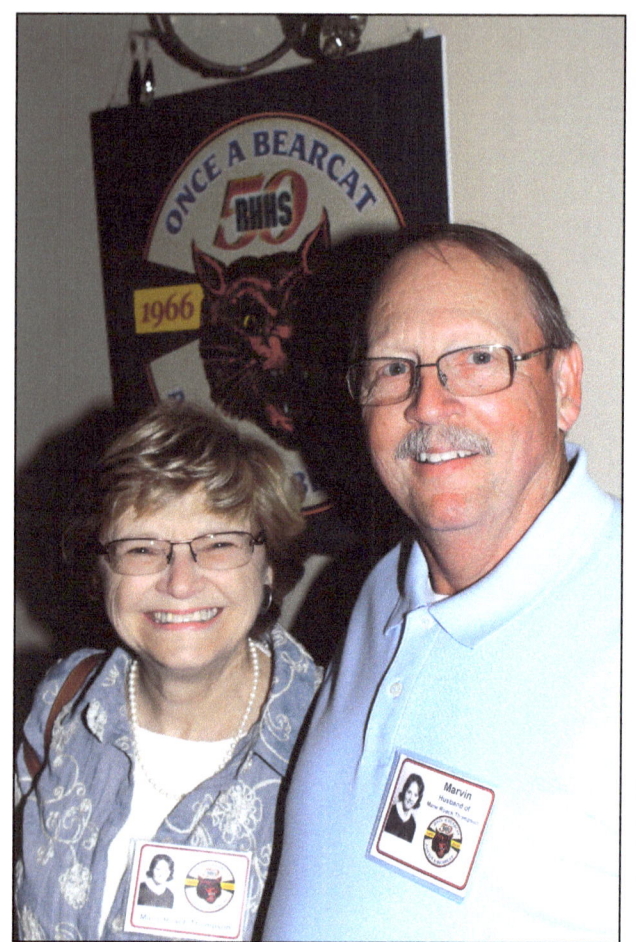

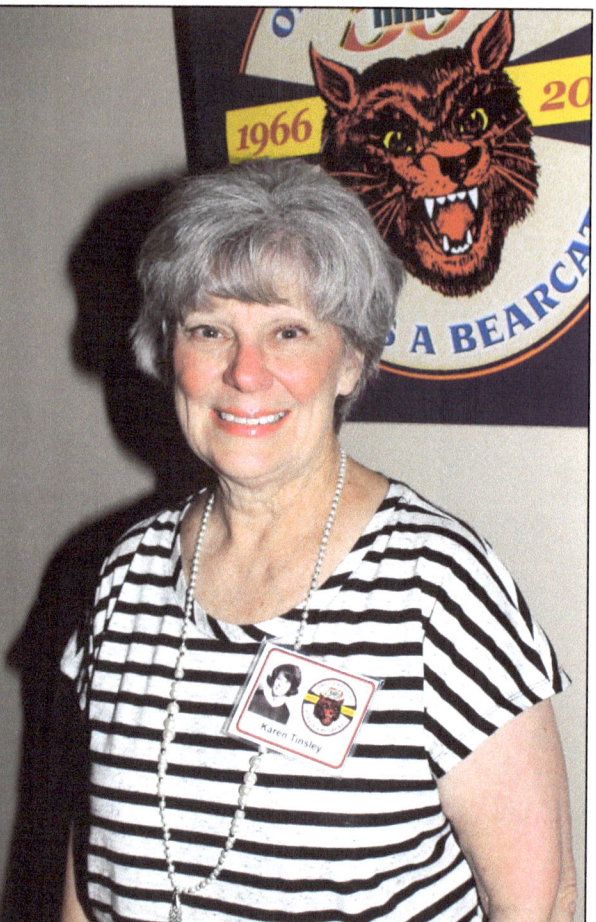

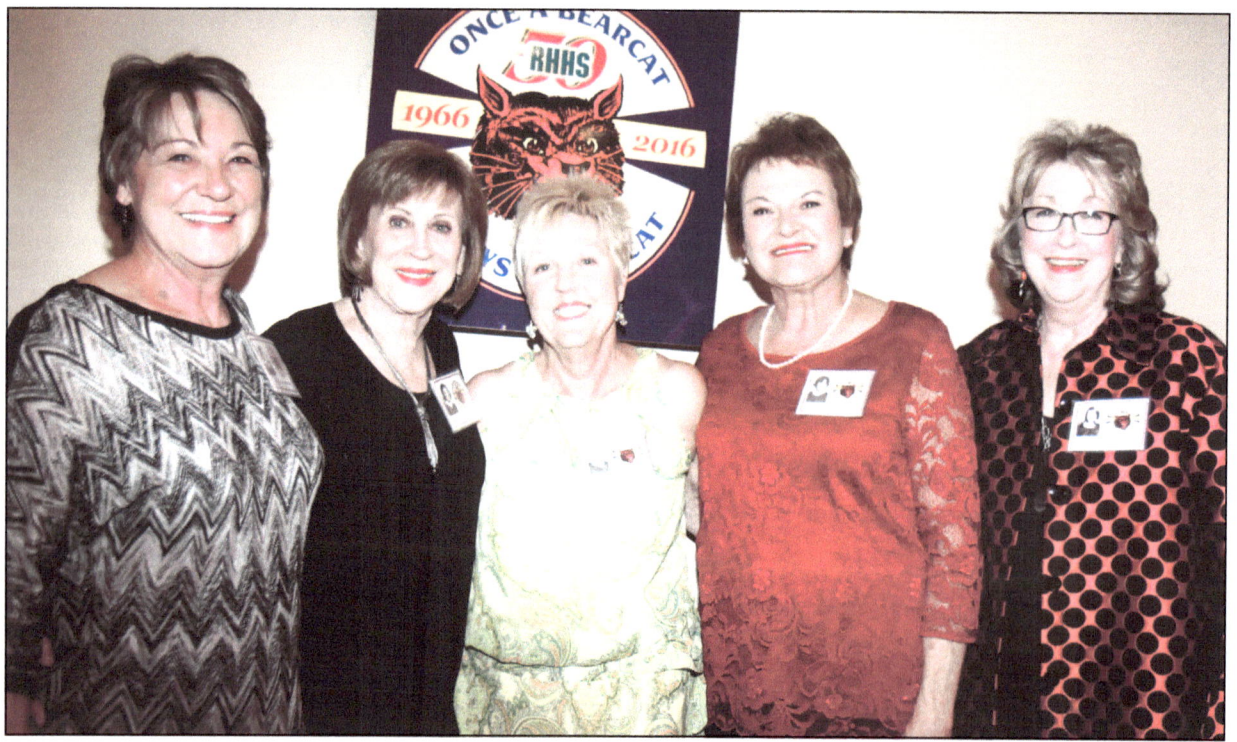

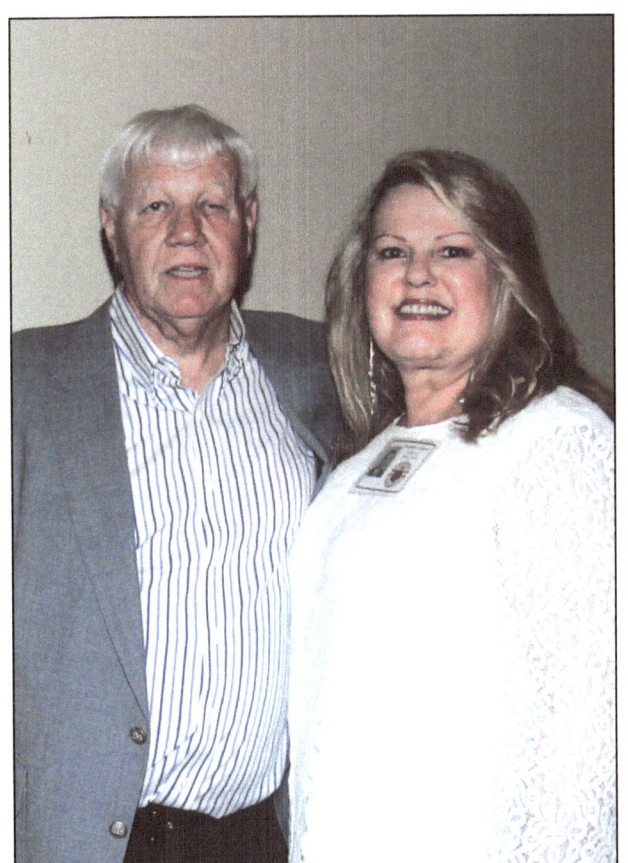

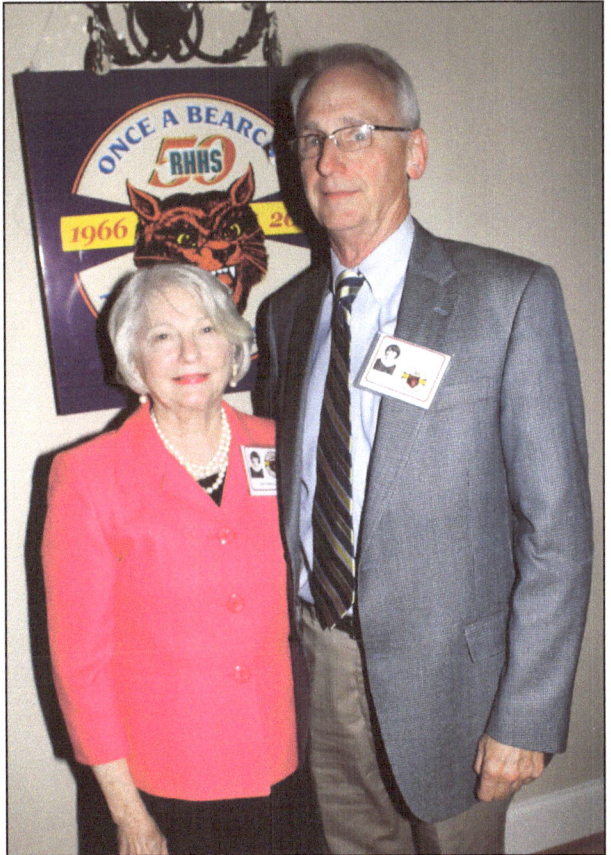

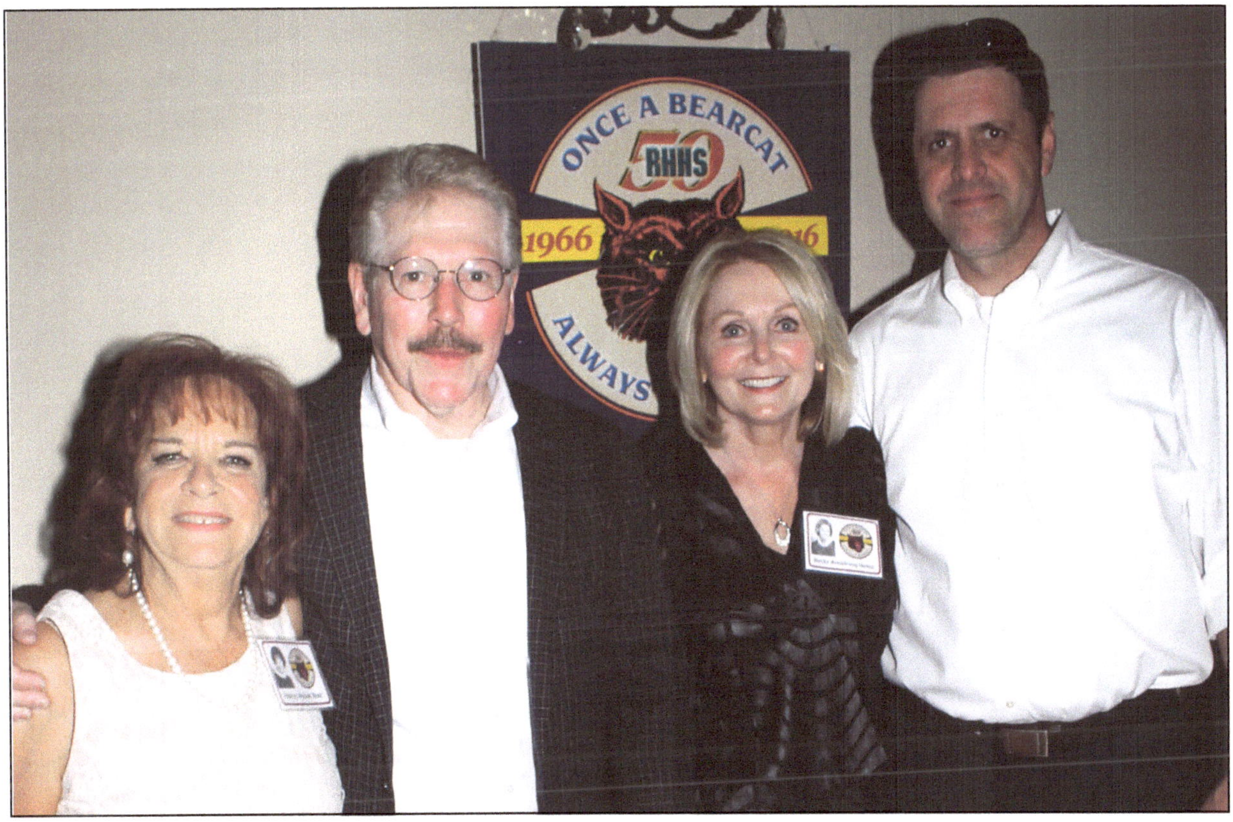

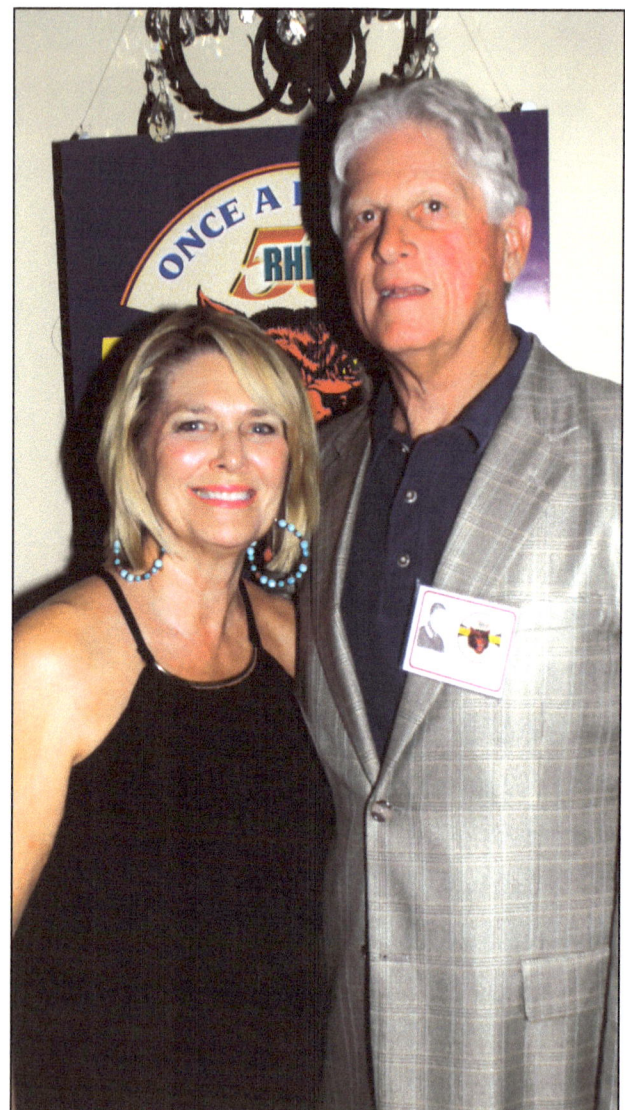

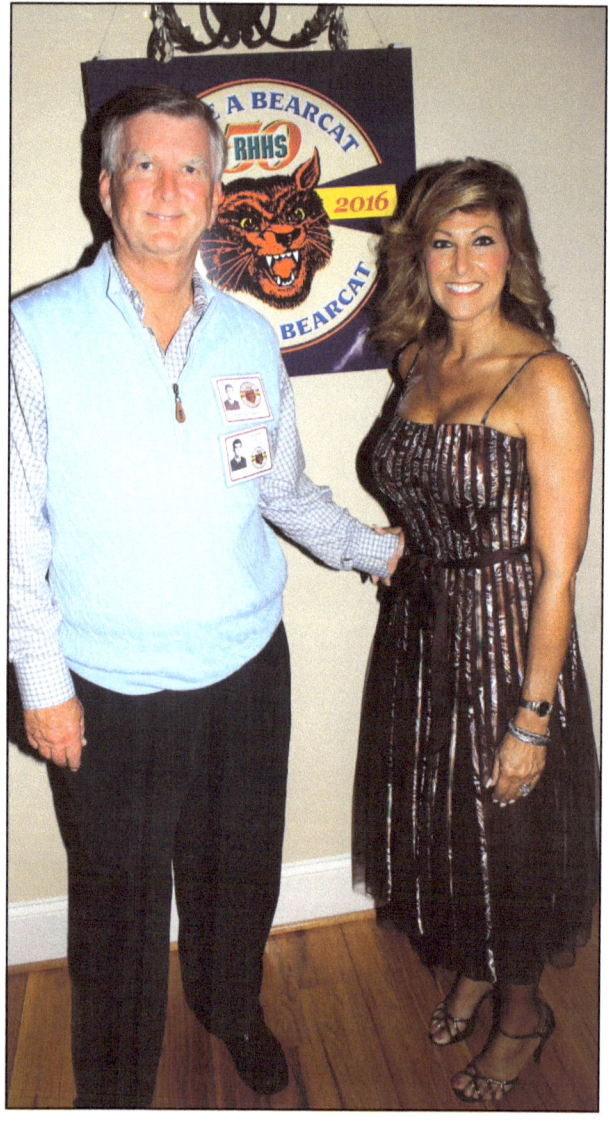

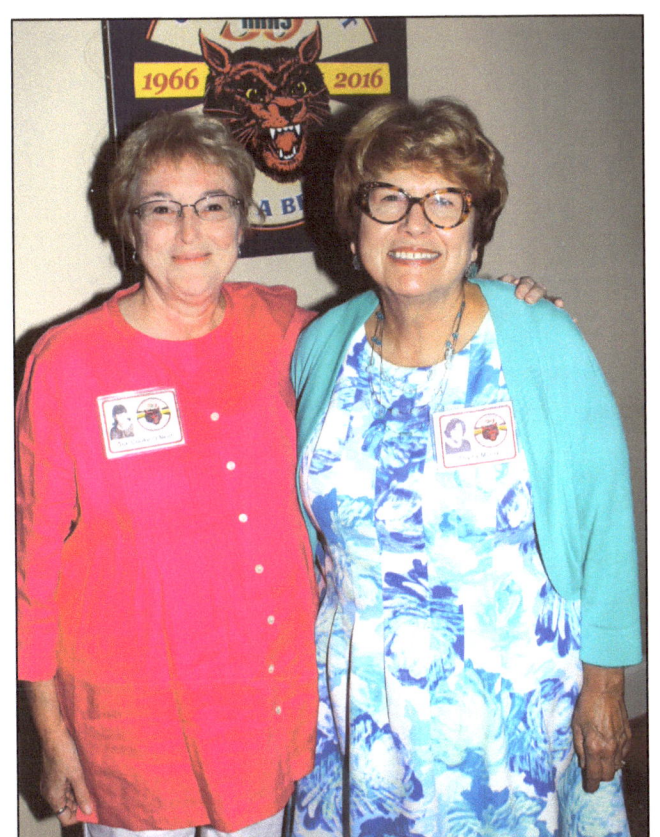

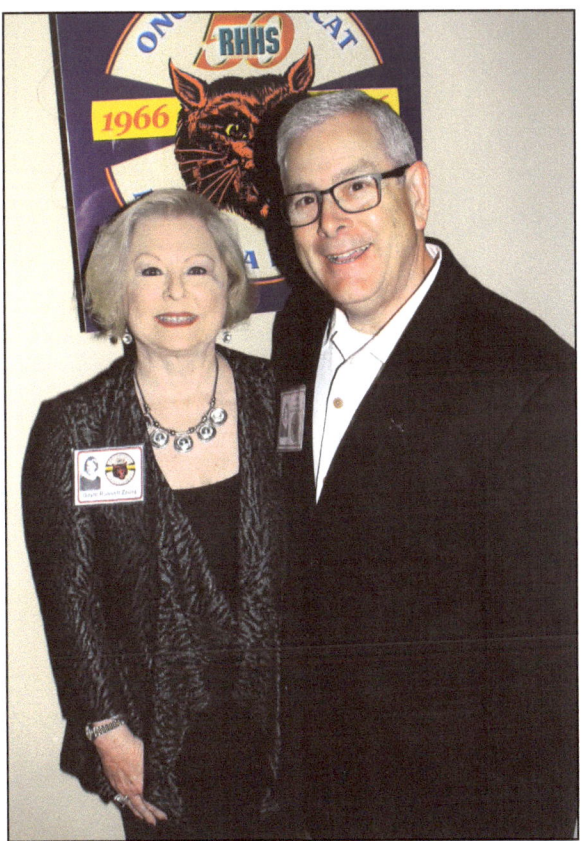

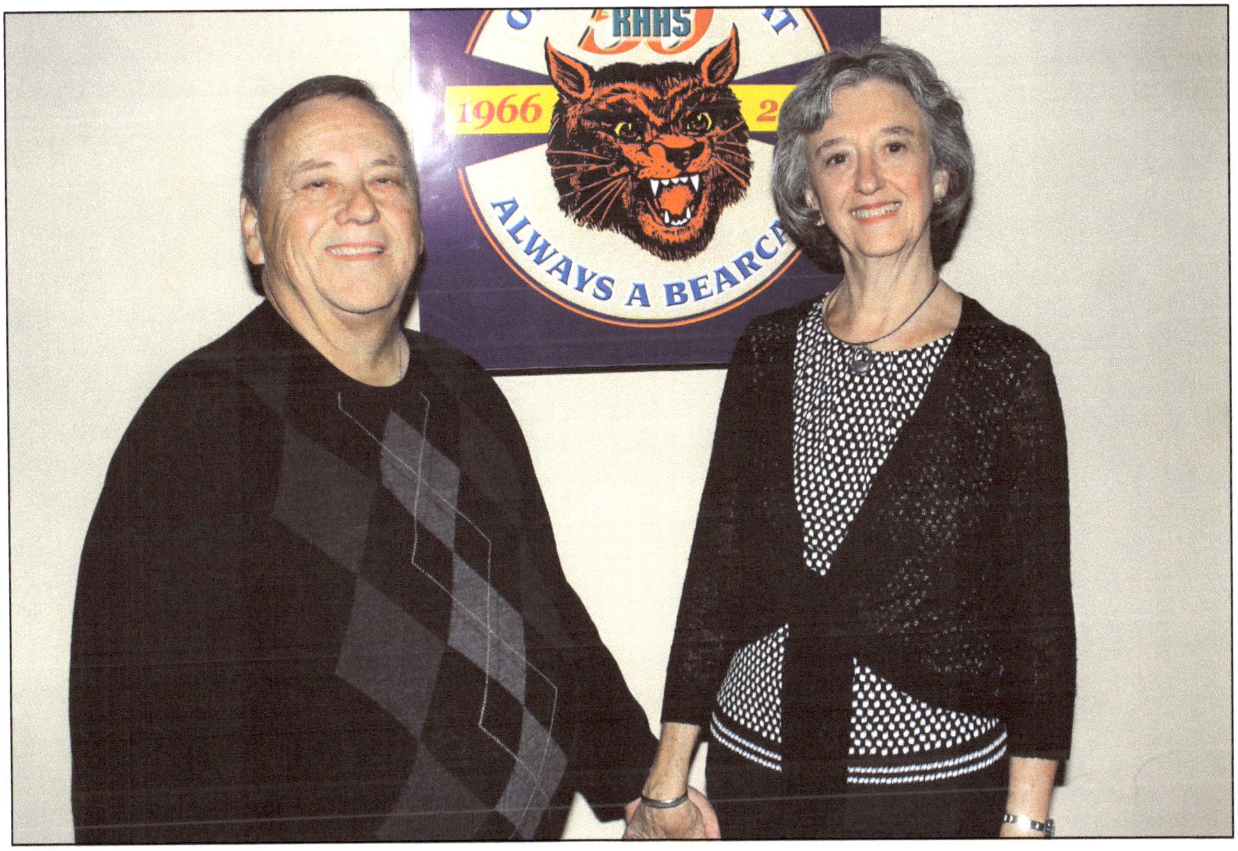

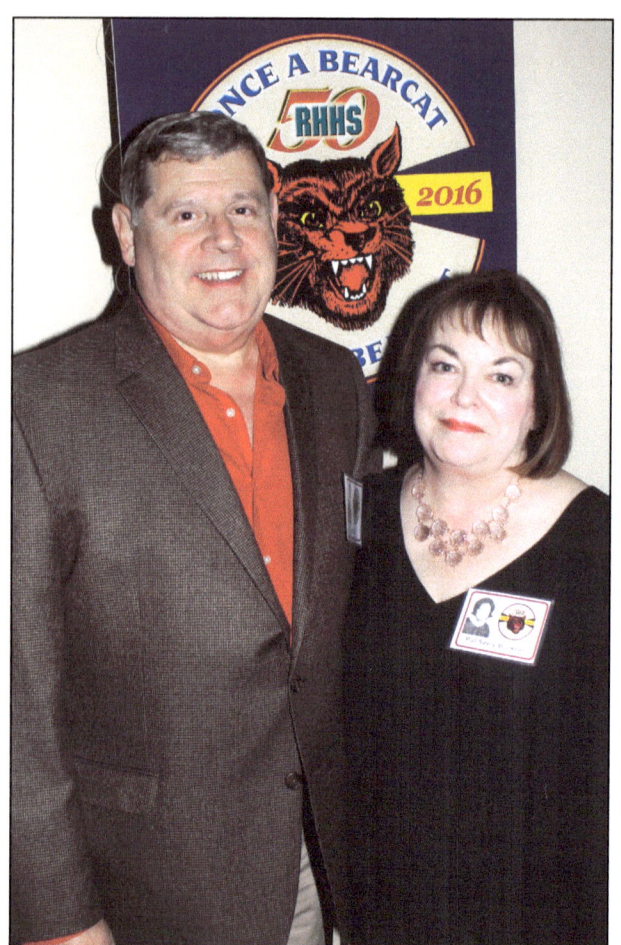

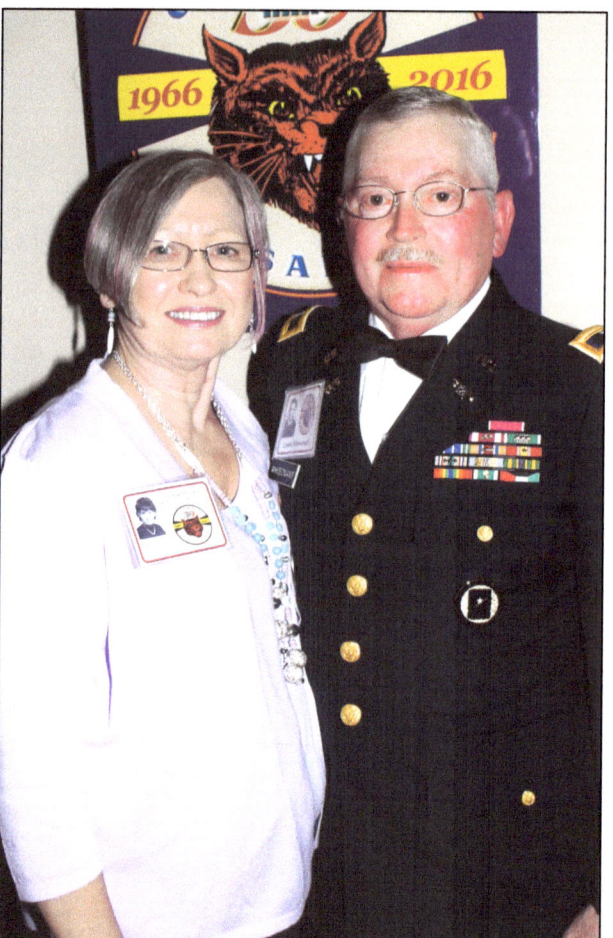

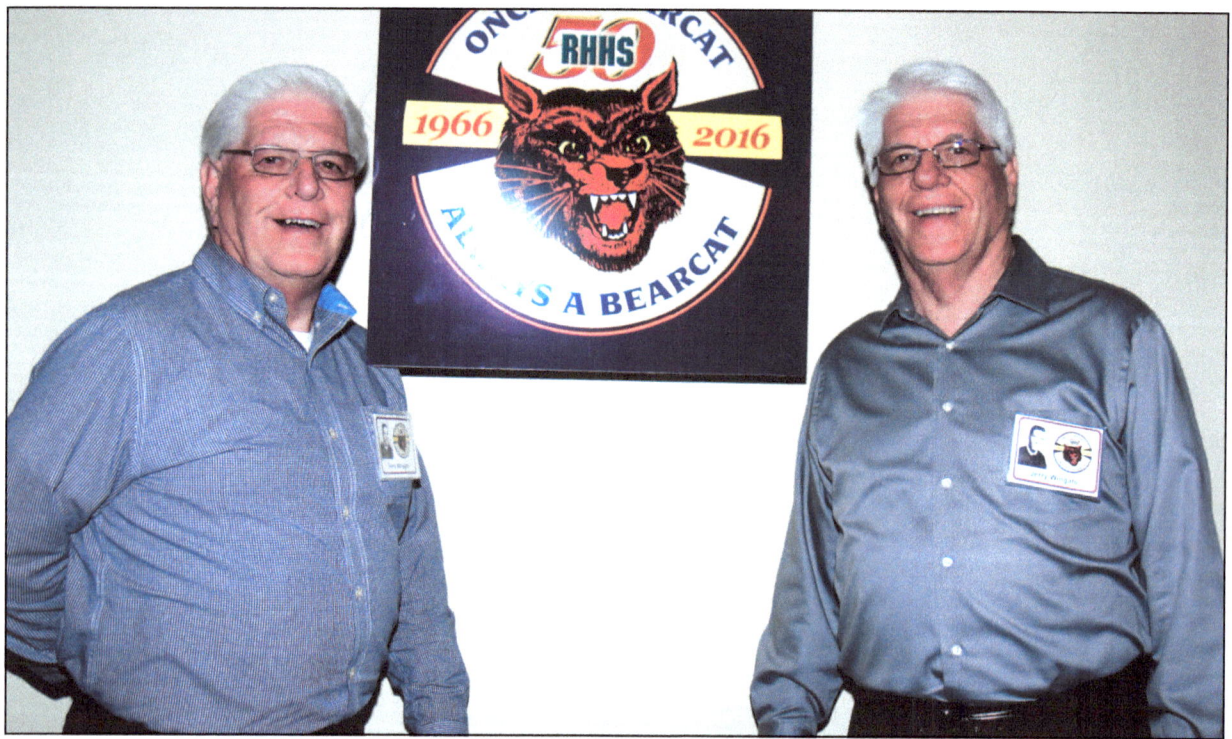

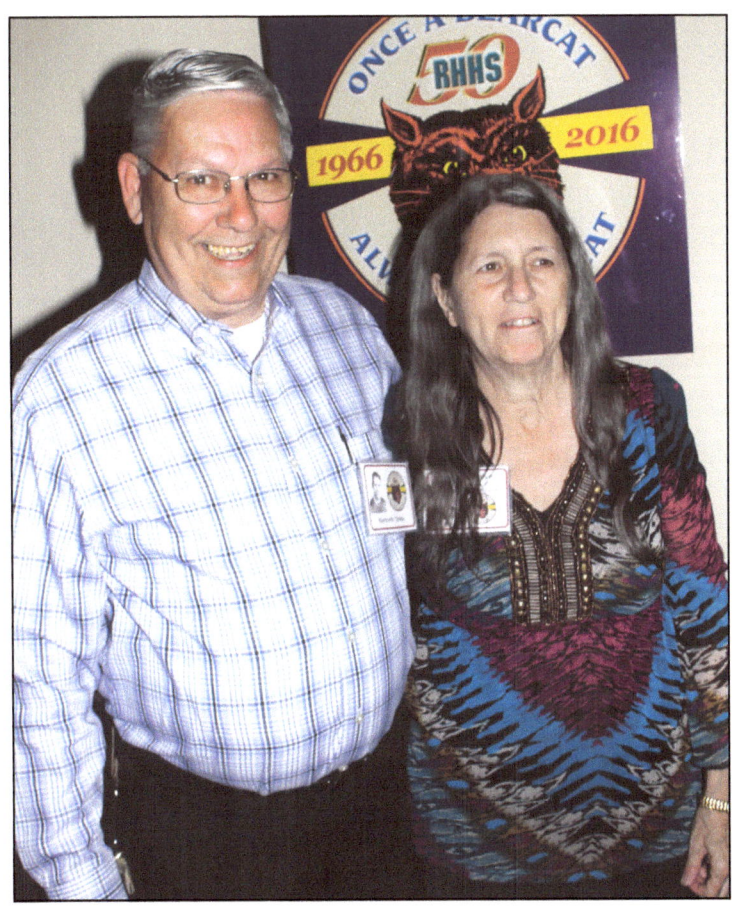

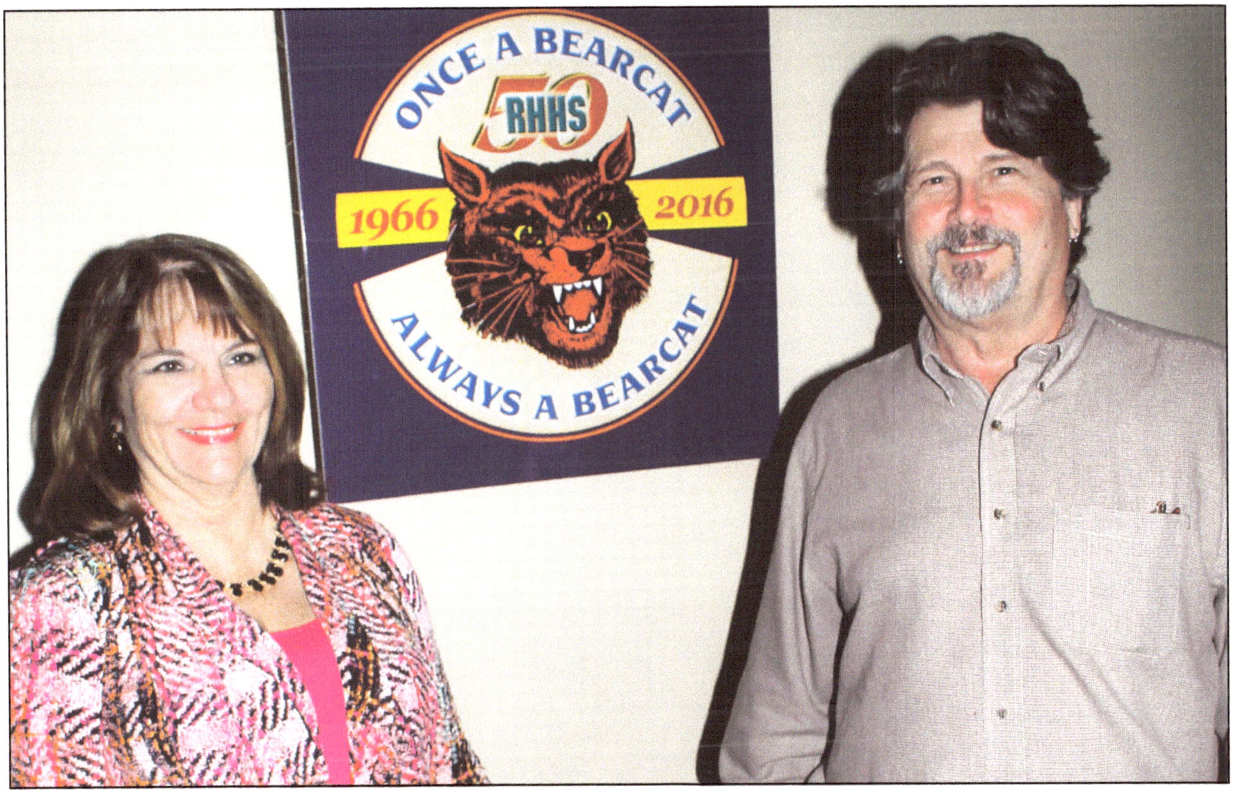

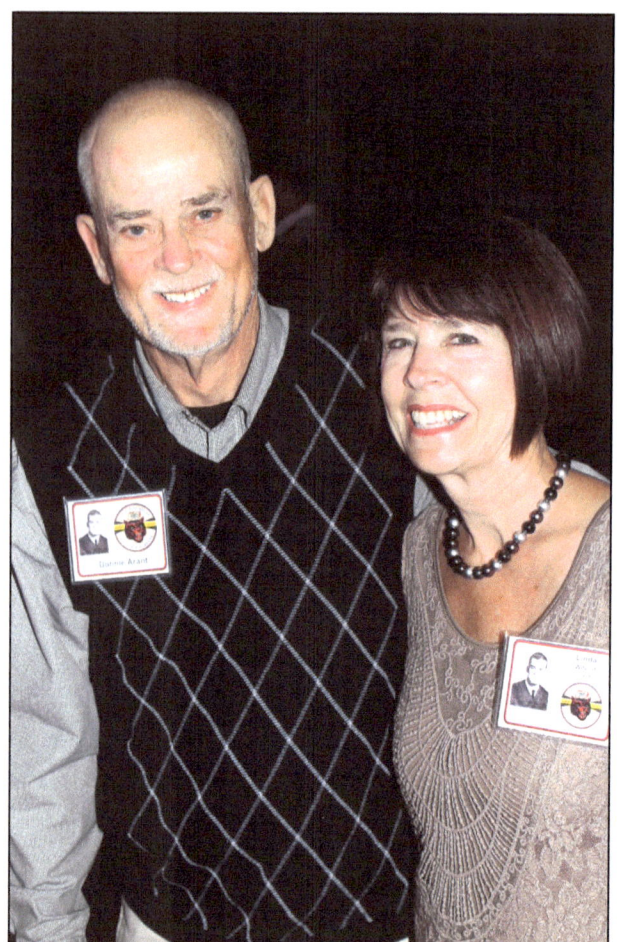

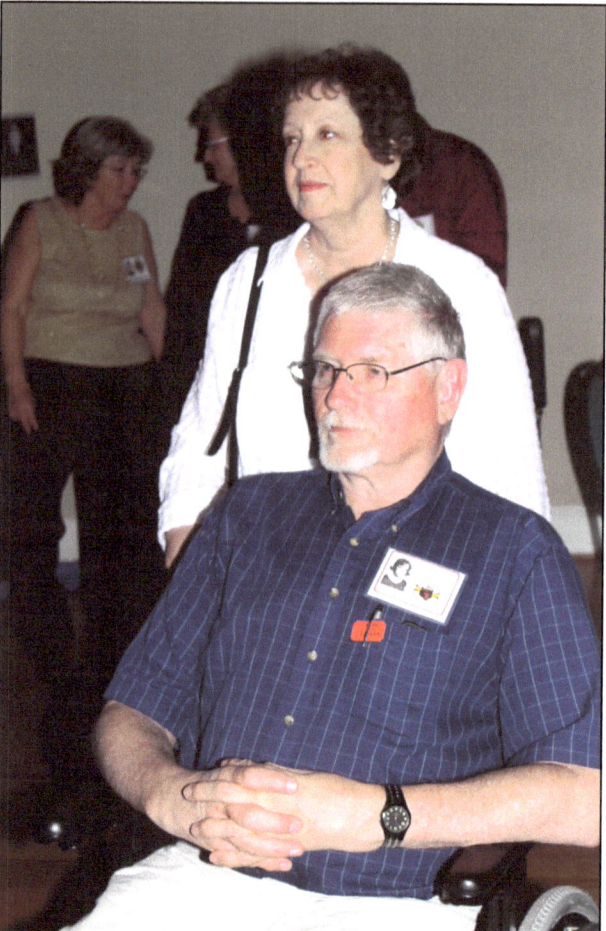

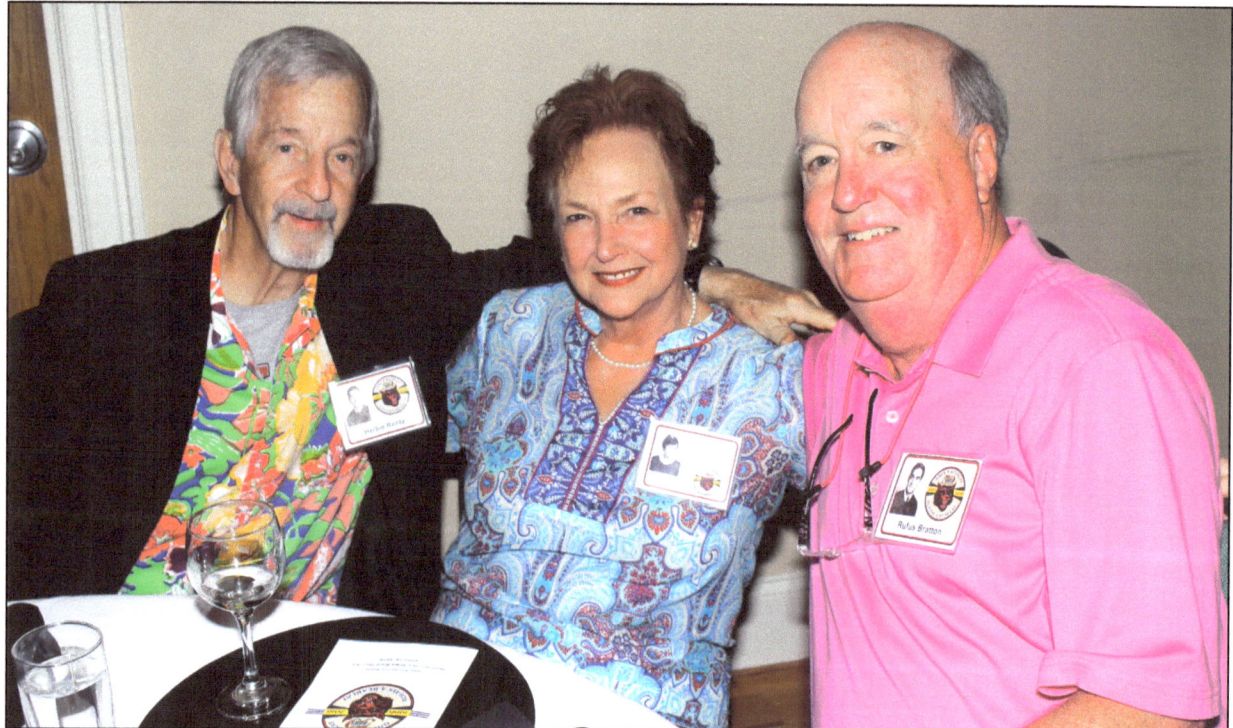

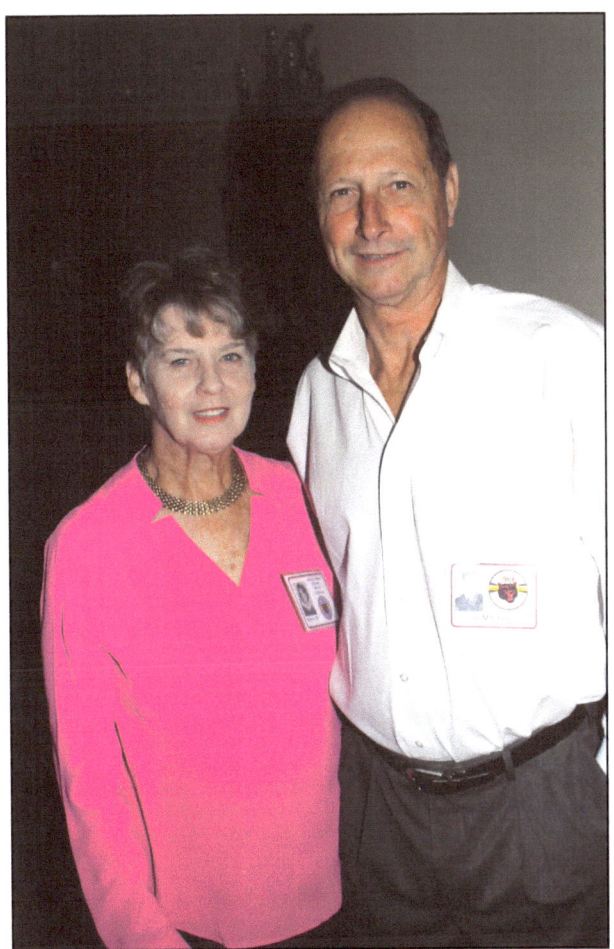

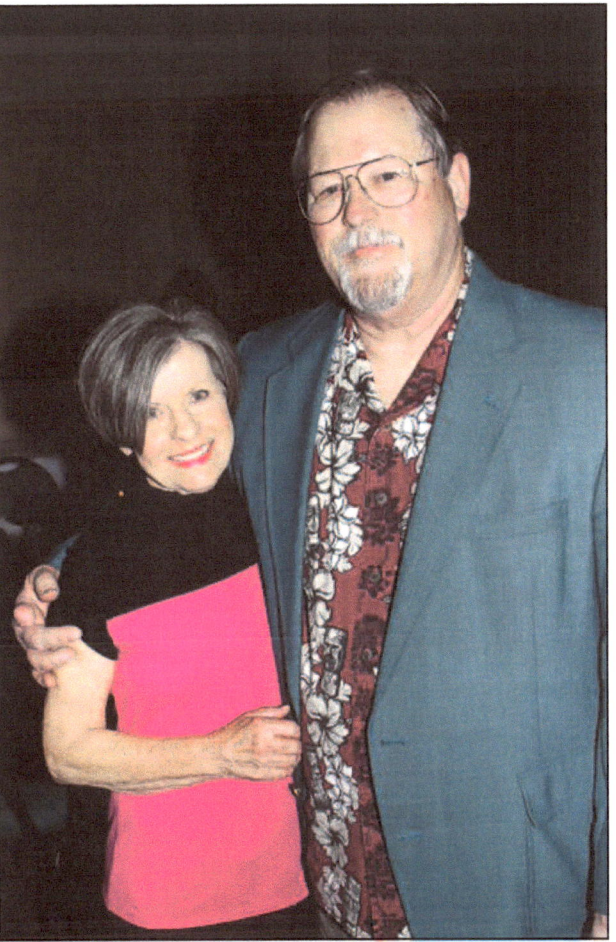

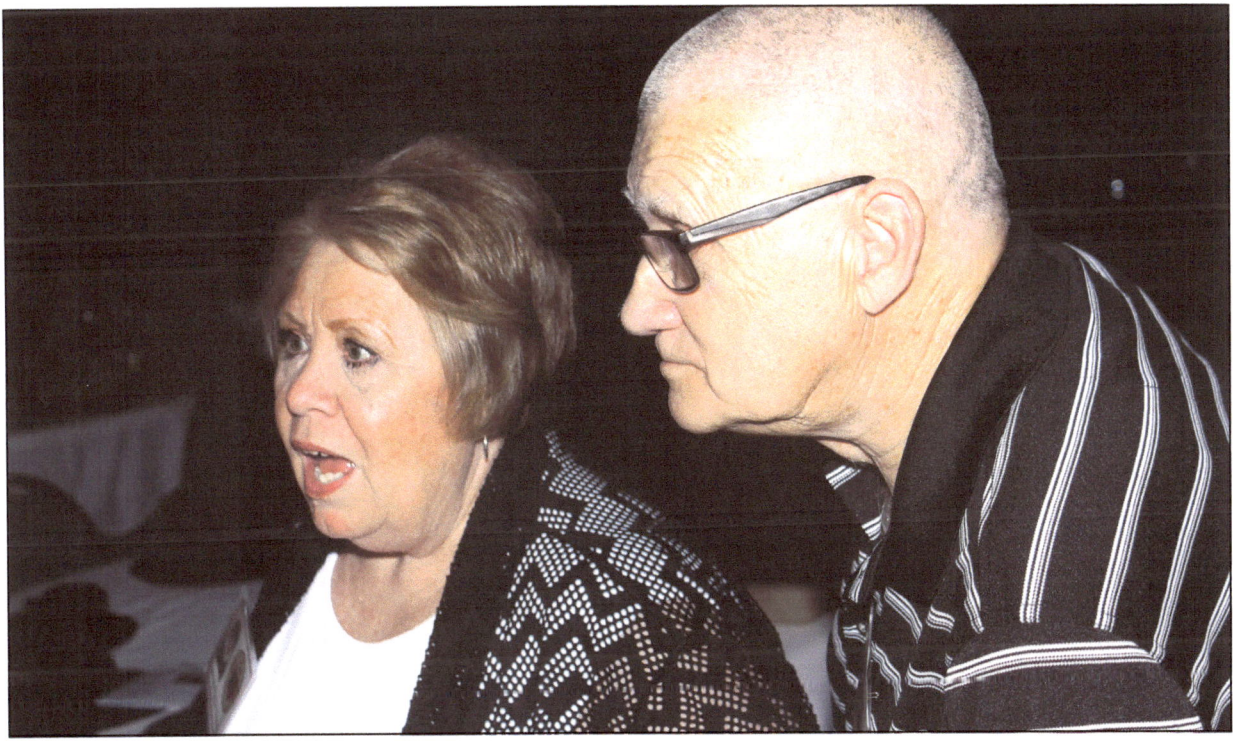

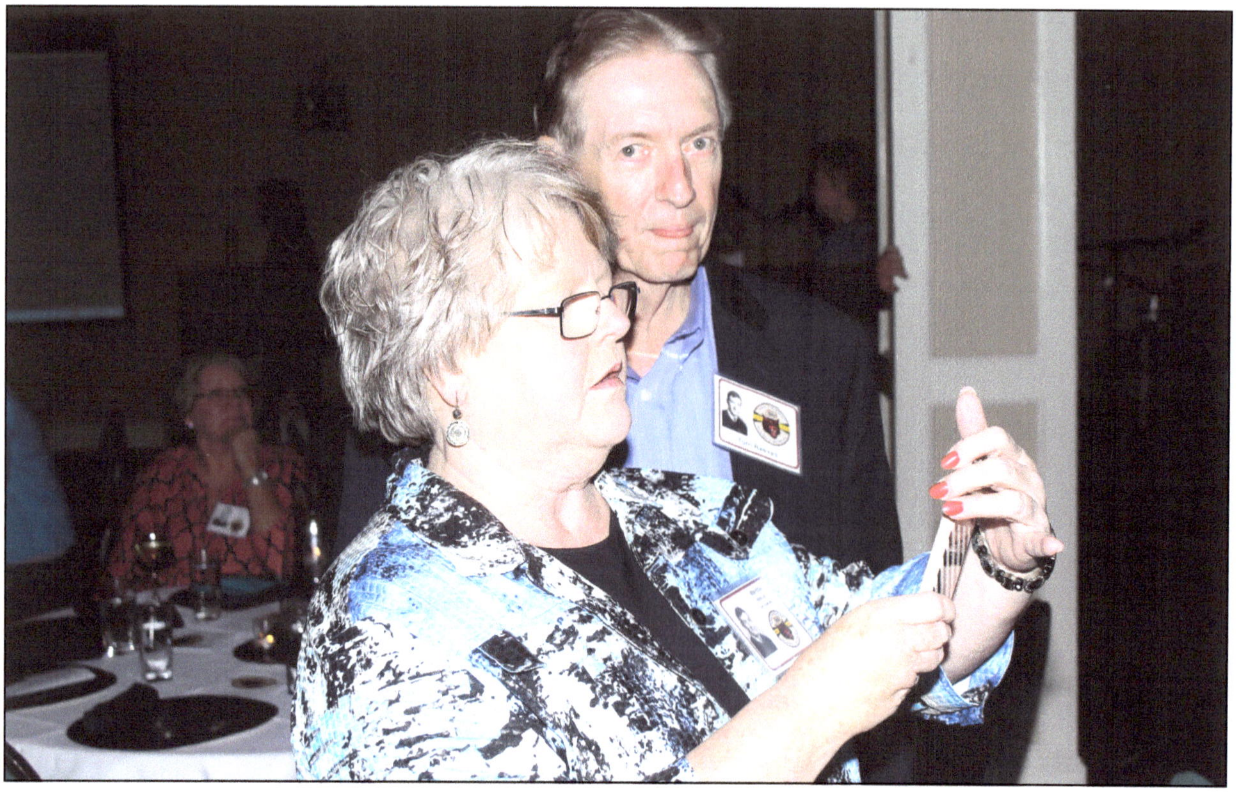

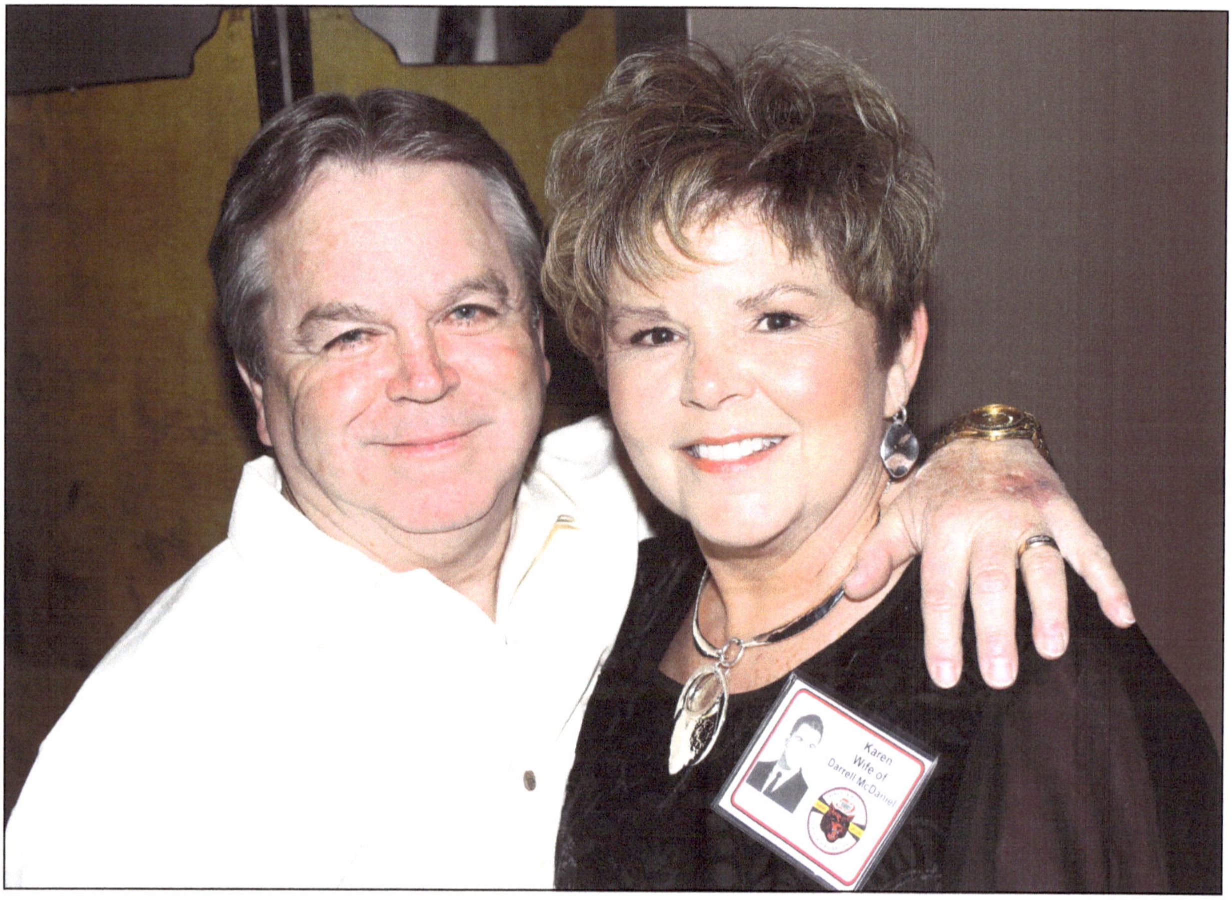
Karen
Wife of
Darrell McDaniel

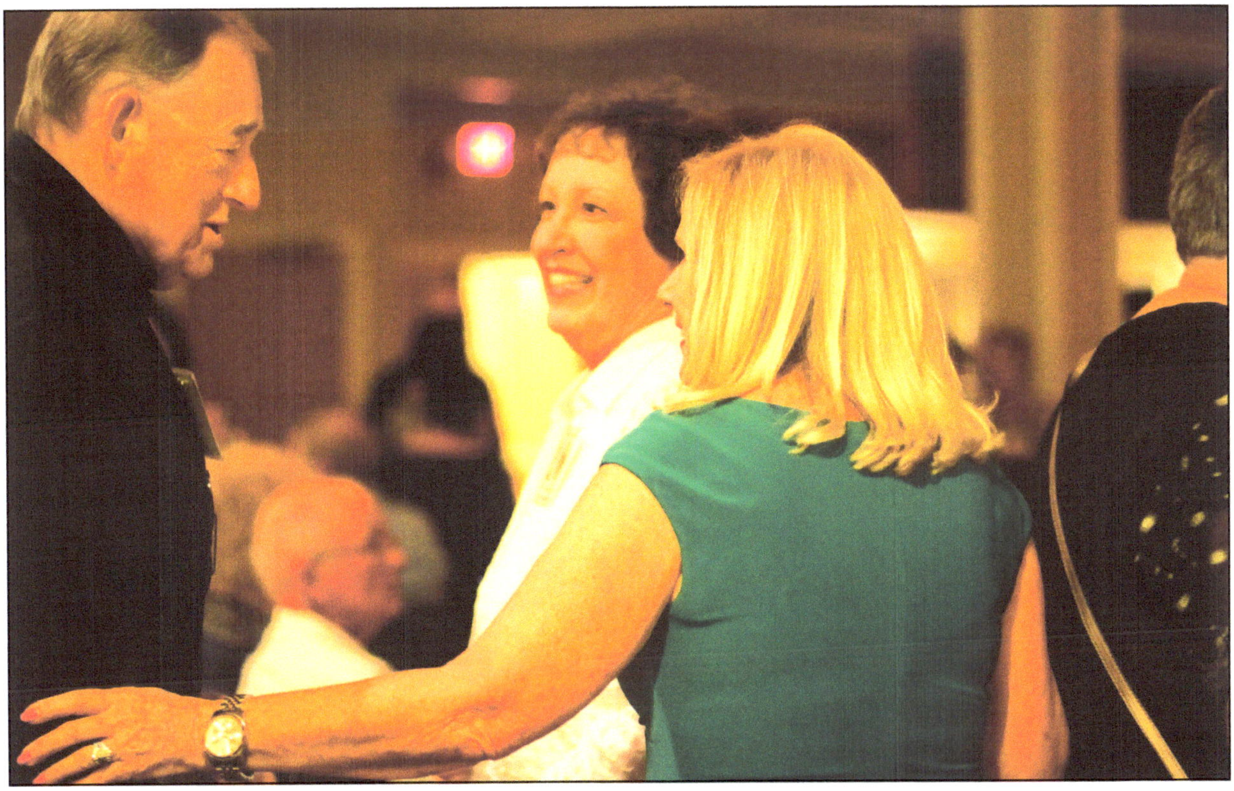

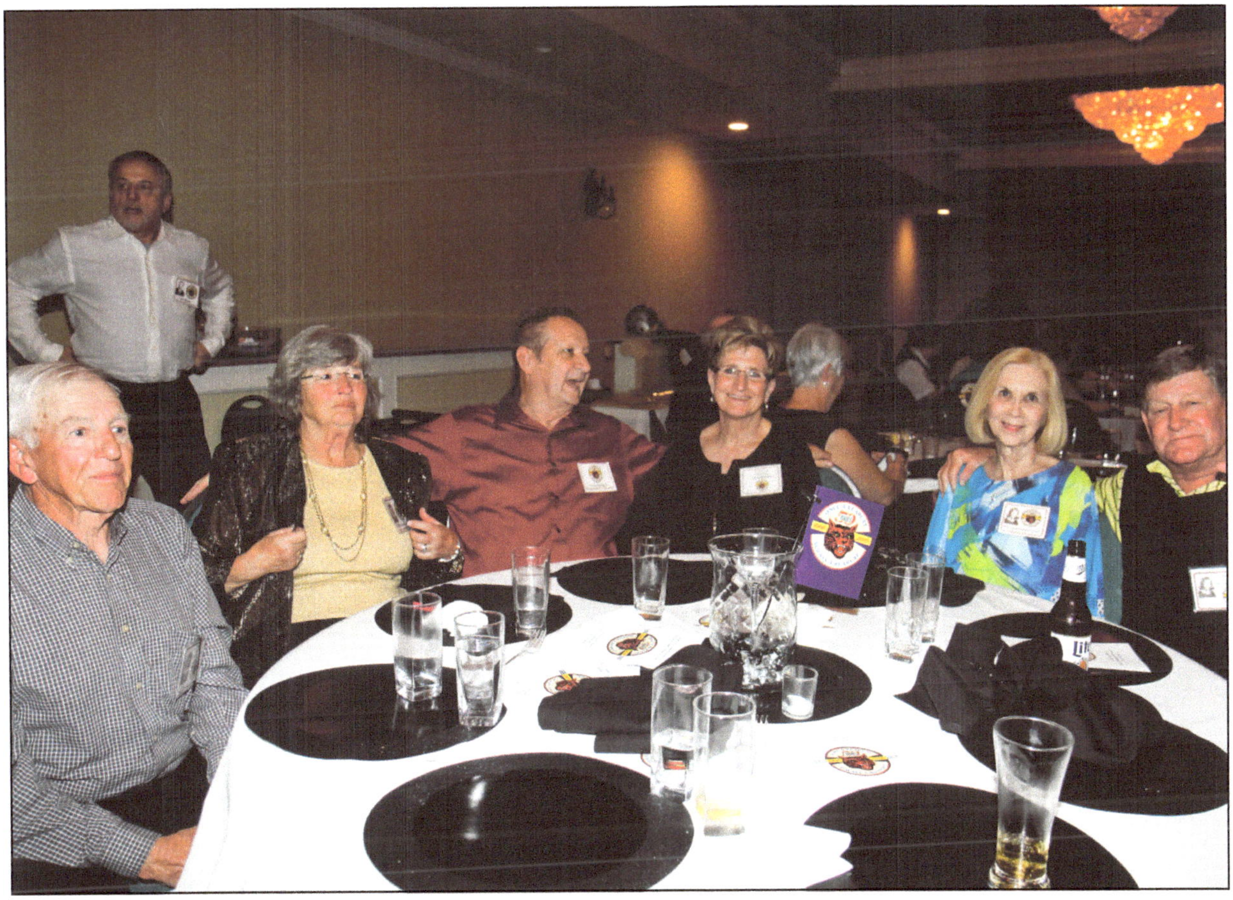

REUNION PHOTOS: OFFICIAL PHOTOS & CANDID SHOTS

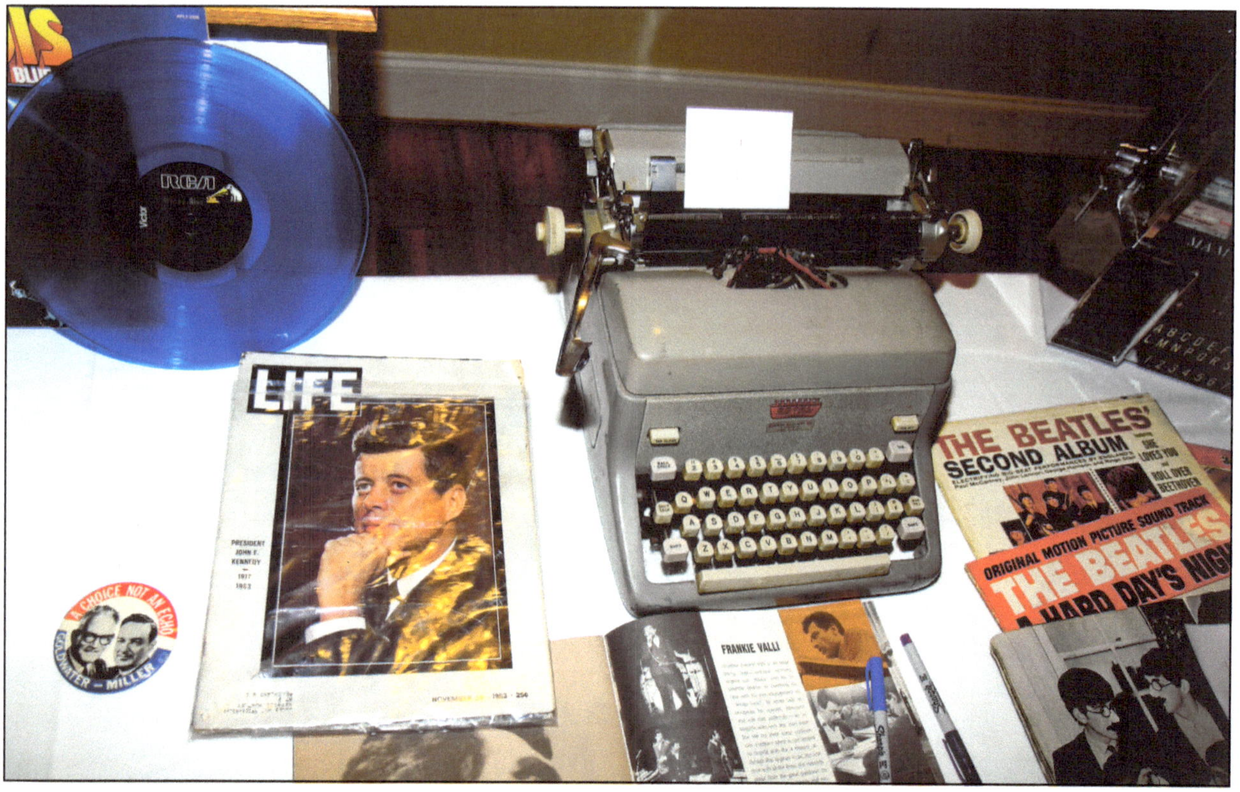
LIFE
PRESIDENT
JOHN F.
KENNEDY
1917
1963
A CHOICE NOT AN ECHO
GOLDWATER — MILLER
THE BEATLES'
SECOND ALBUM
SHE LOVES YOU
ROLL OVER BEETHOVEN
ORIGINAL MOTION PICTURE SOUND TRACK
THE BEATLES
A HARD DAY'S NIGH
FRANKIE VALLI
RCA

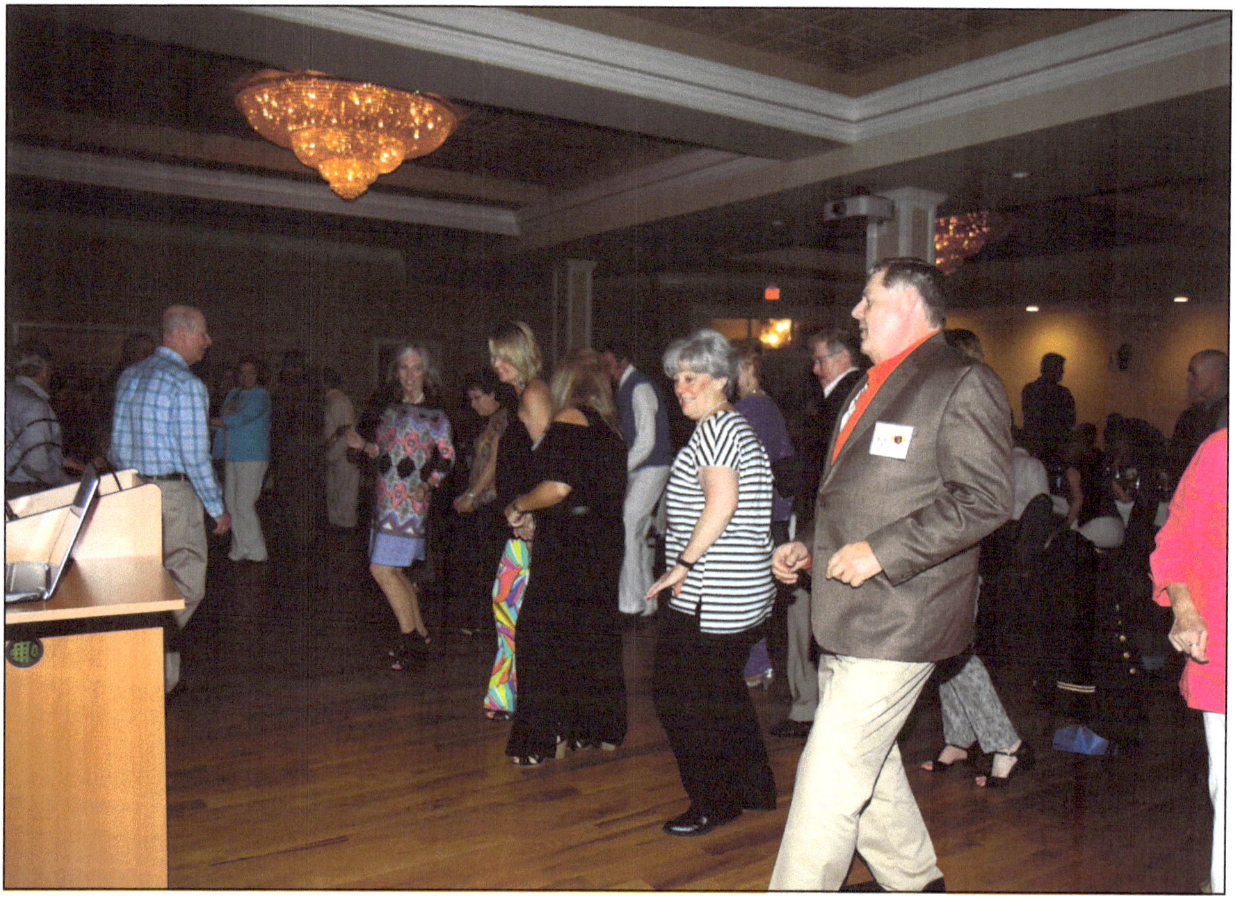

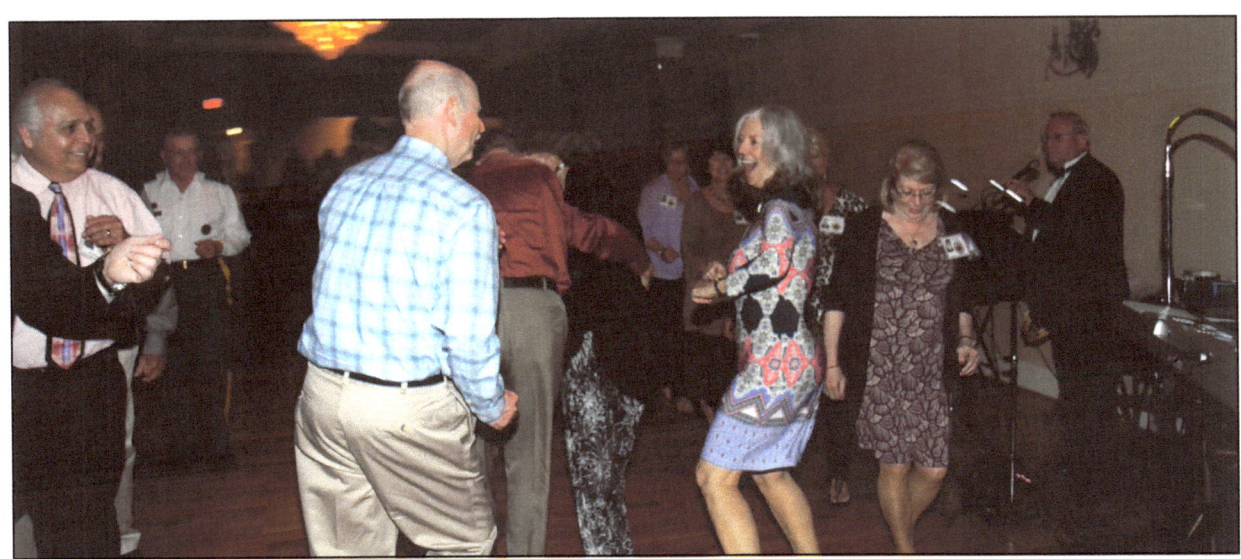

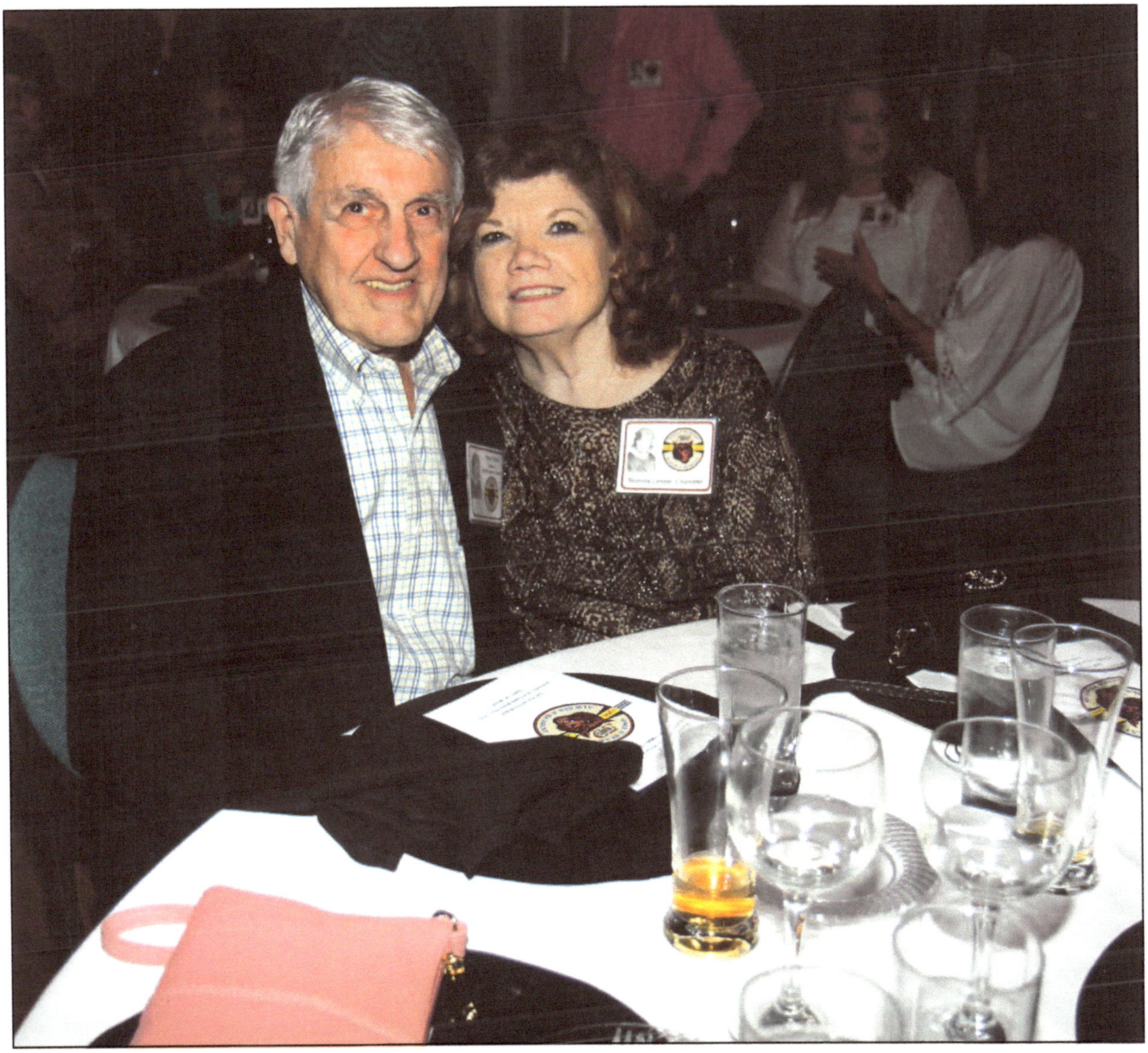

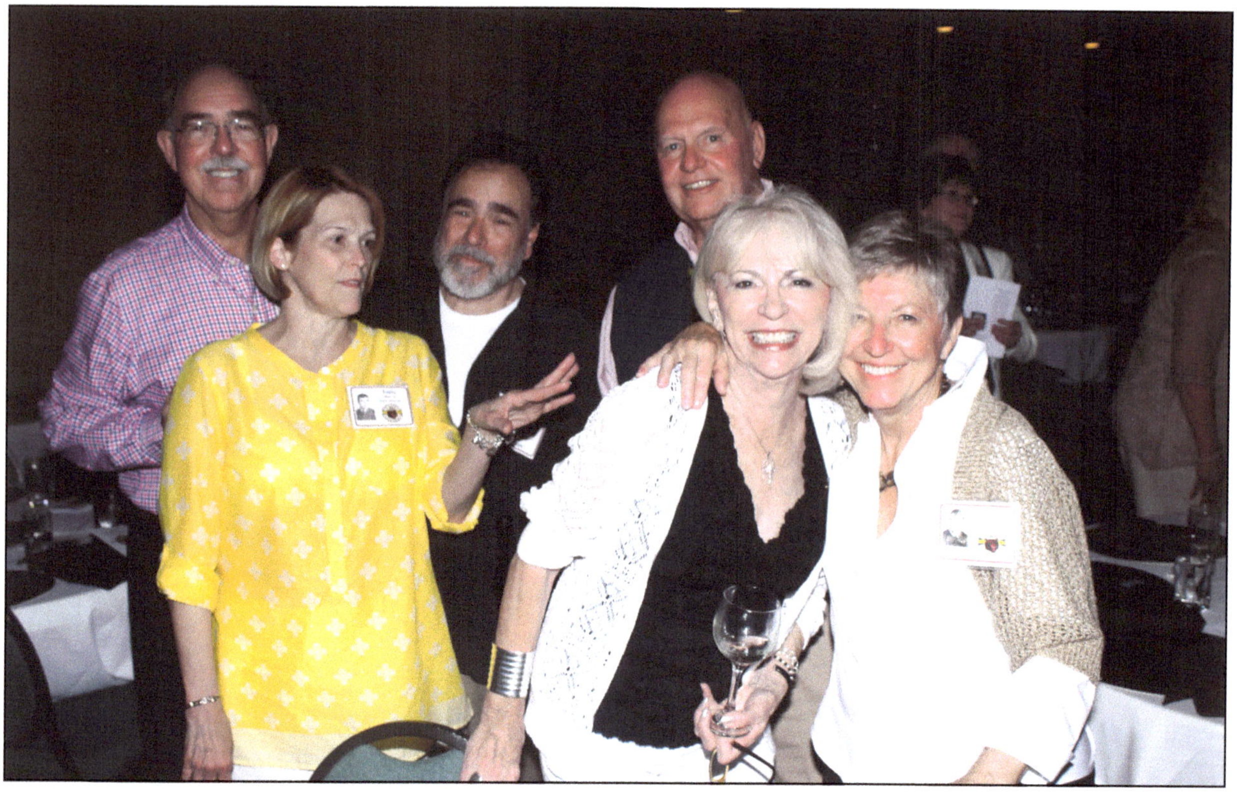

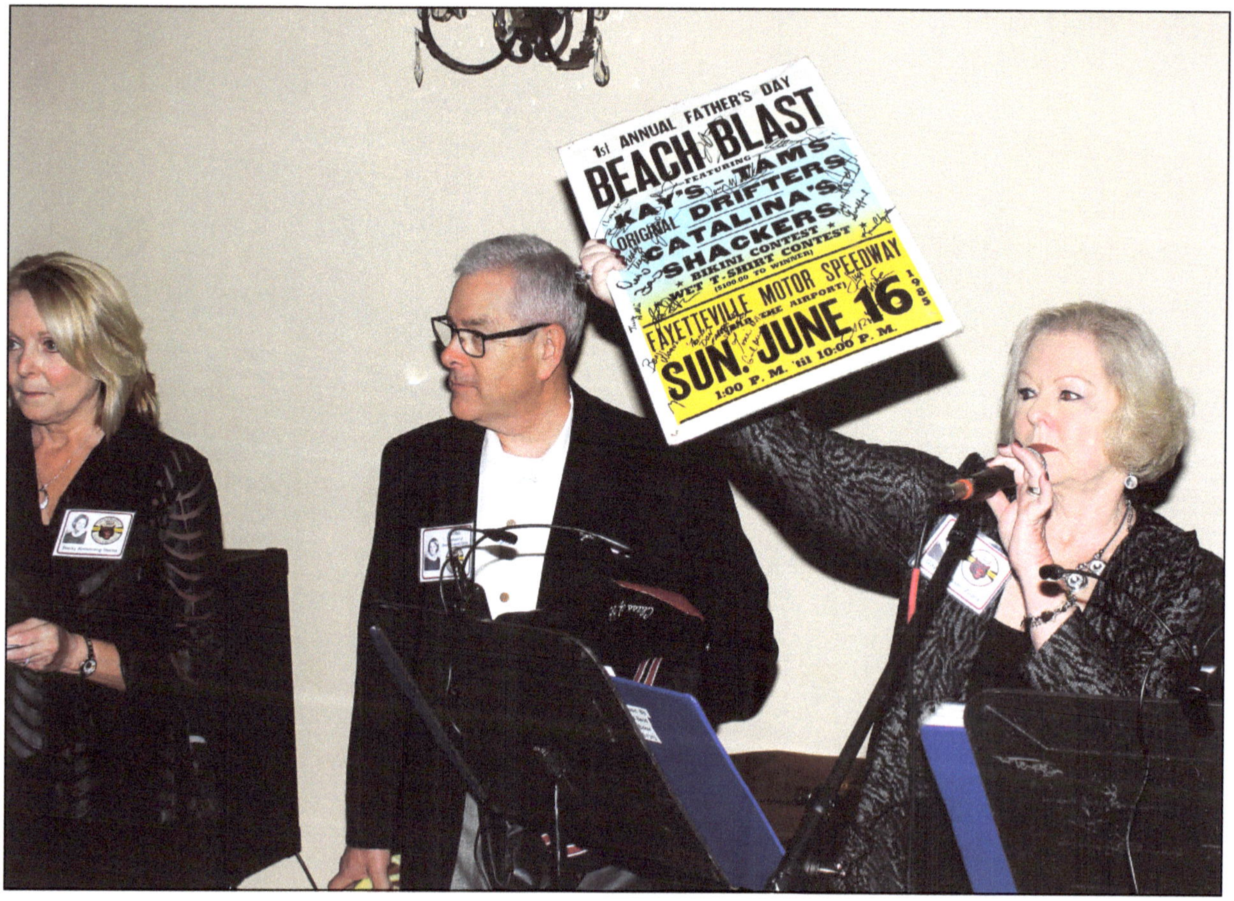

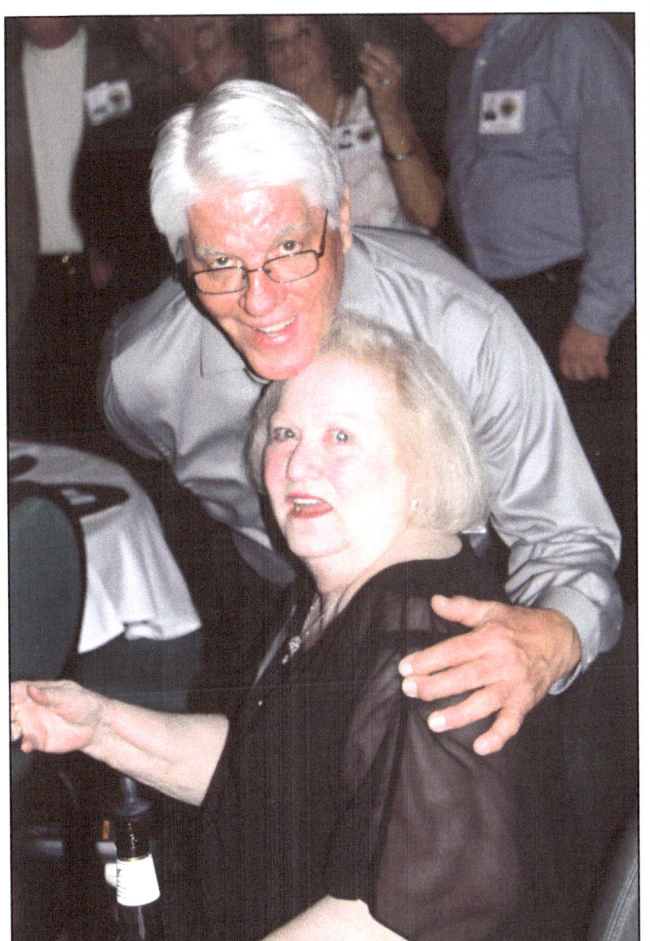

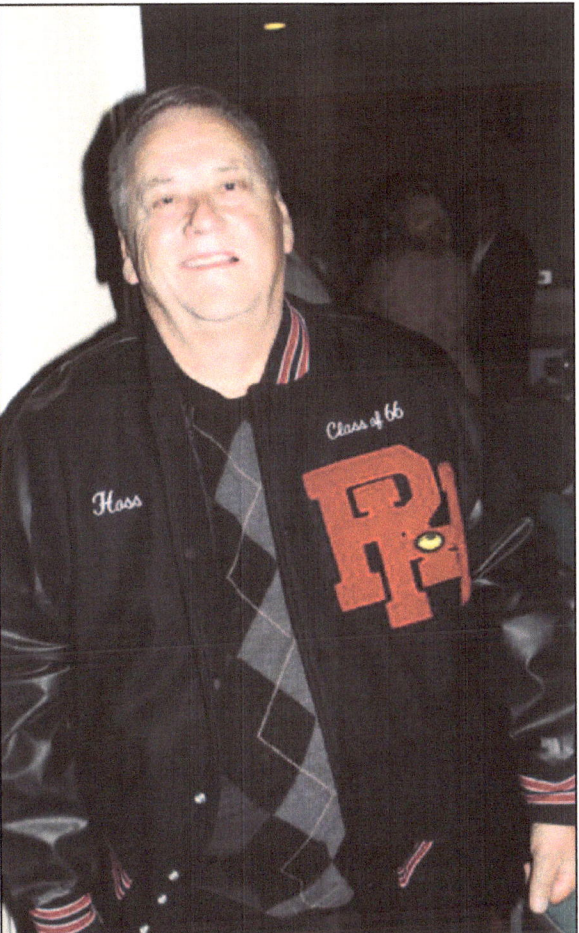

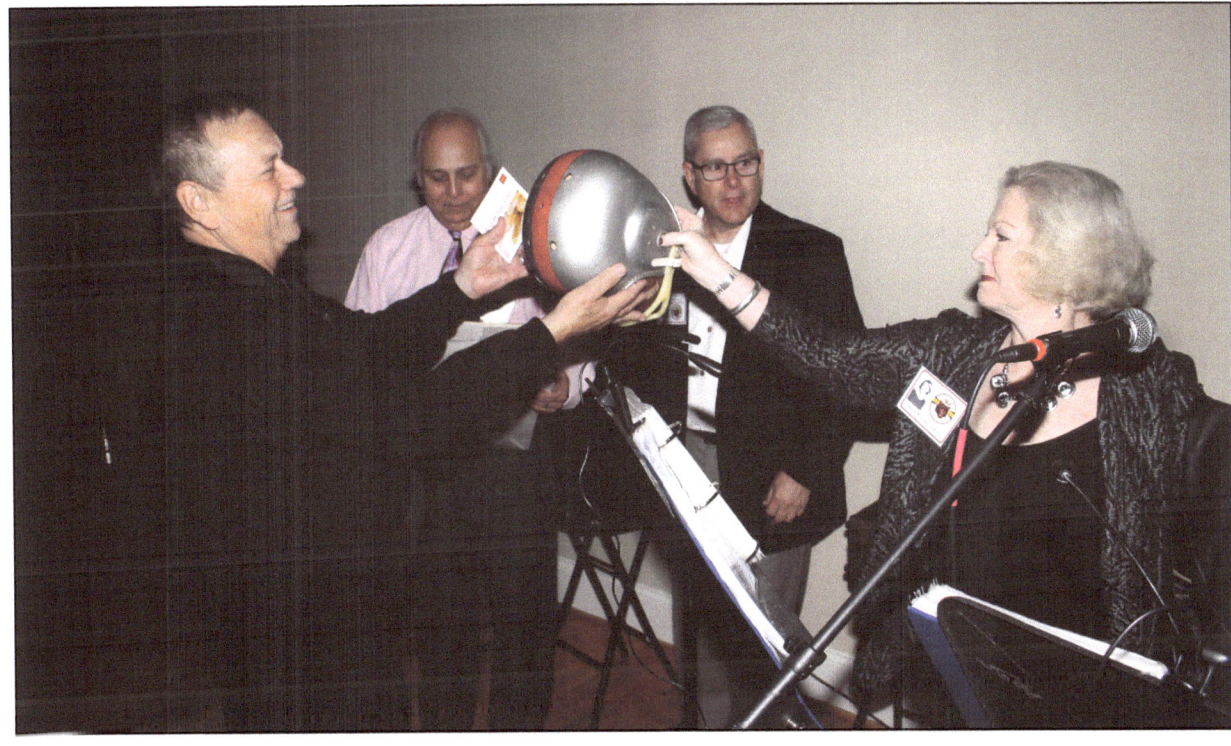

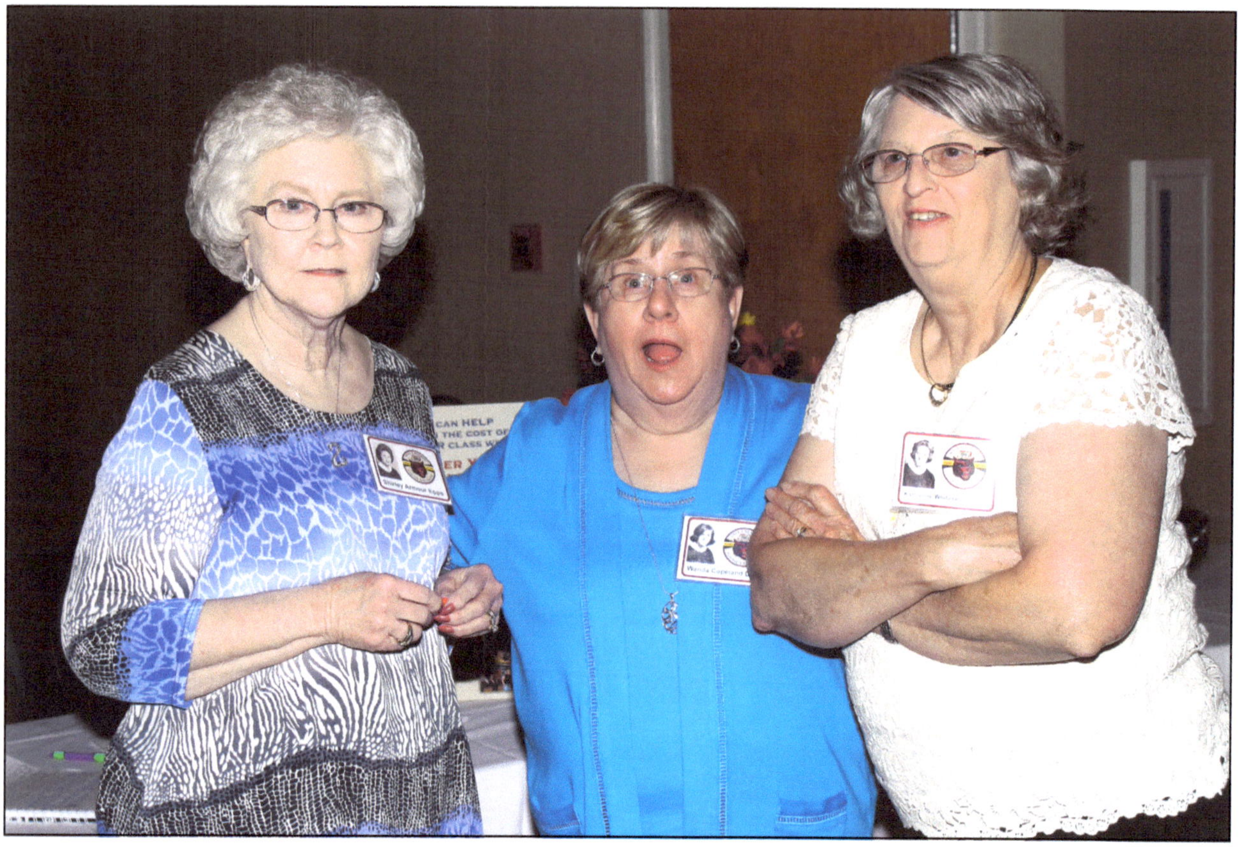

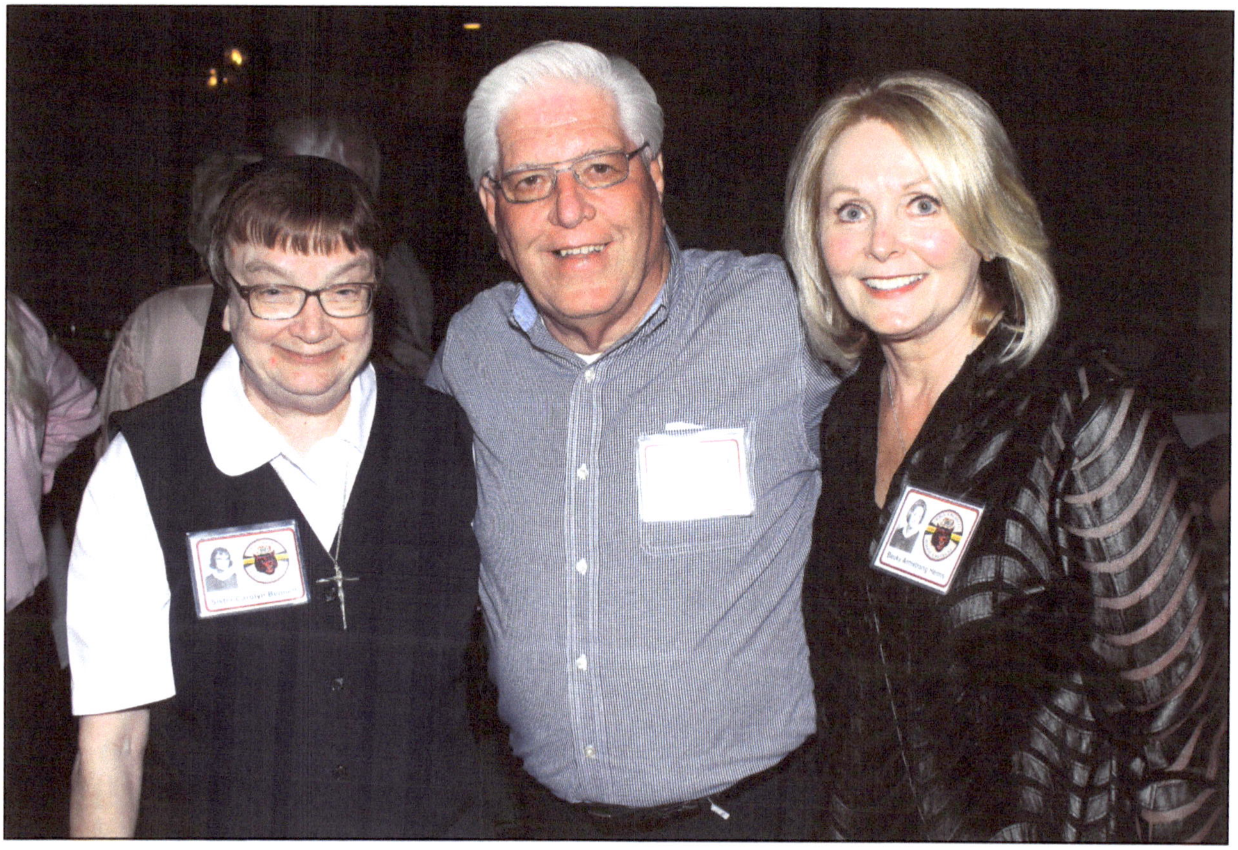

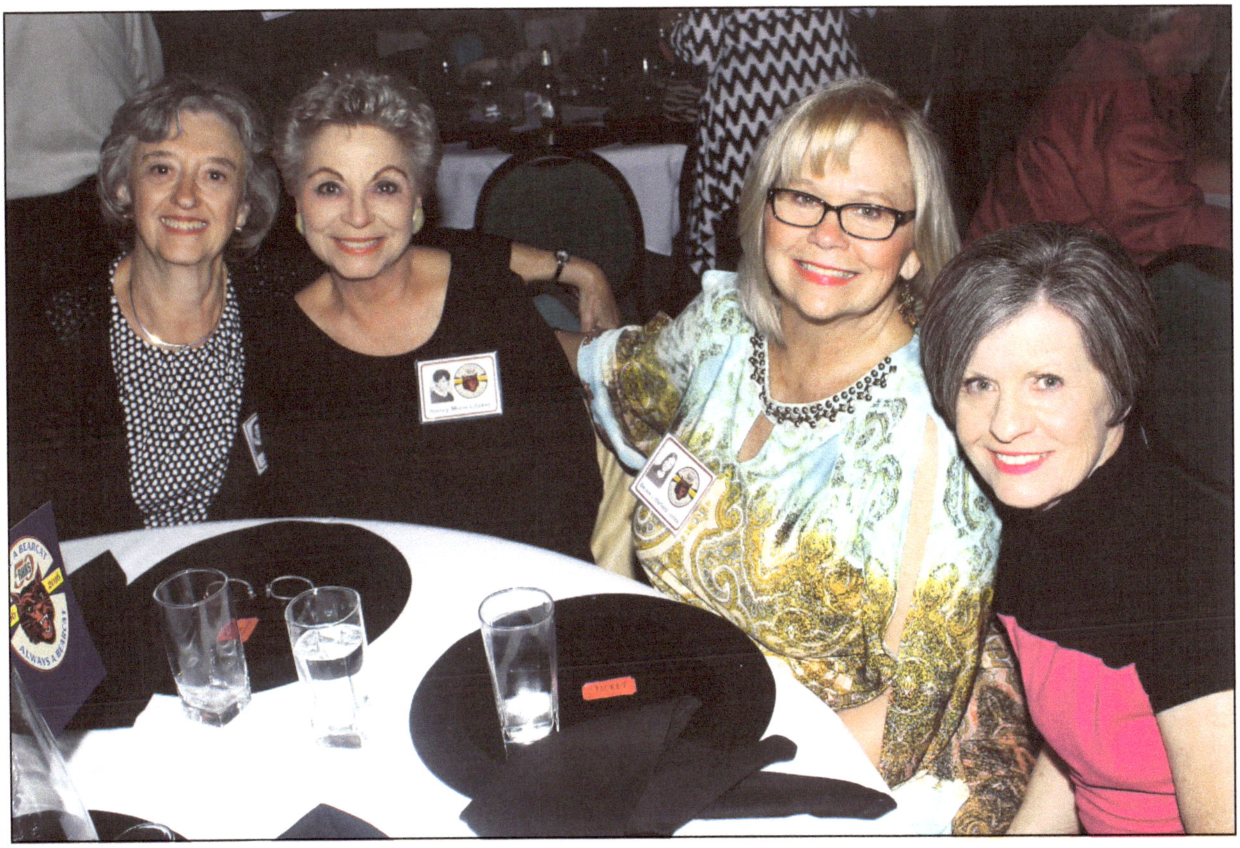

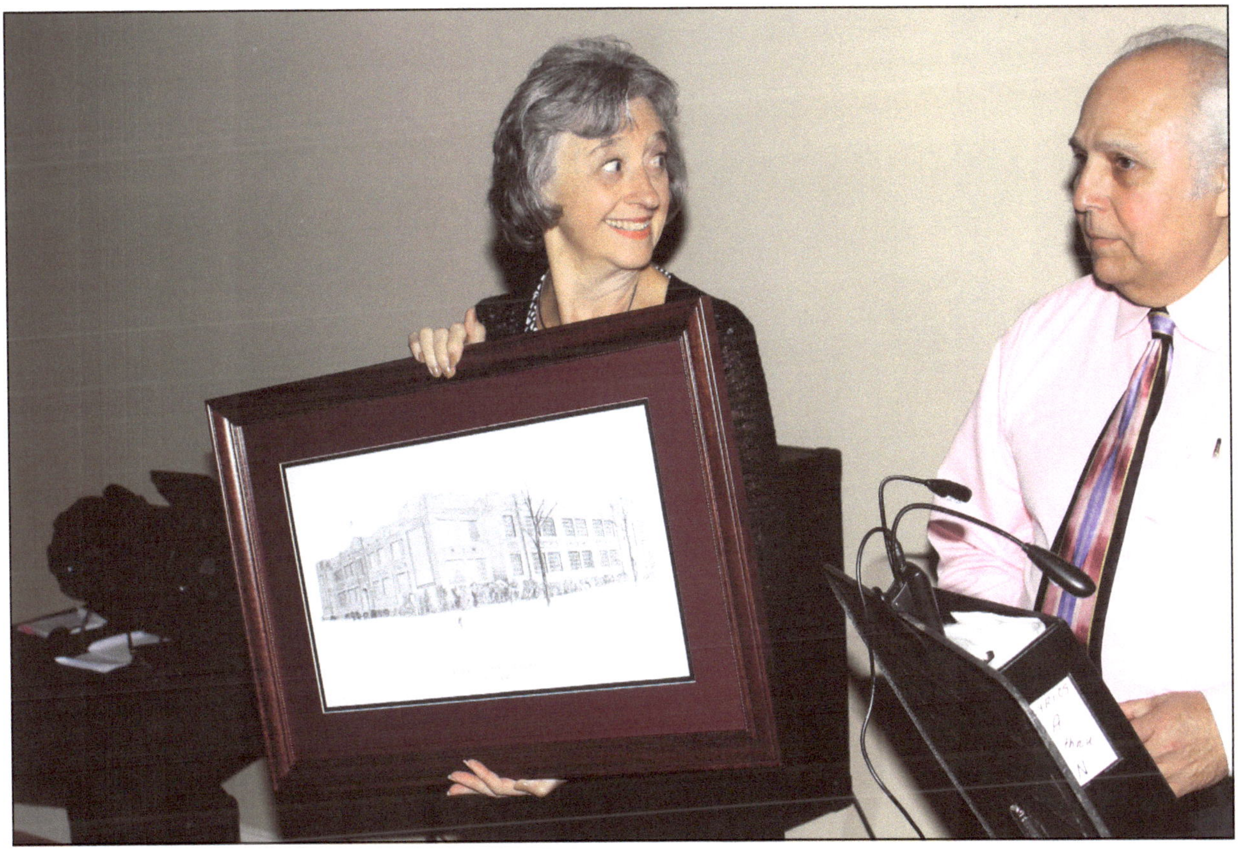

REUNION PHOTOS: OFFICIAL PHOTOS & CANDID SHOTS

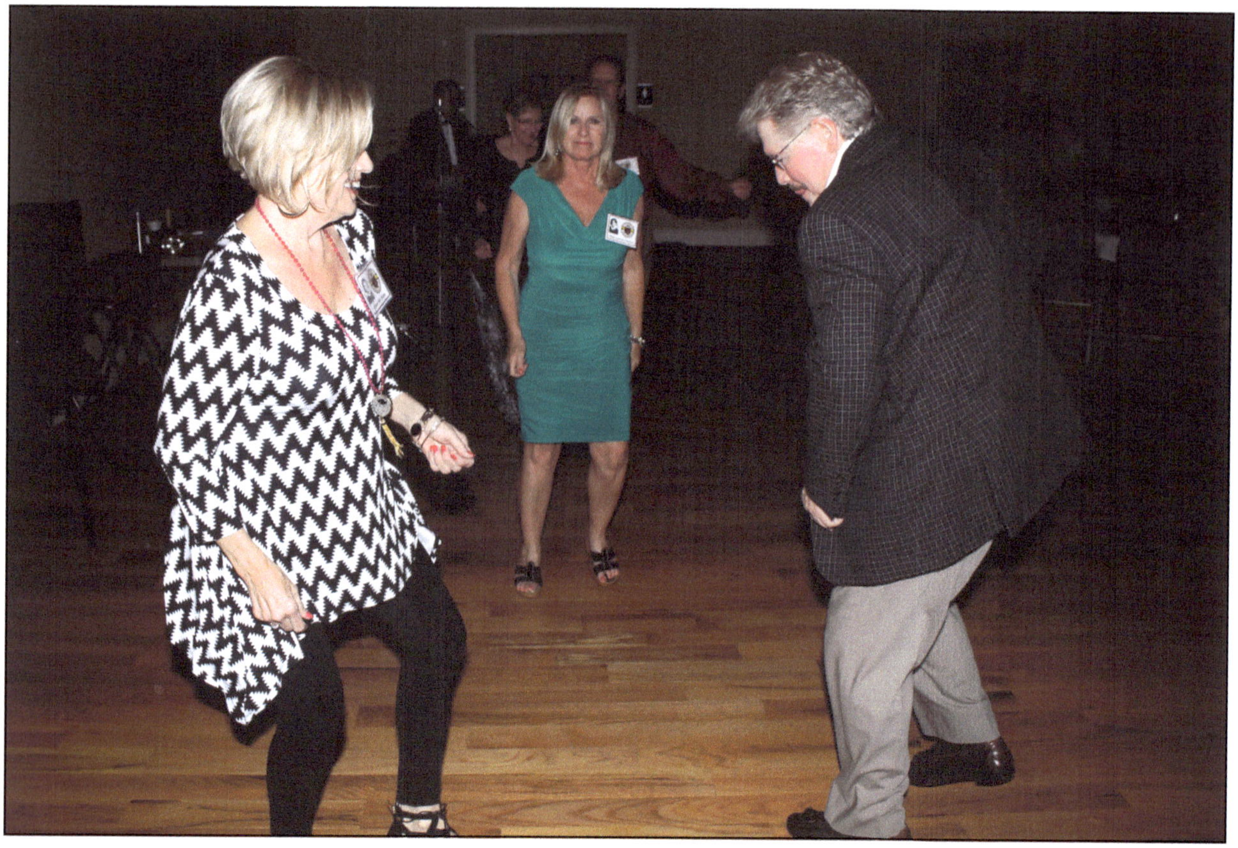

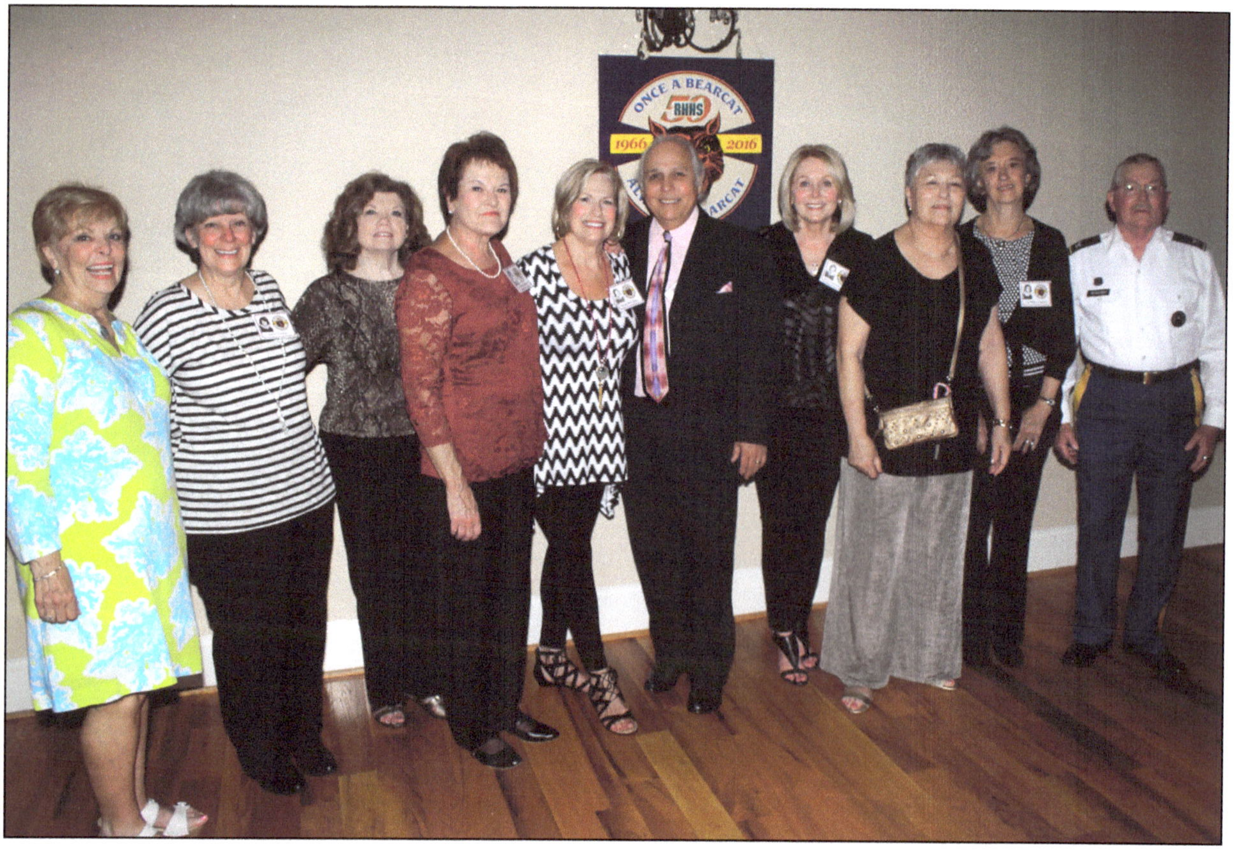
ONCE A BEARCAT
RHHS
1966
2016

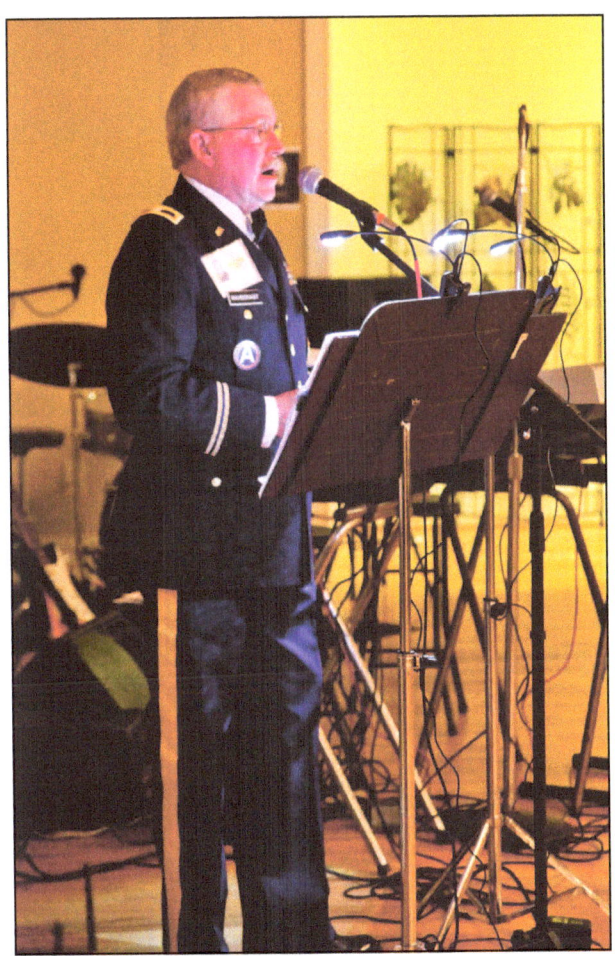

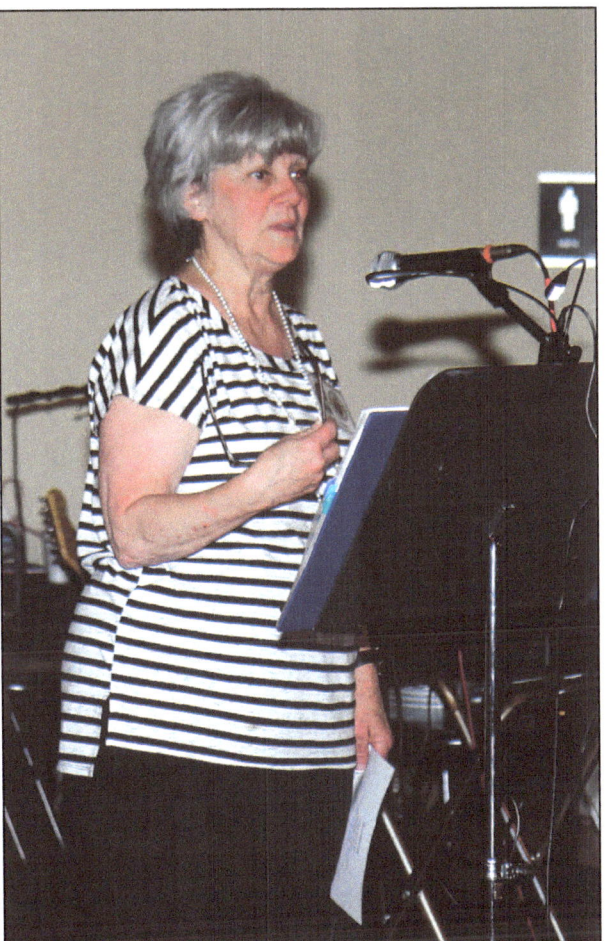

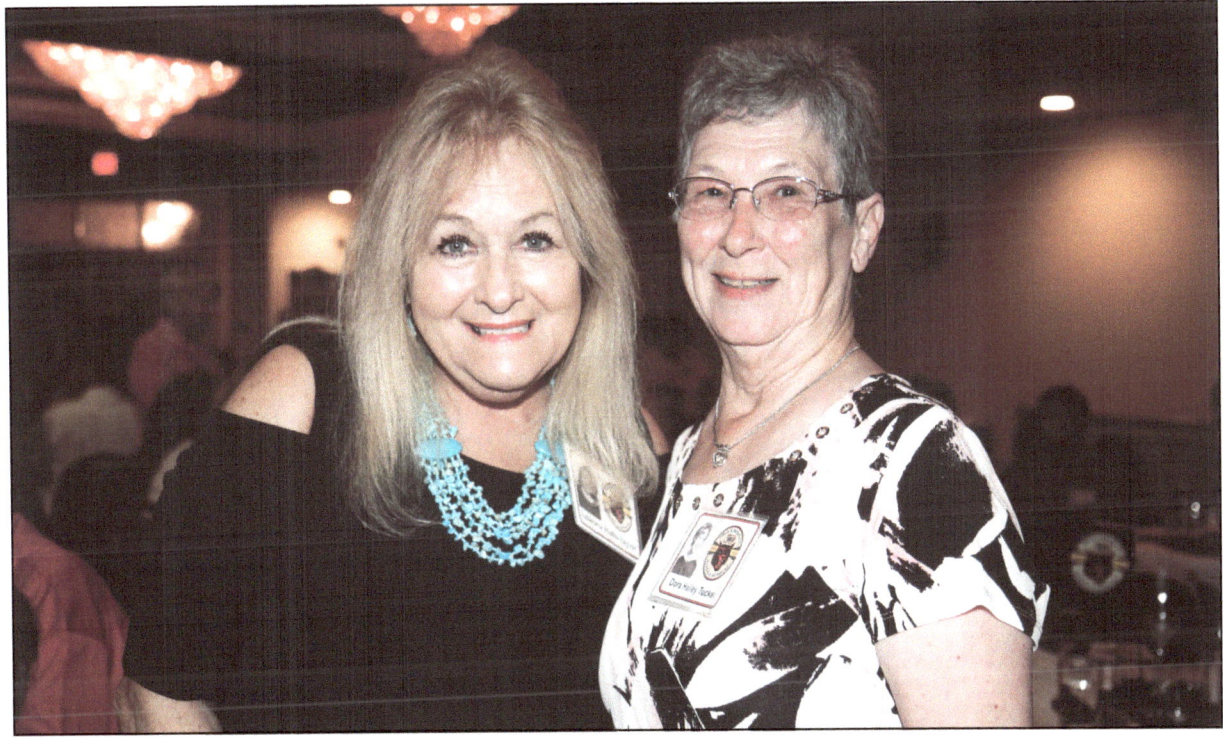

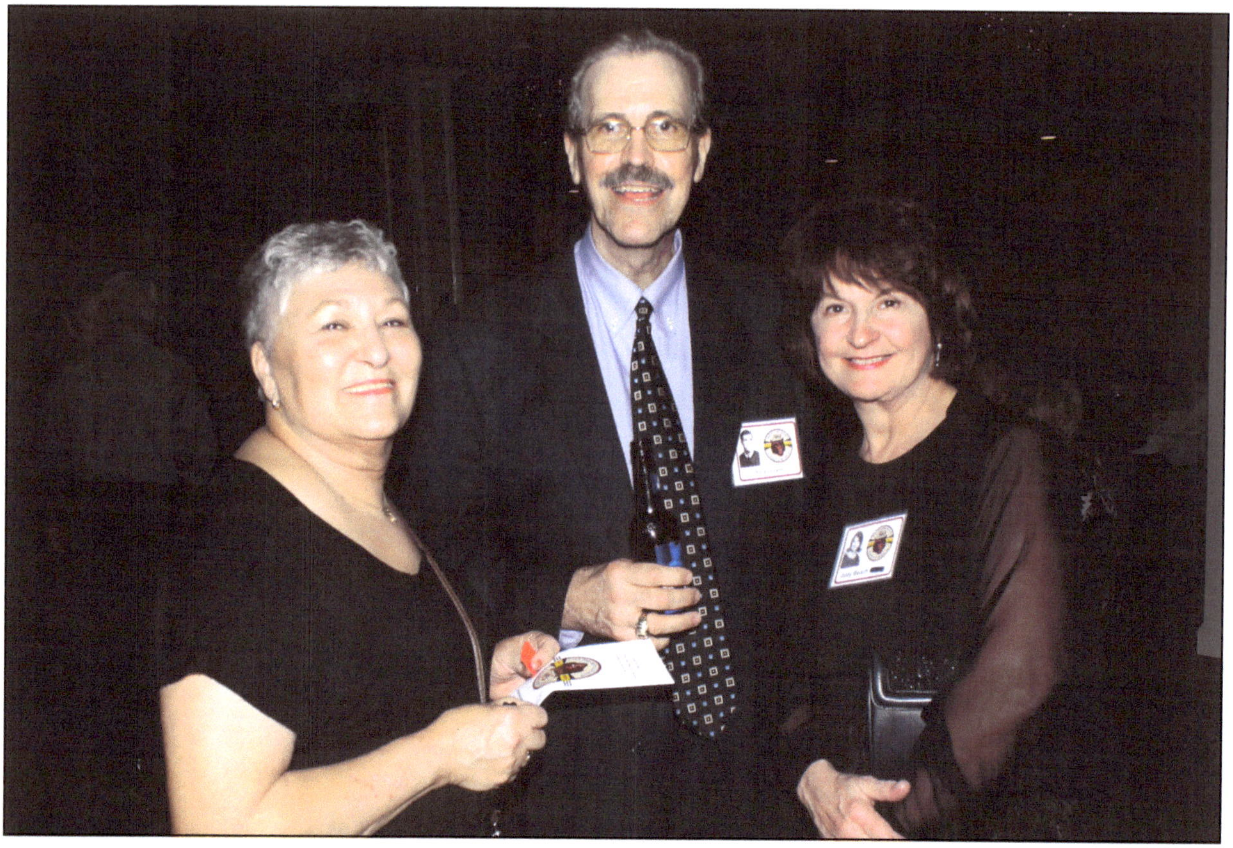

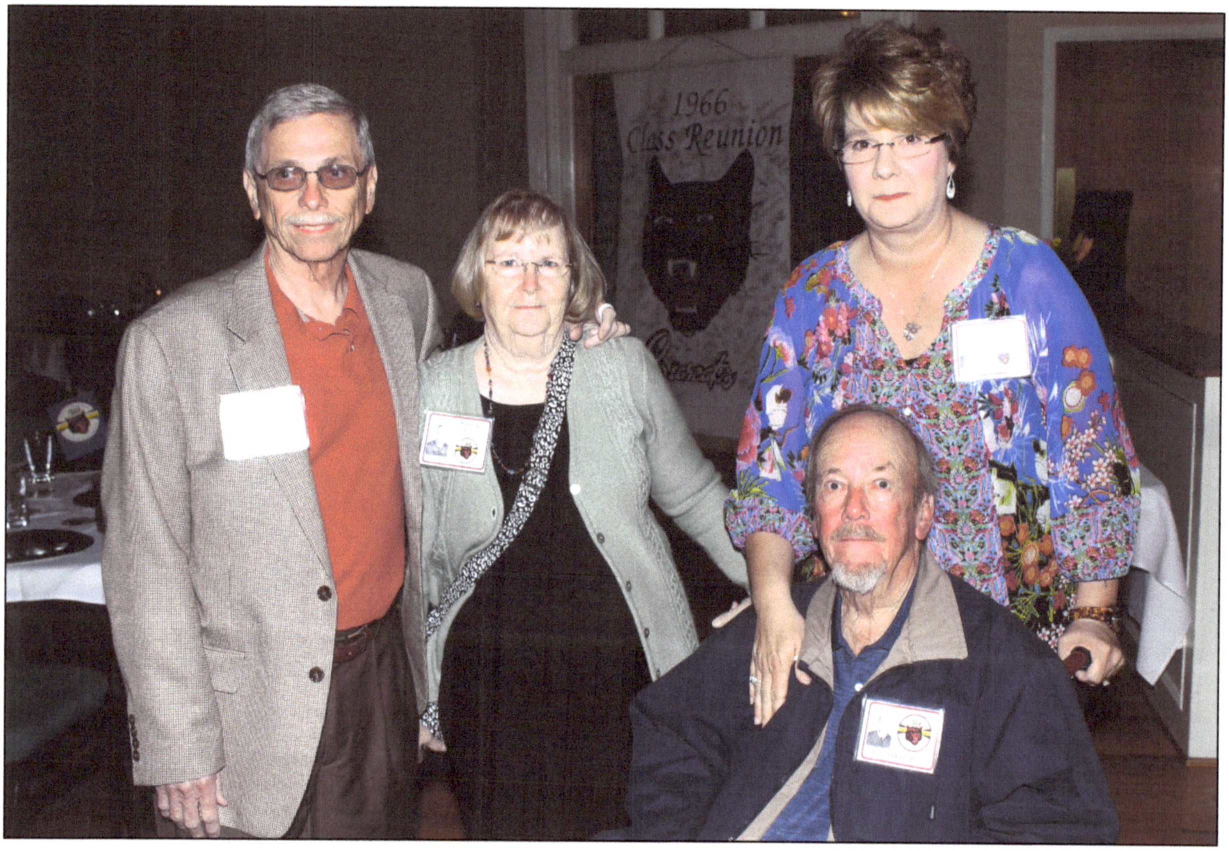
1966
Class Reunion

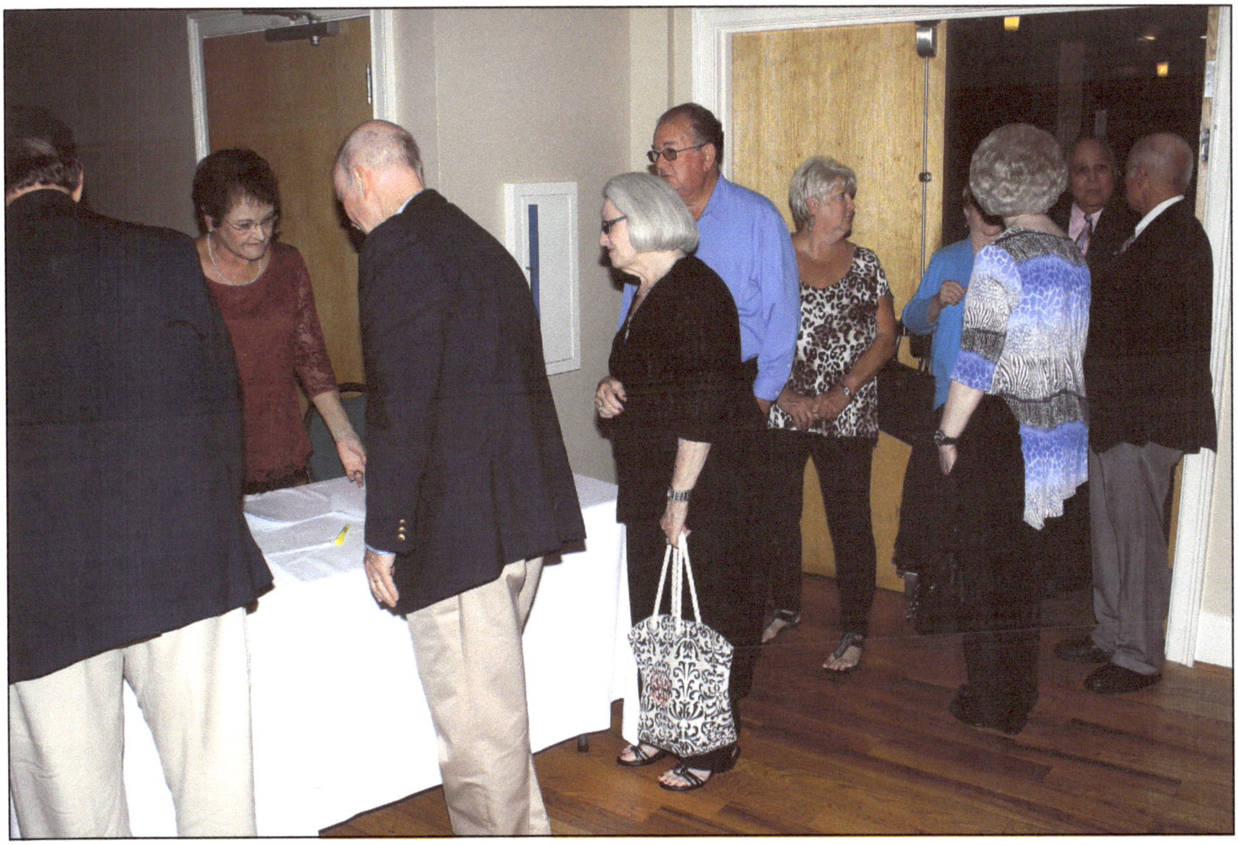

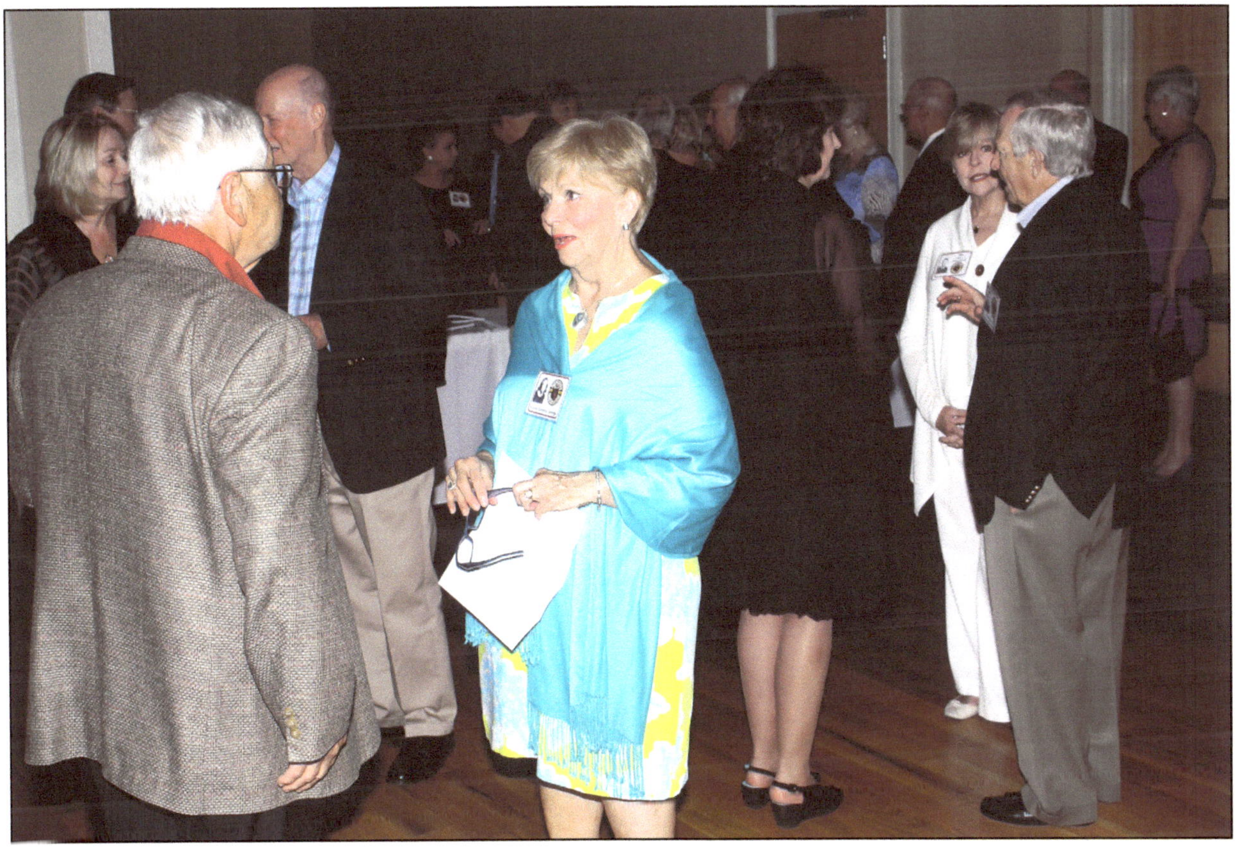

REUNION PHOTOS: OFFICIAL PHOTOS & CANDID SHOTS

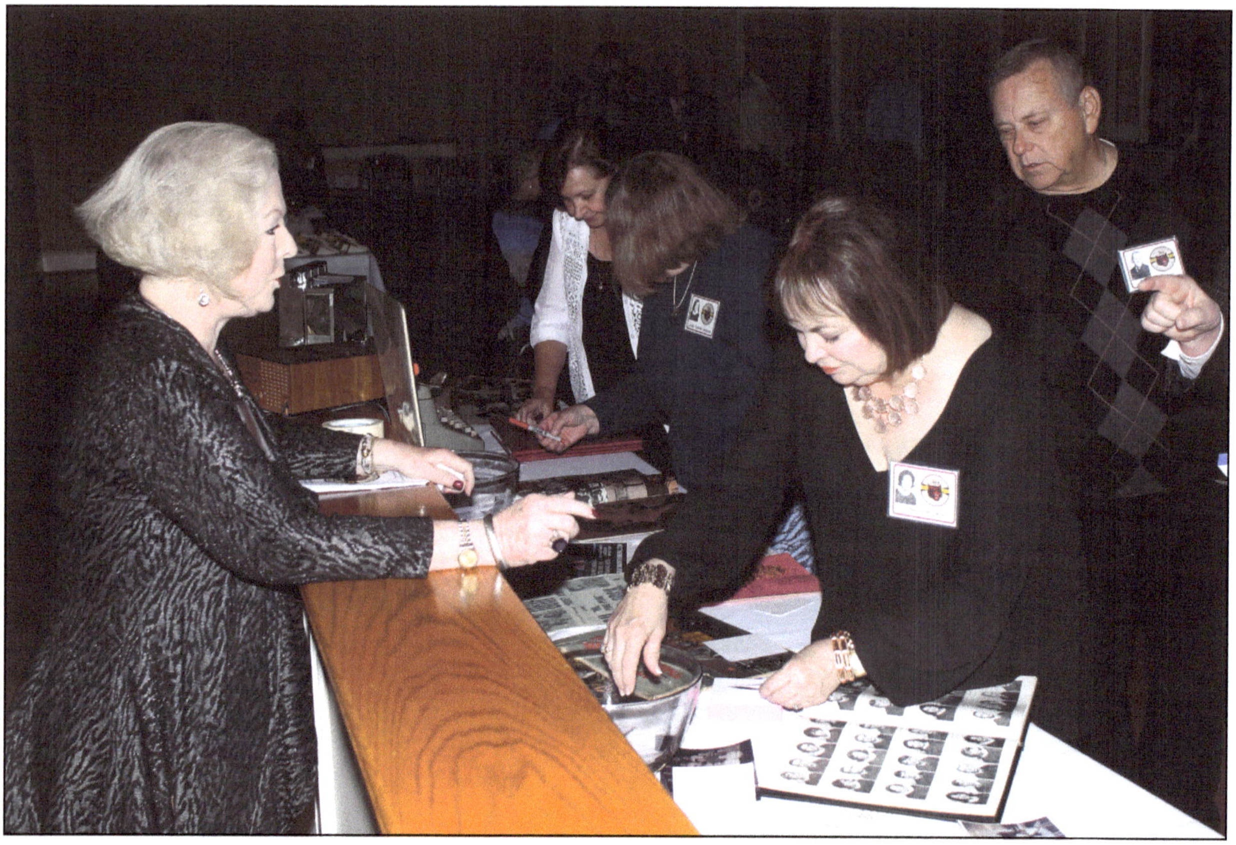

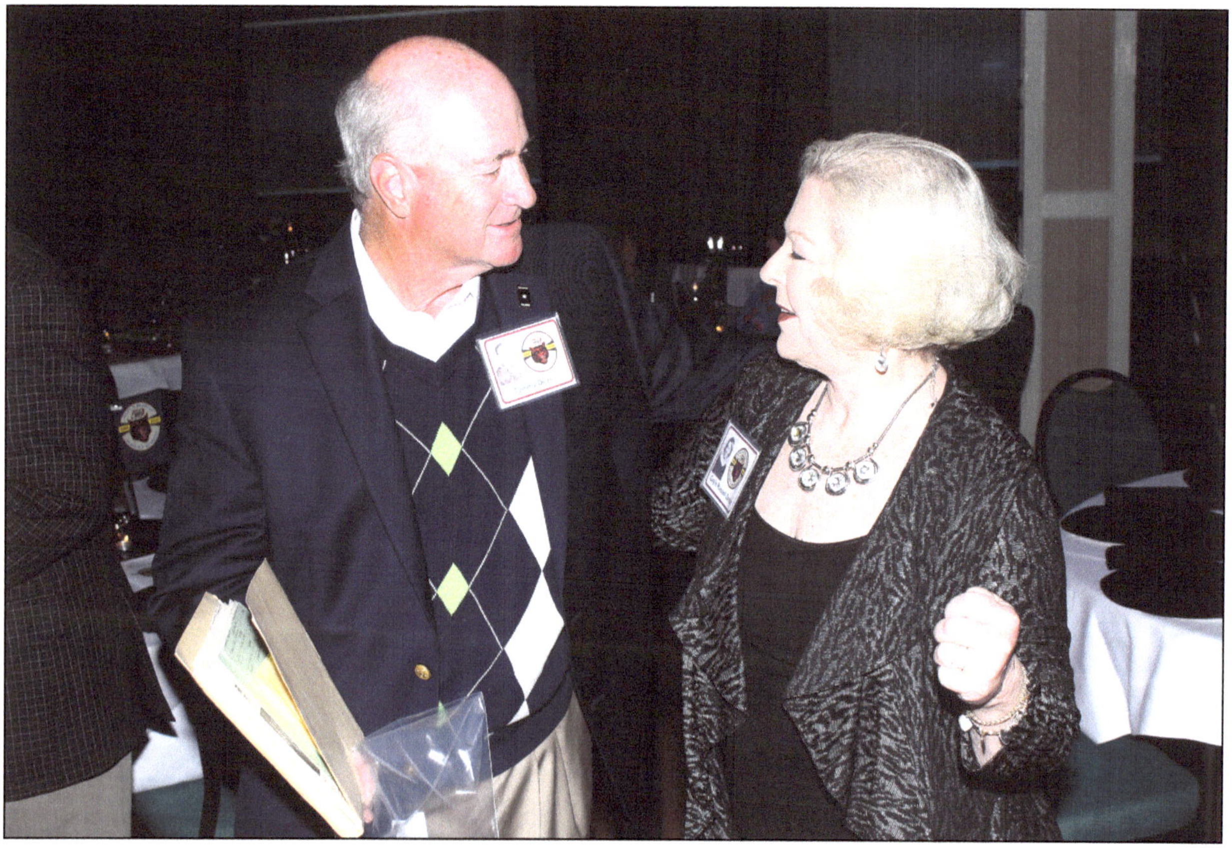

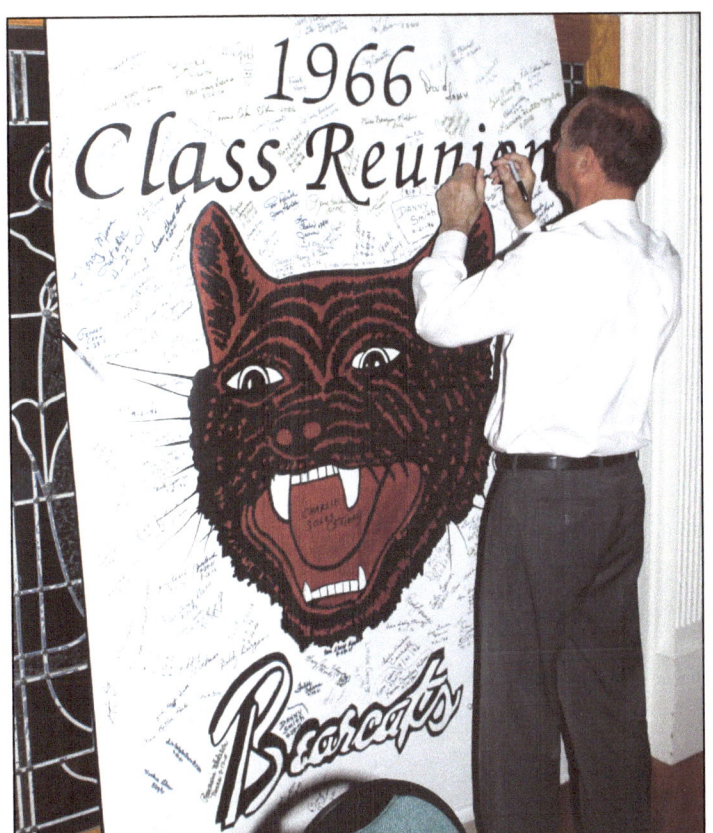

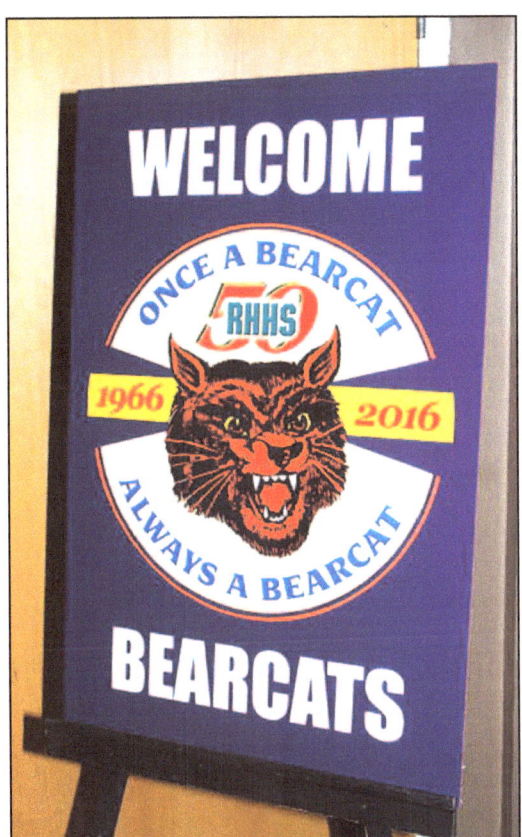

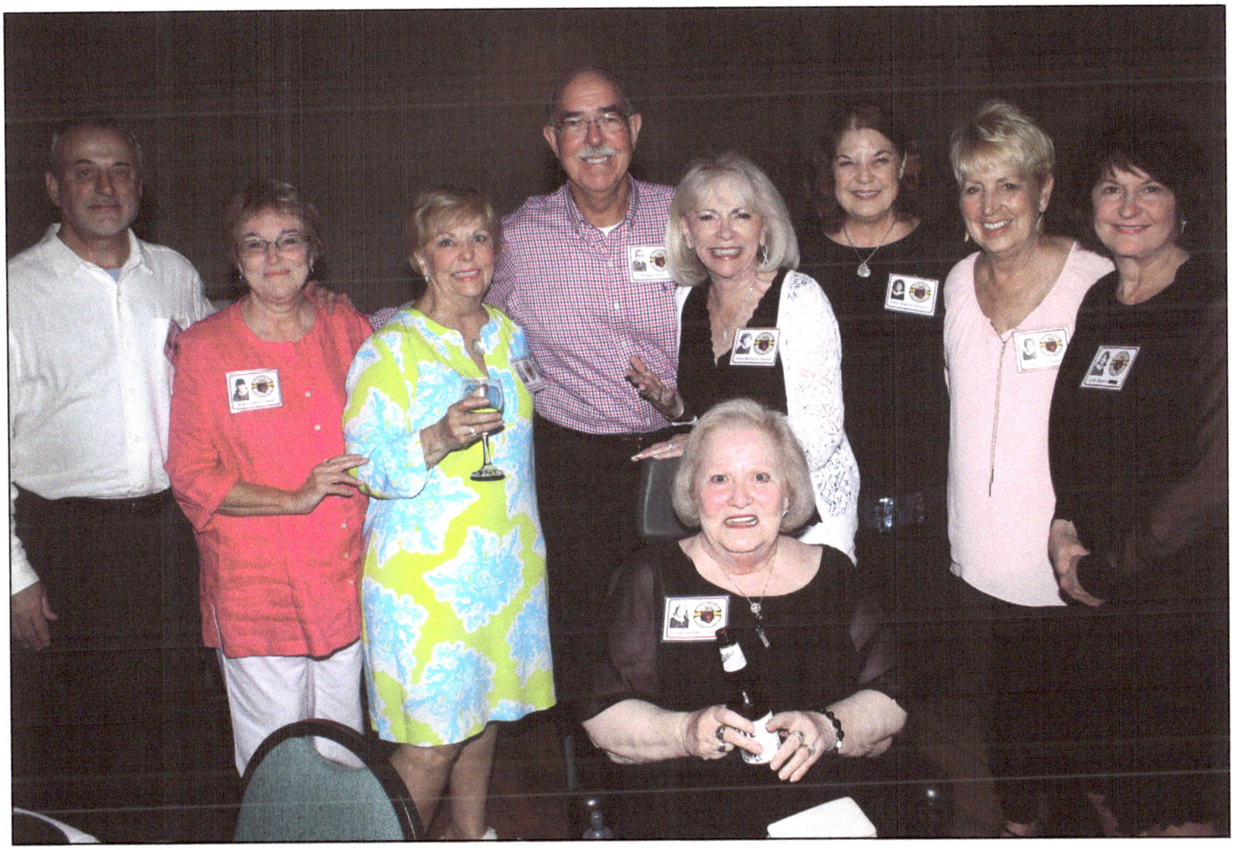

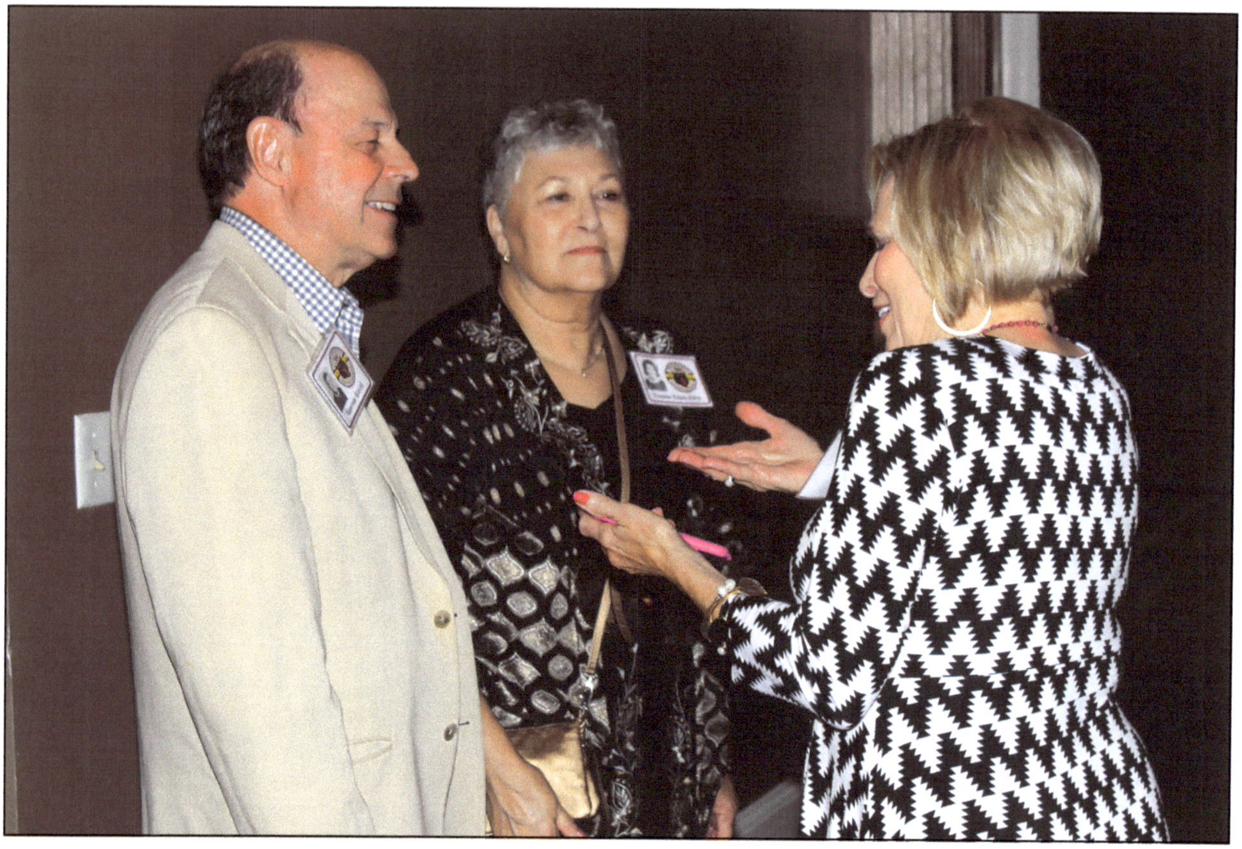

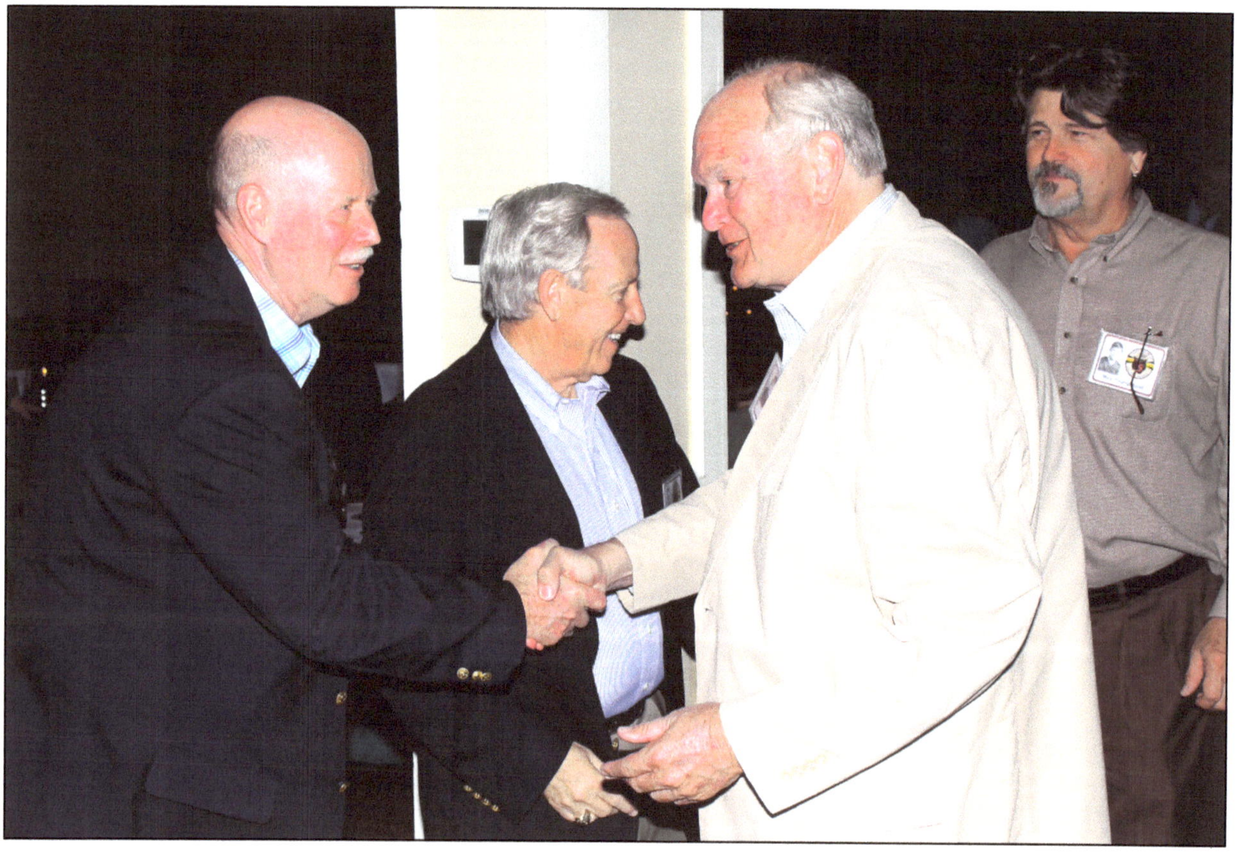

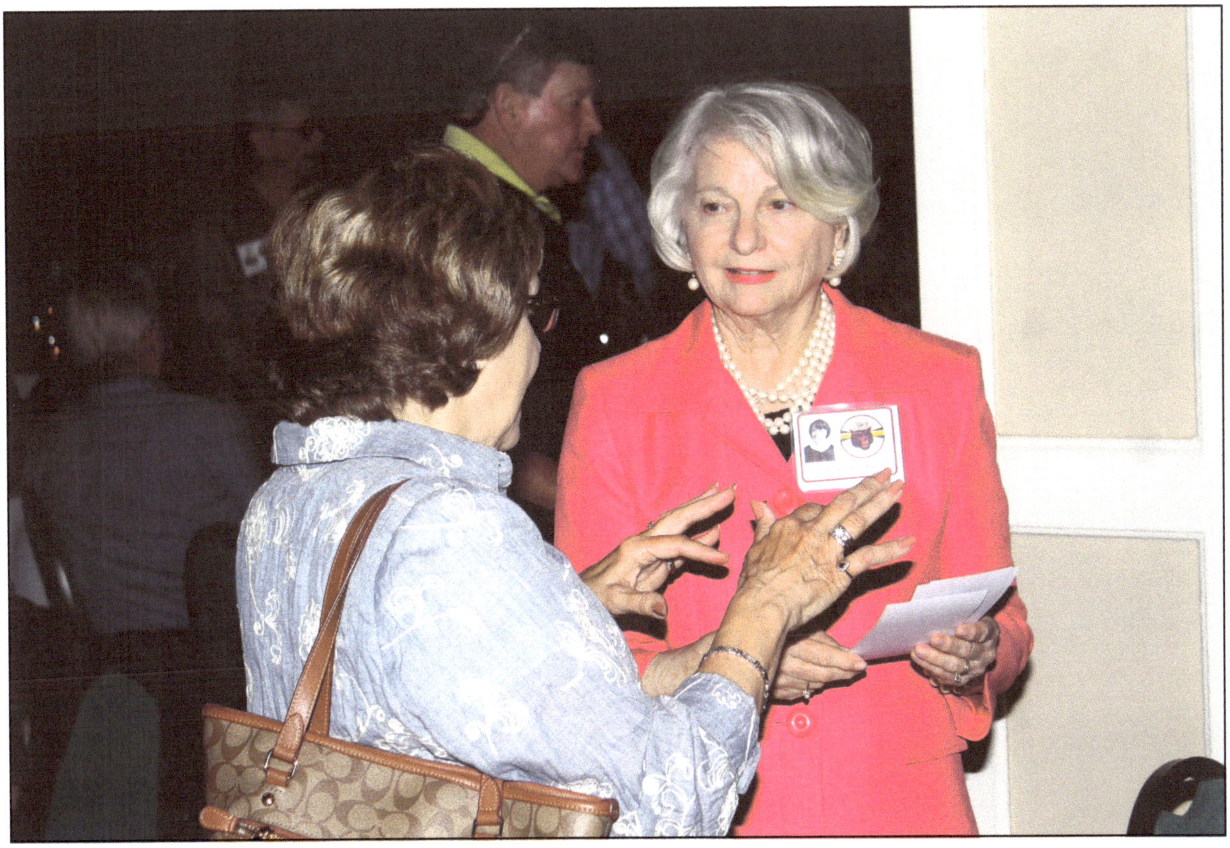

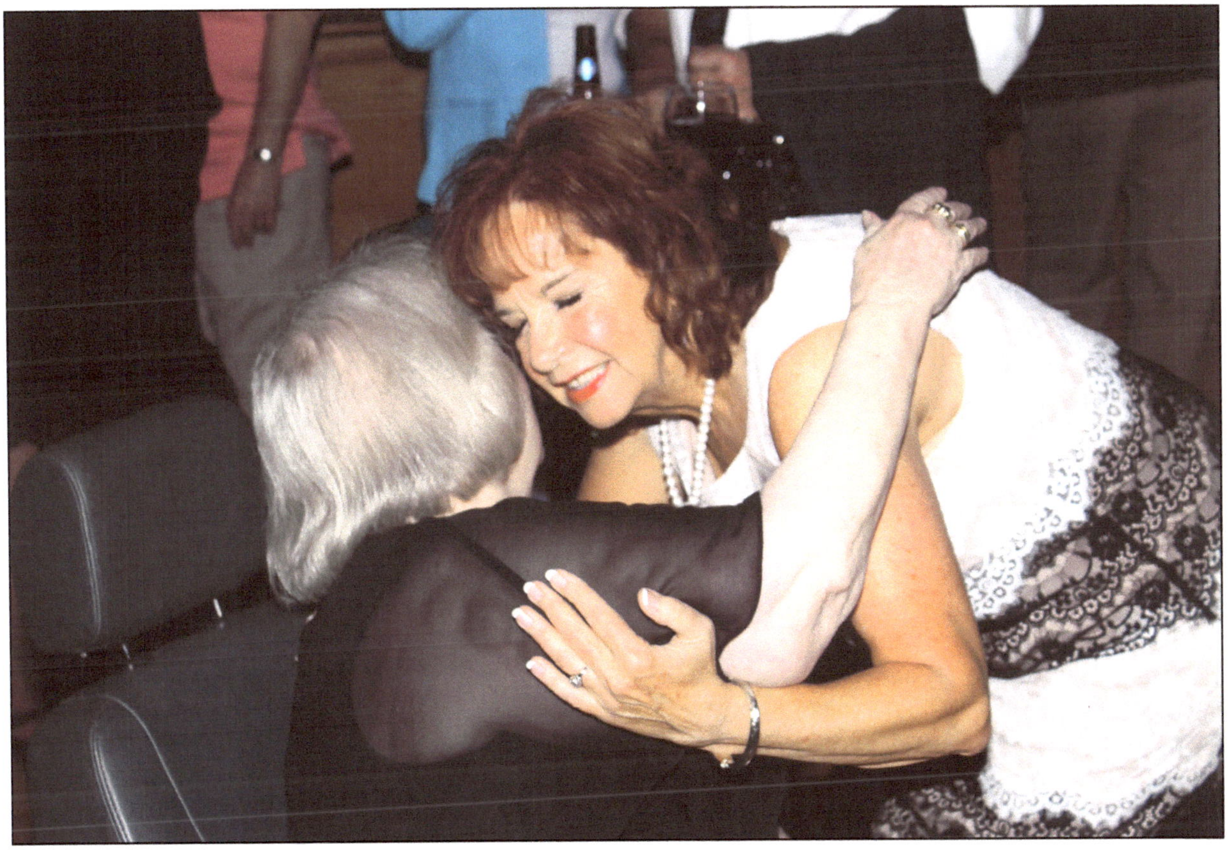

REUNION PHOTOS: OFFICIAL PHOTOS & CANDID SHOTS

41

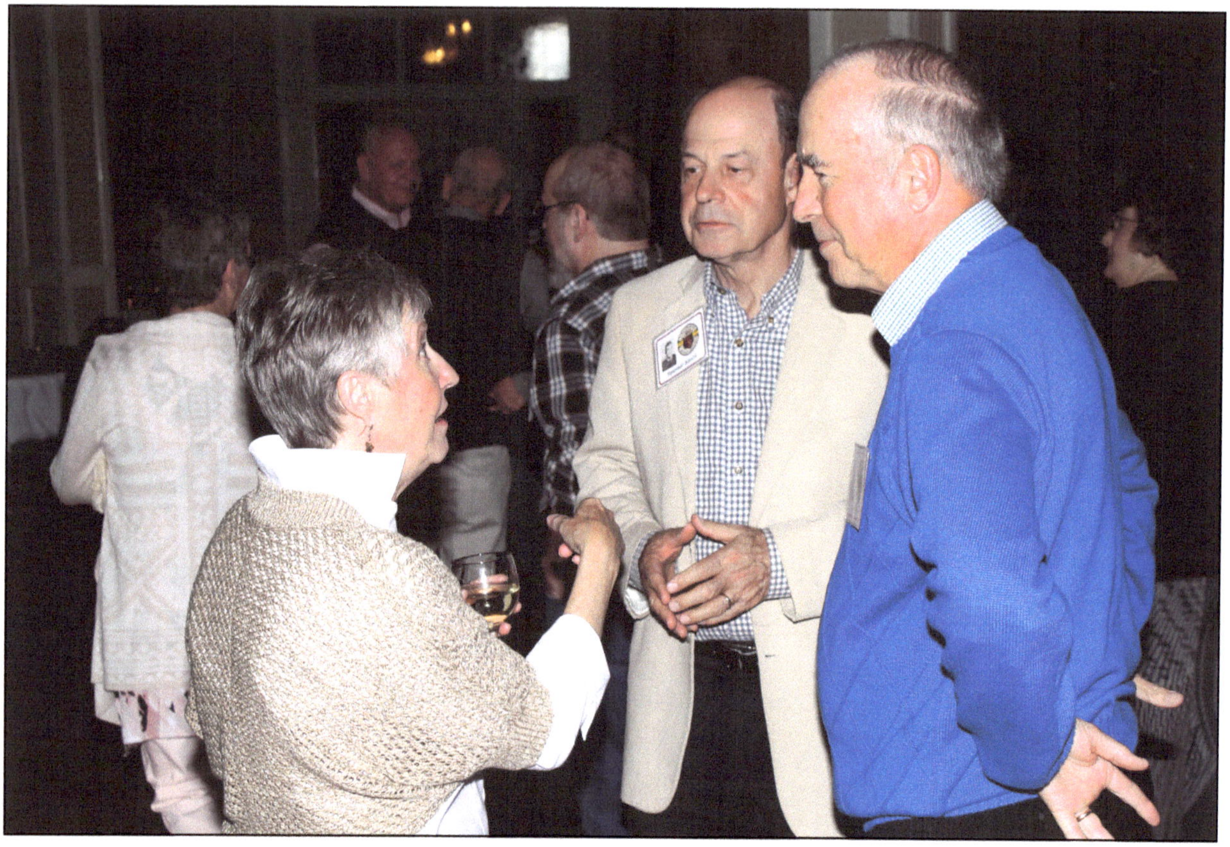

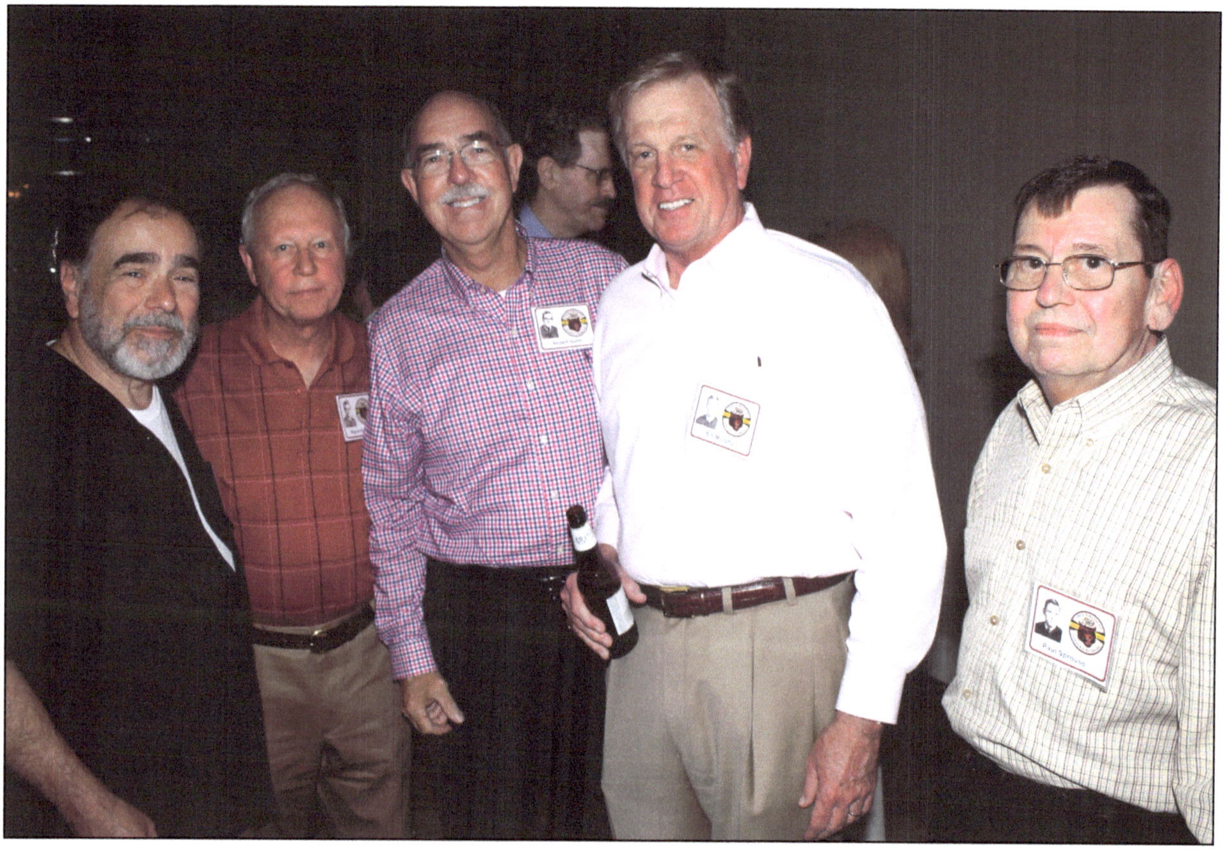

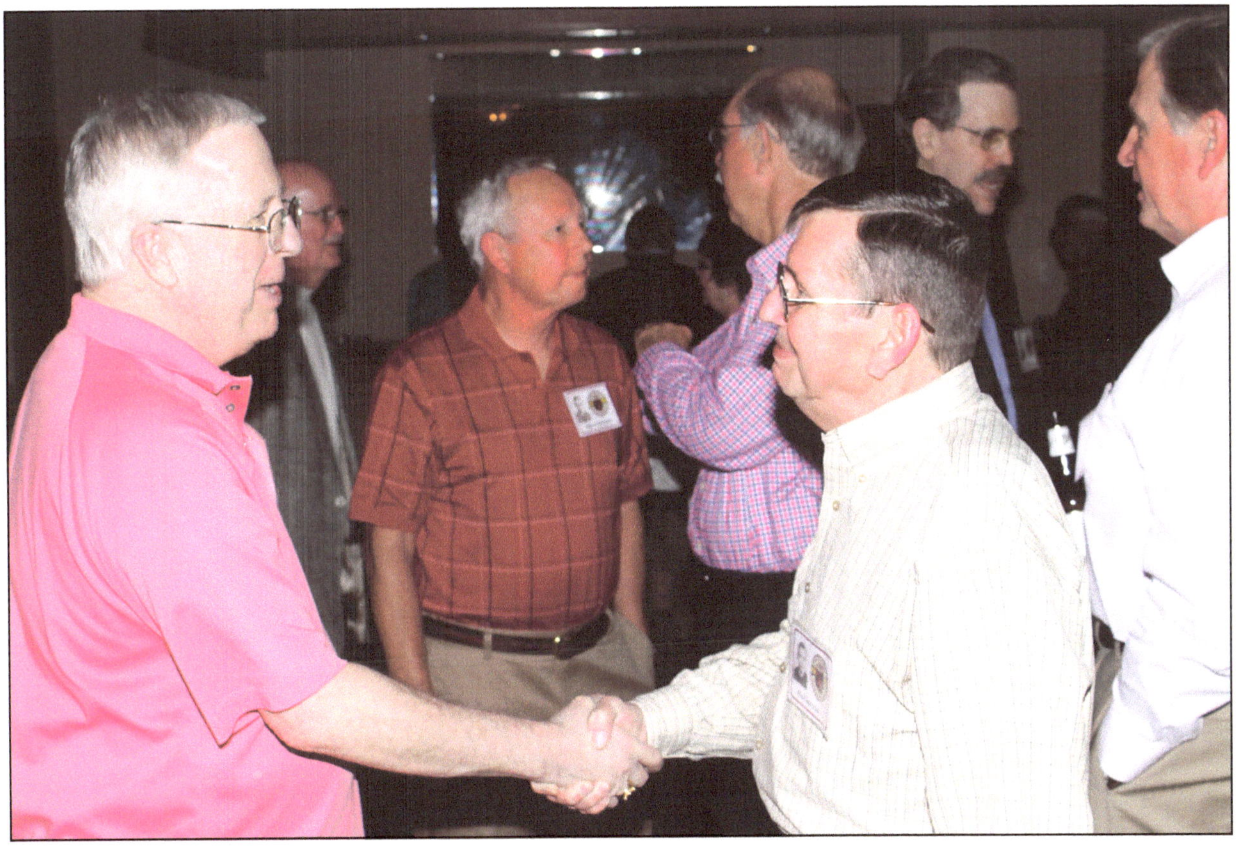

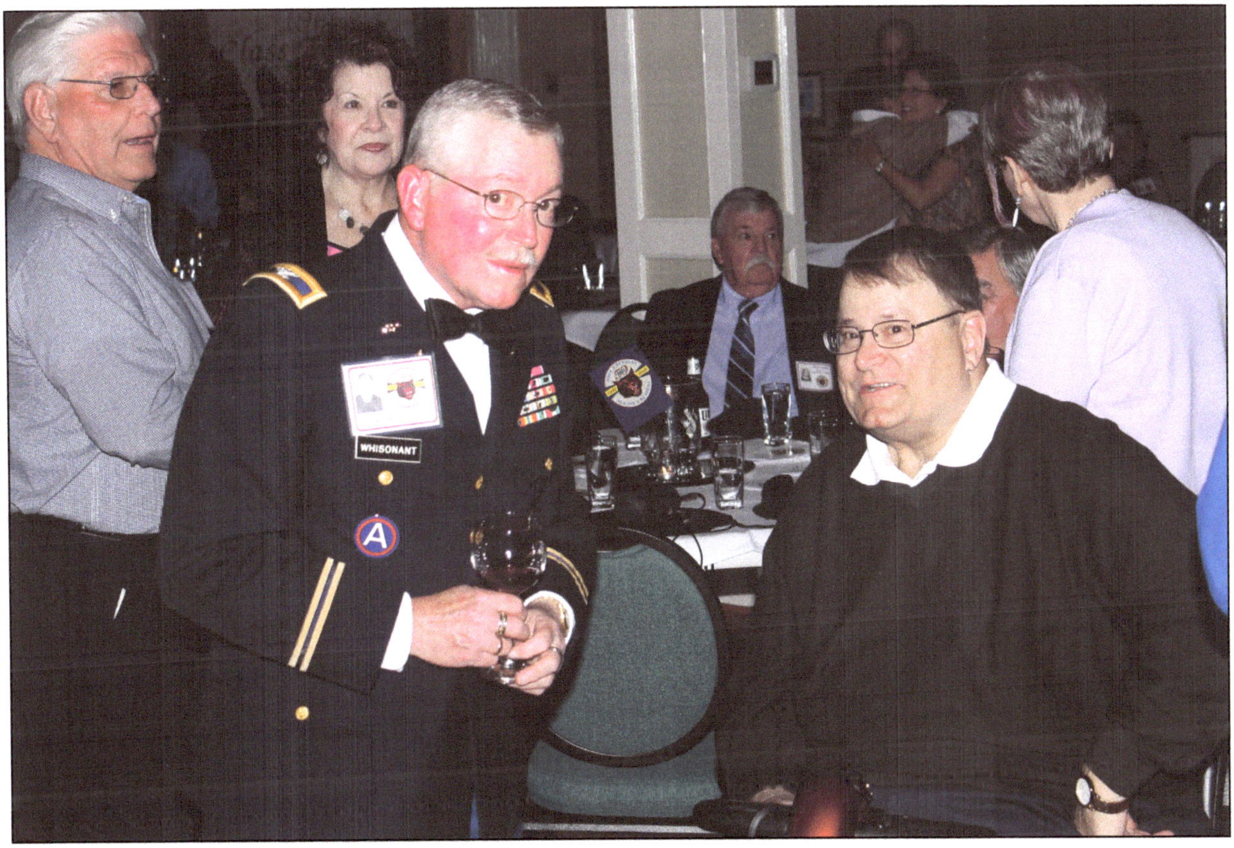
WHISONANT

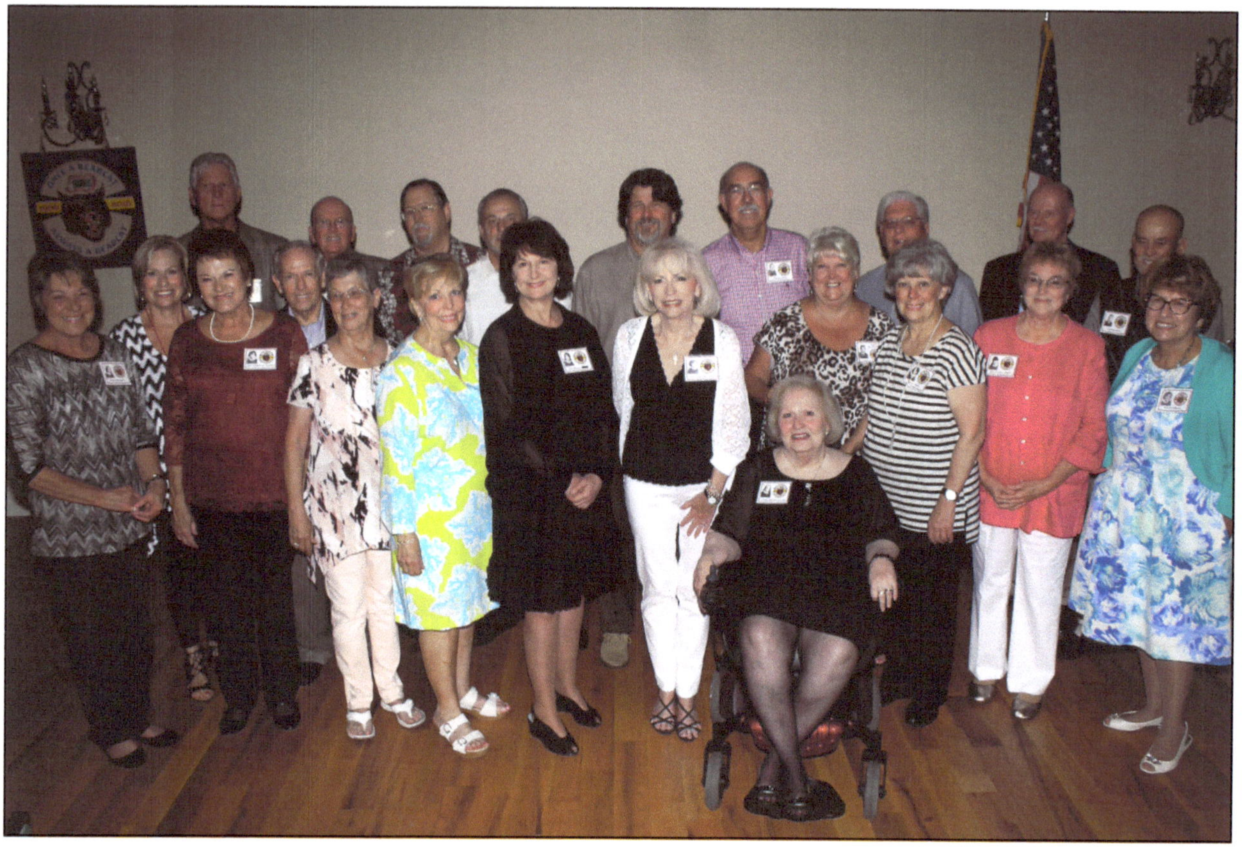

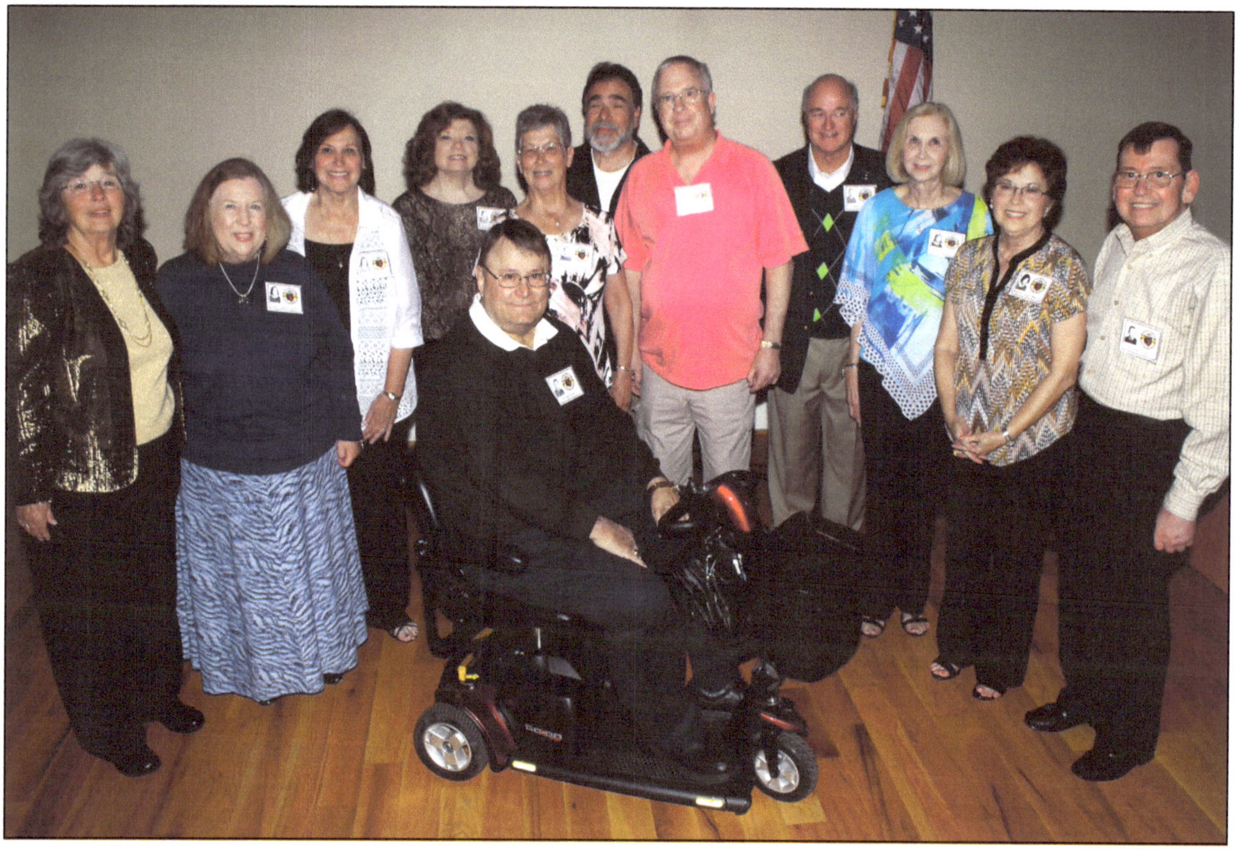

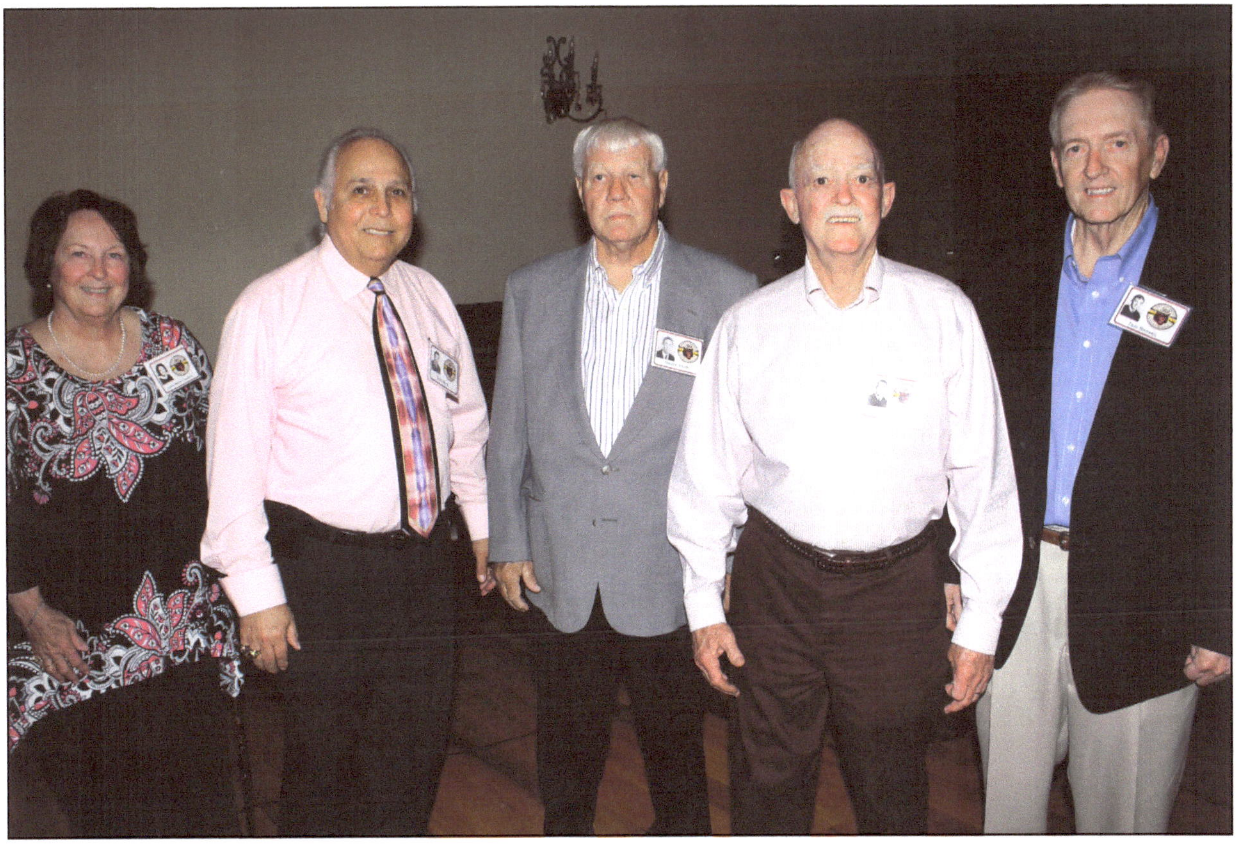

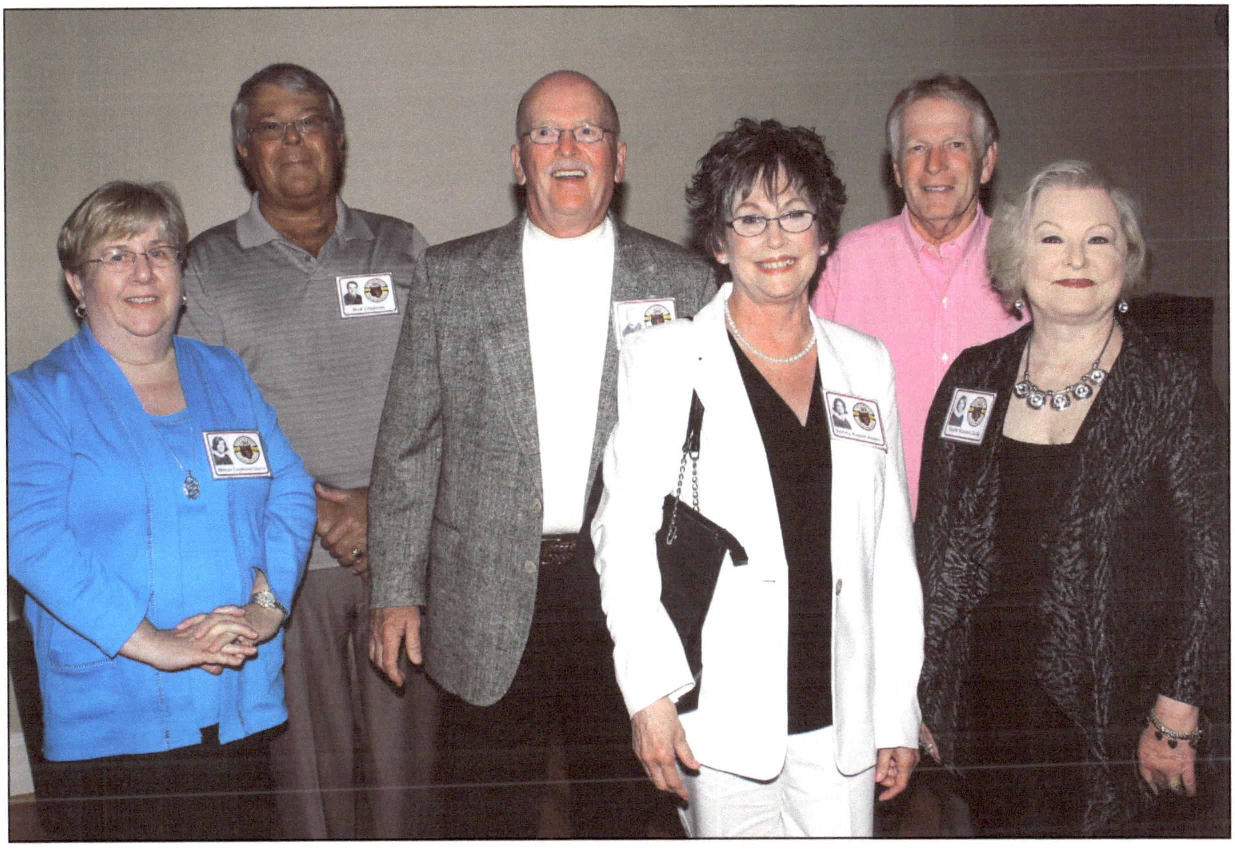

REUNION PHOTOS: OFFICIAL PHOTOS & CANDID SHOTS

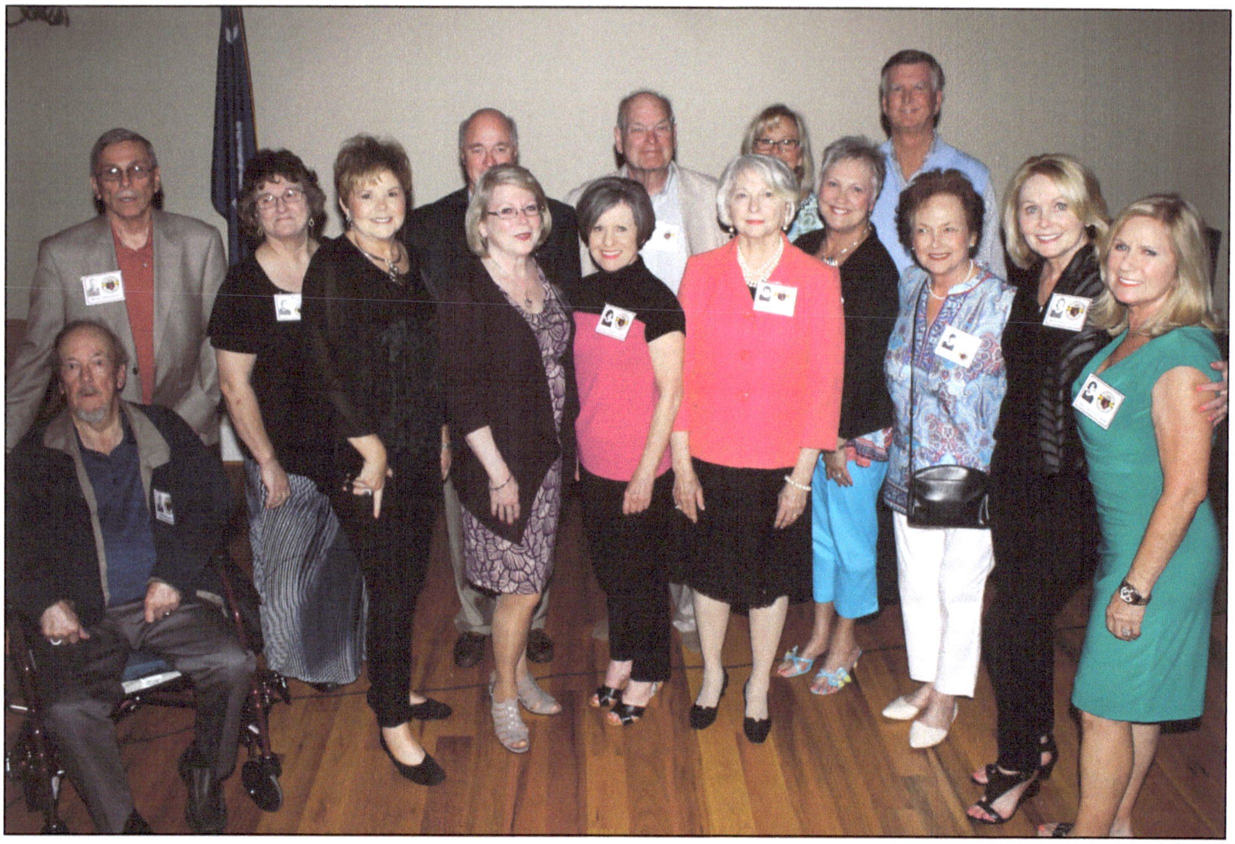

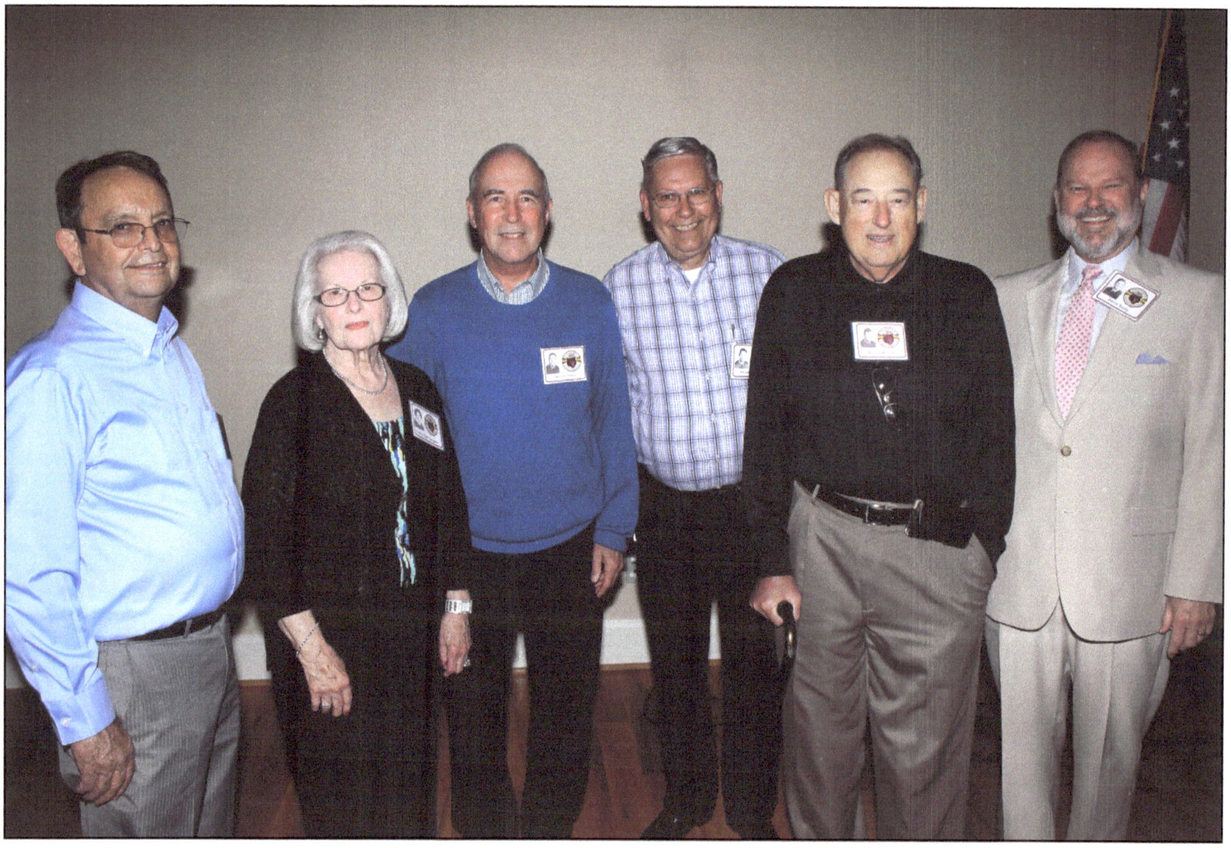

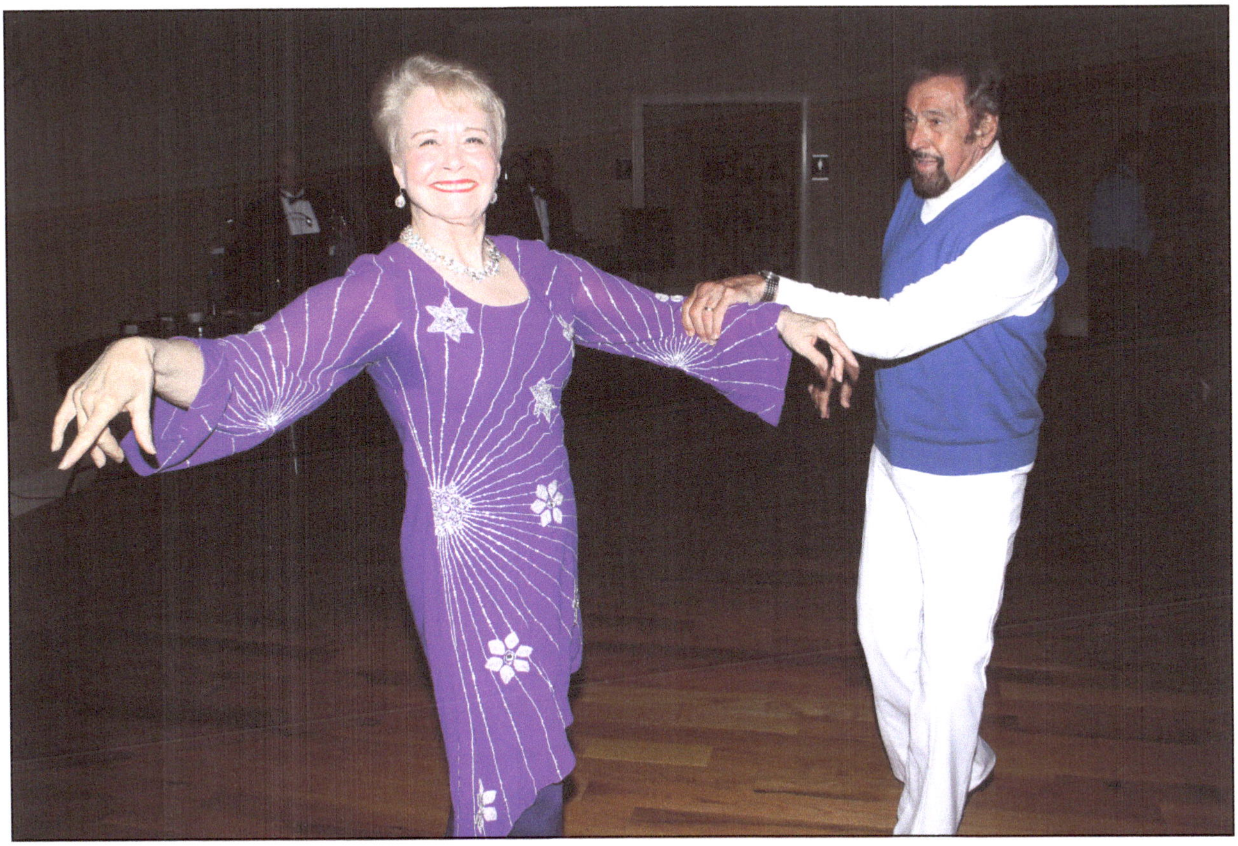

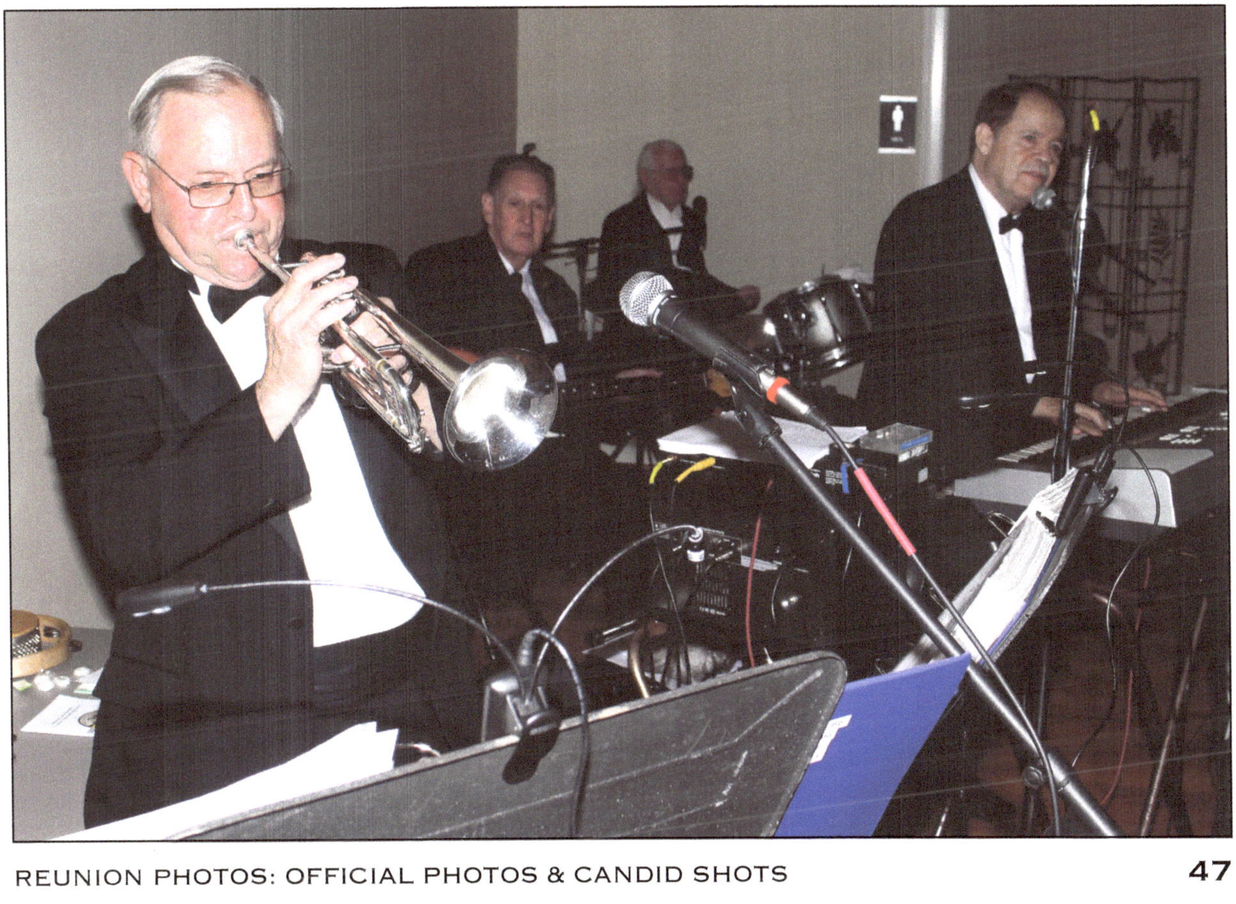

REUNION PHOTOS: OFFICIAL PHOTOS & CANDID SHOTS

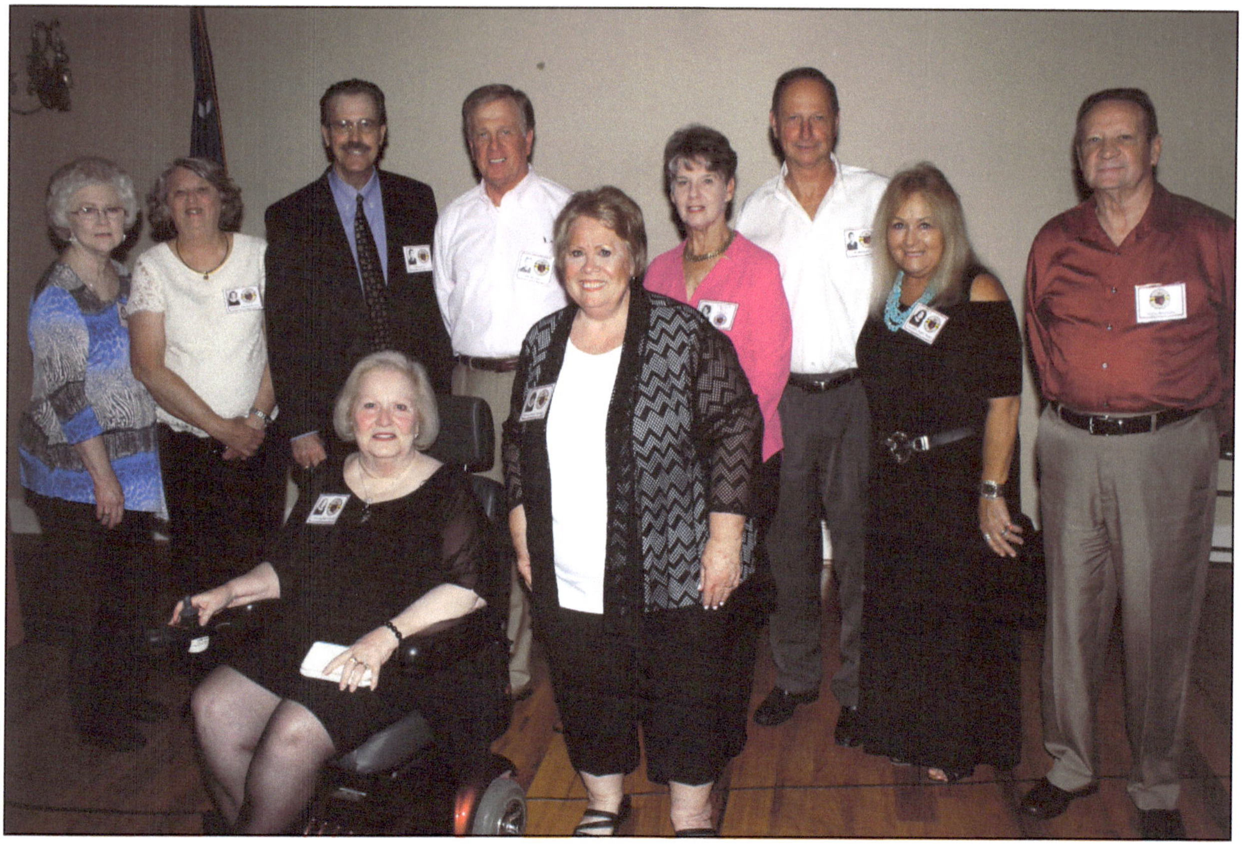

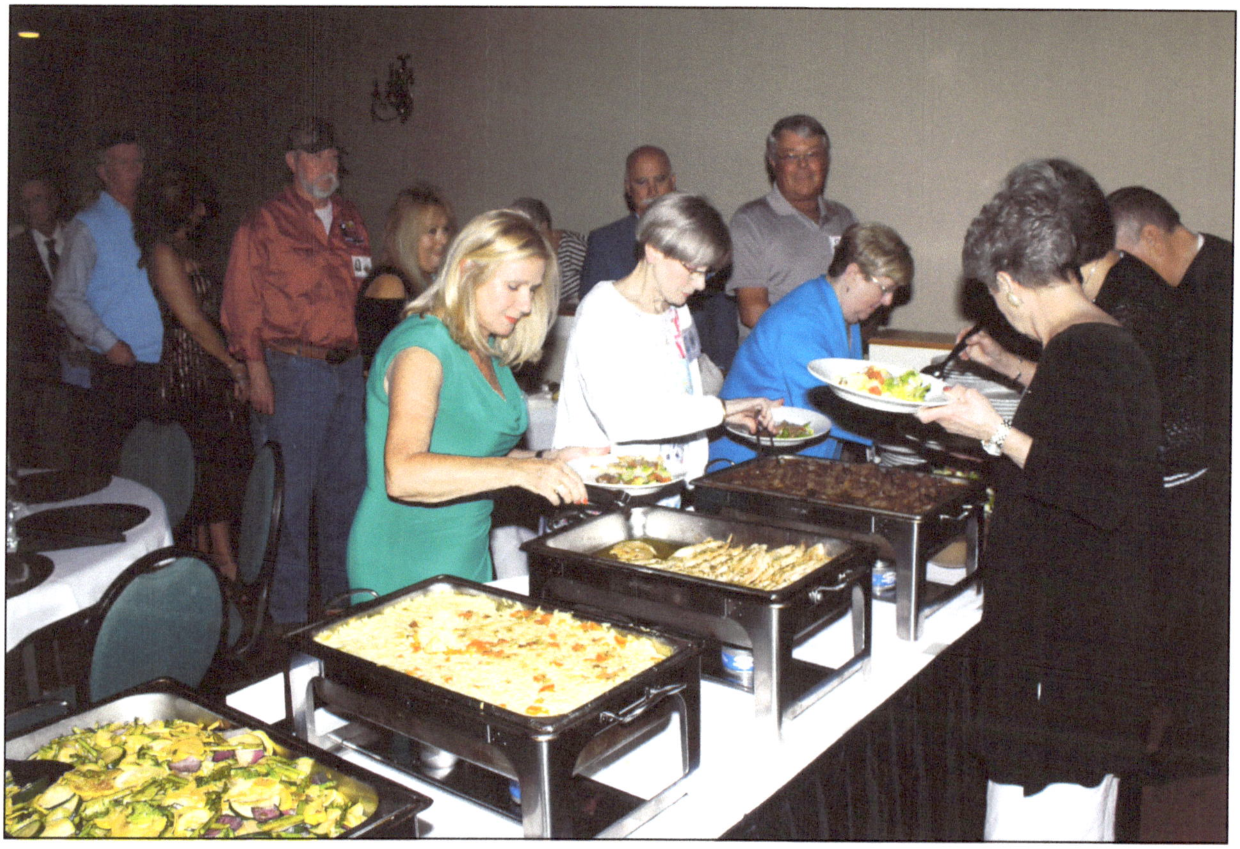

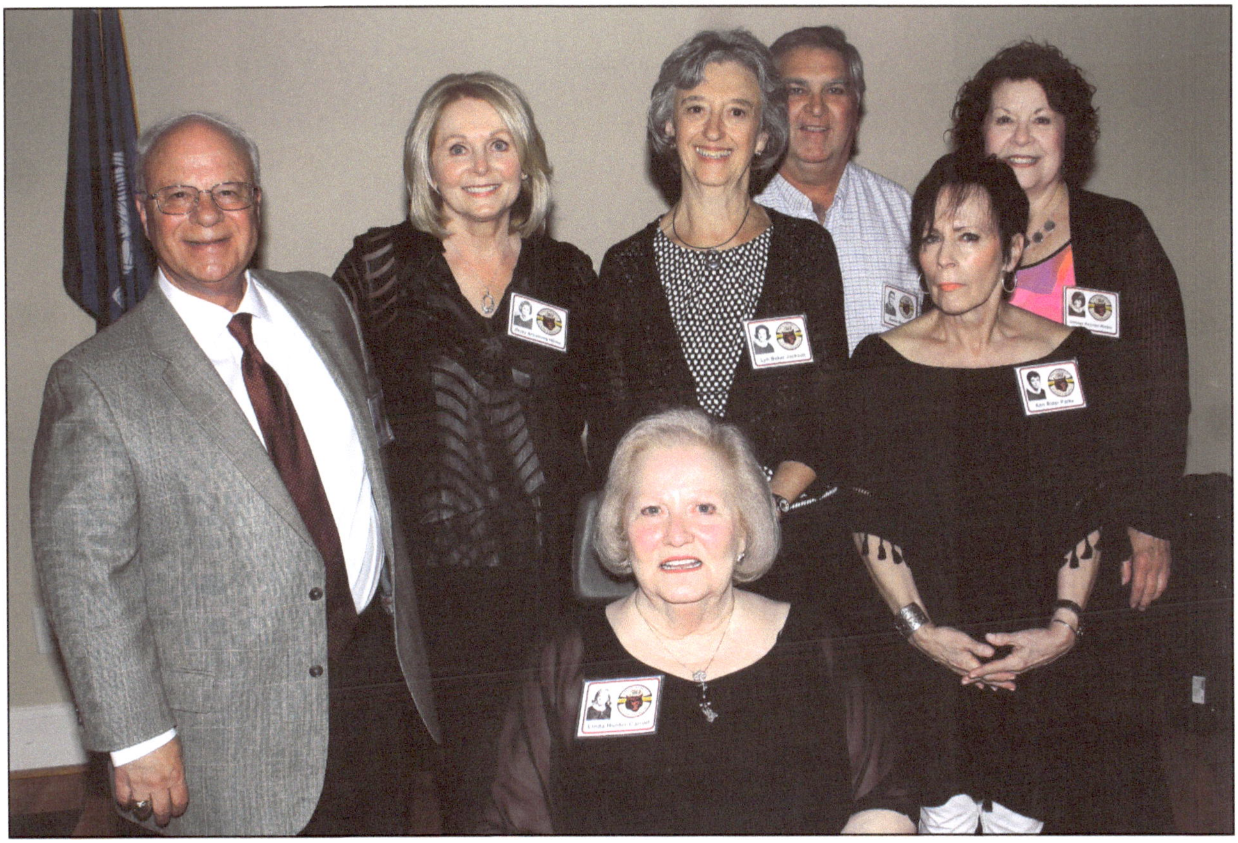

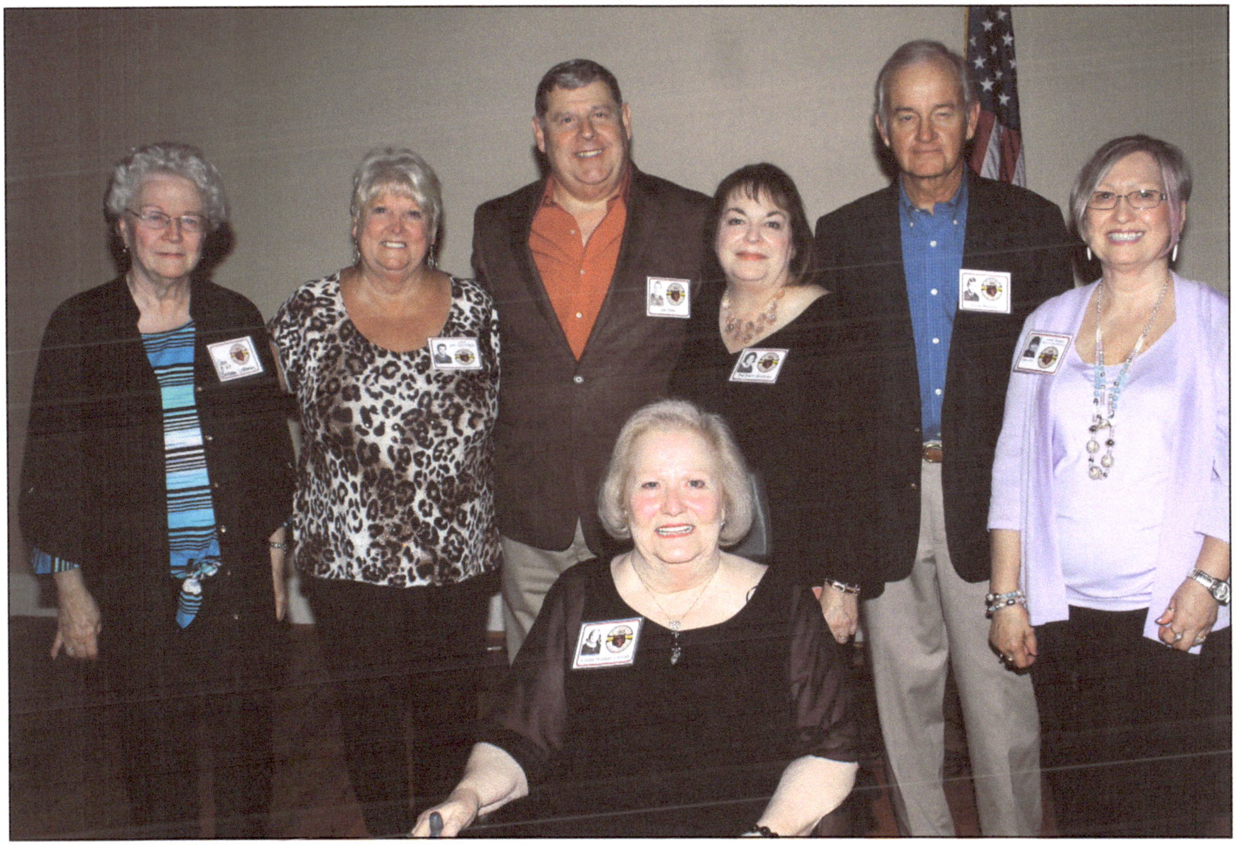

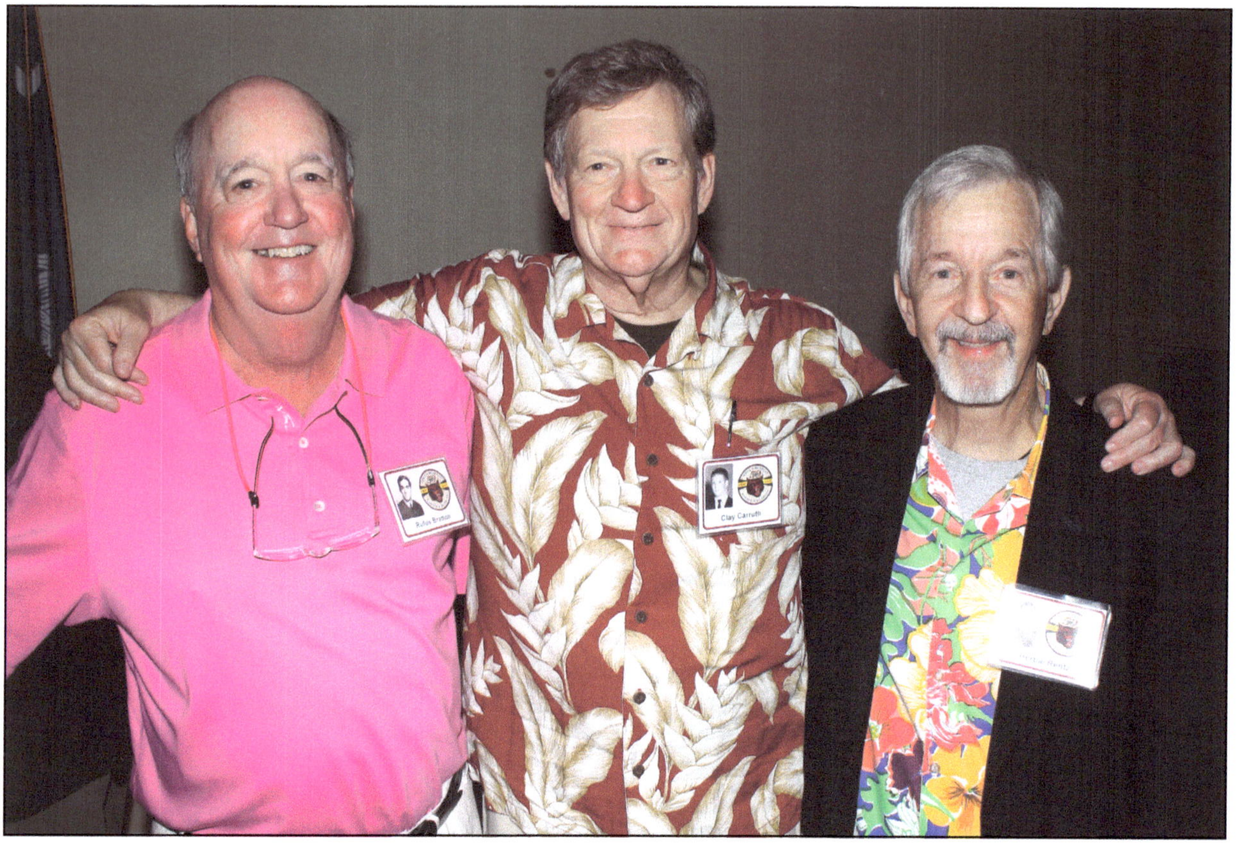

50 Rock Hill High School Class of 1966 50th Reunion

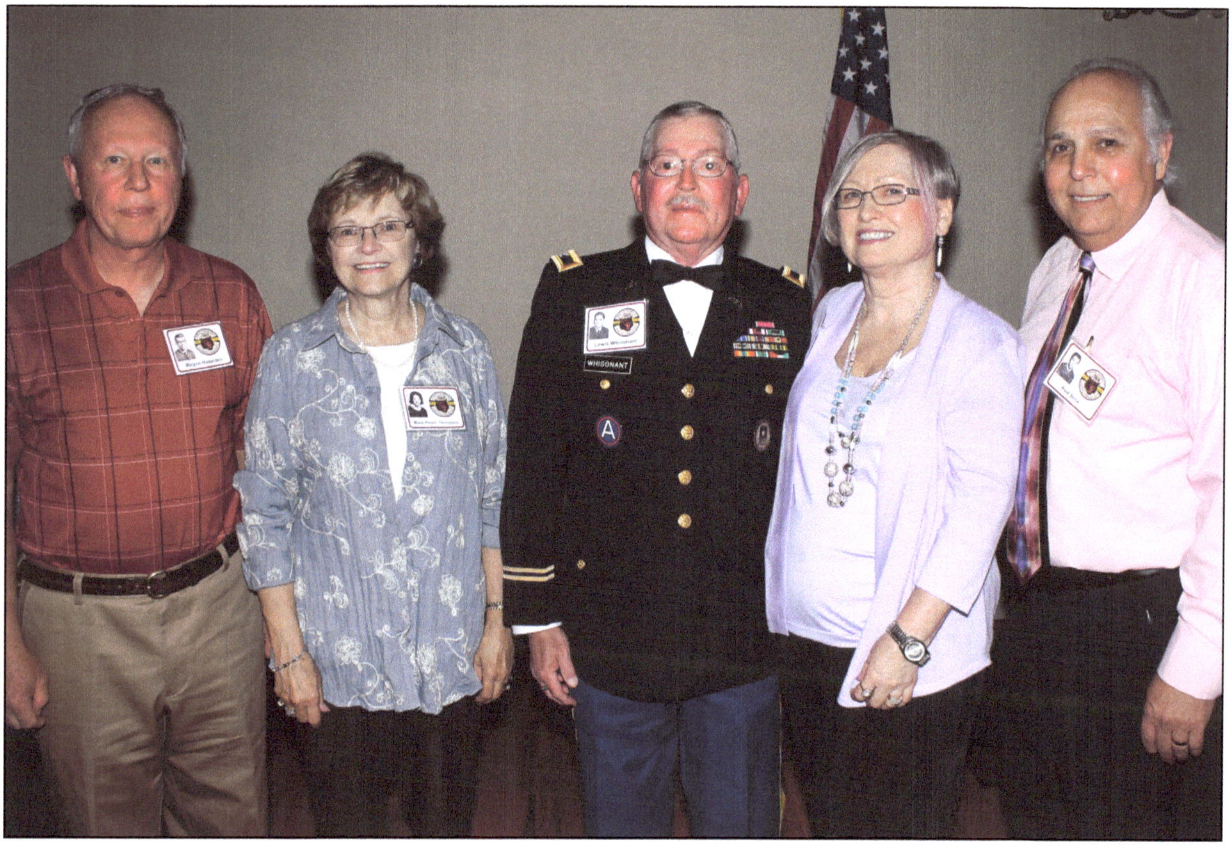

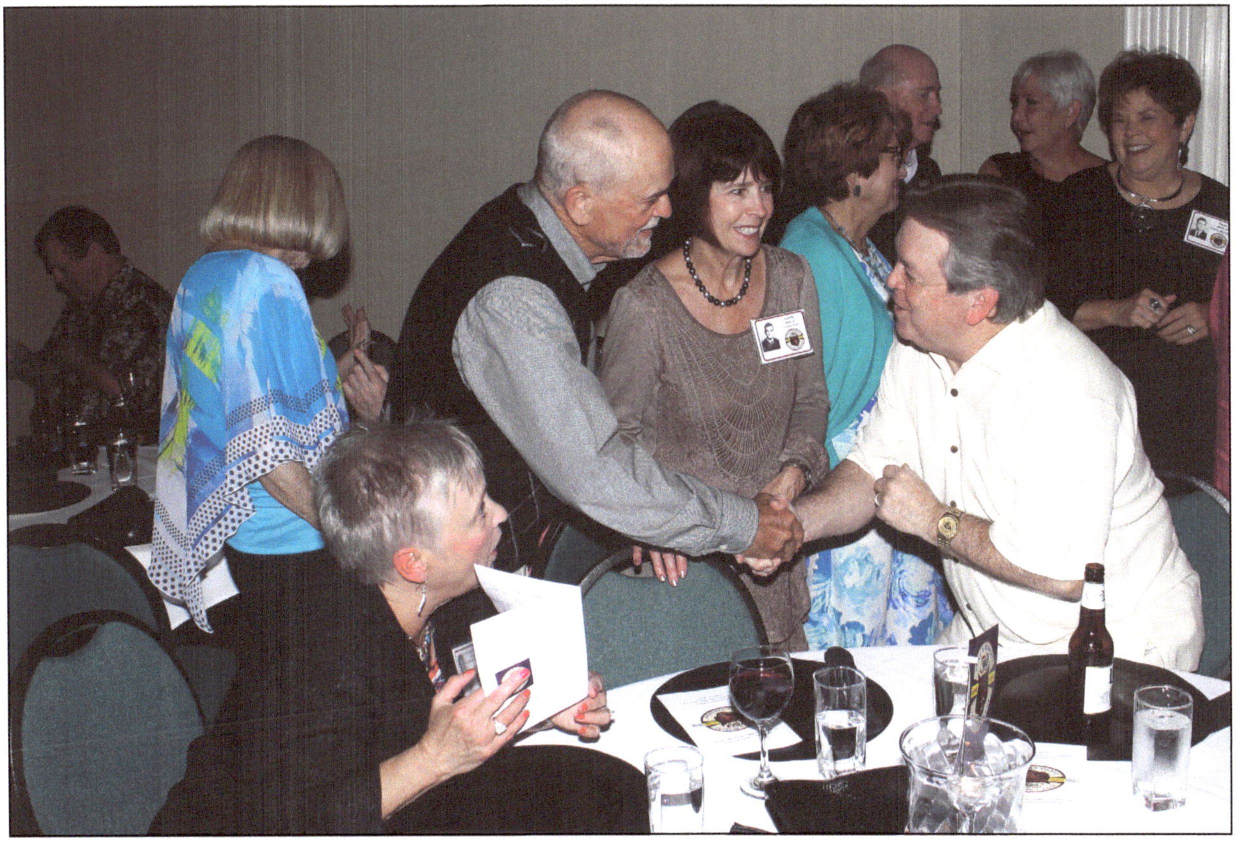

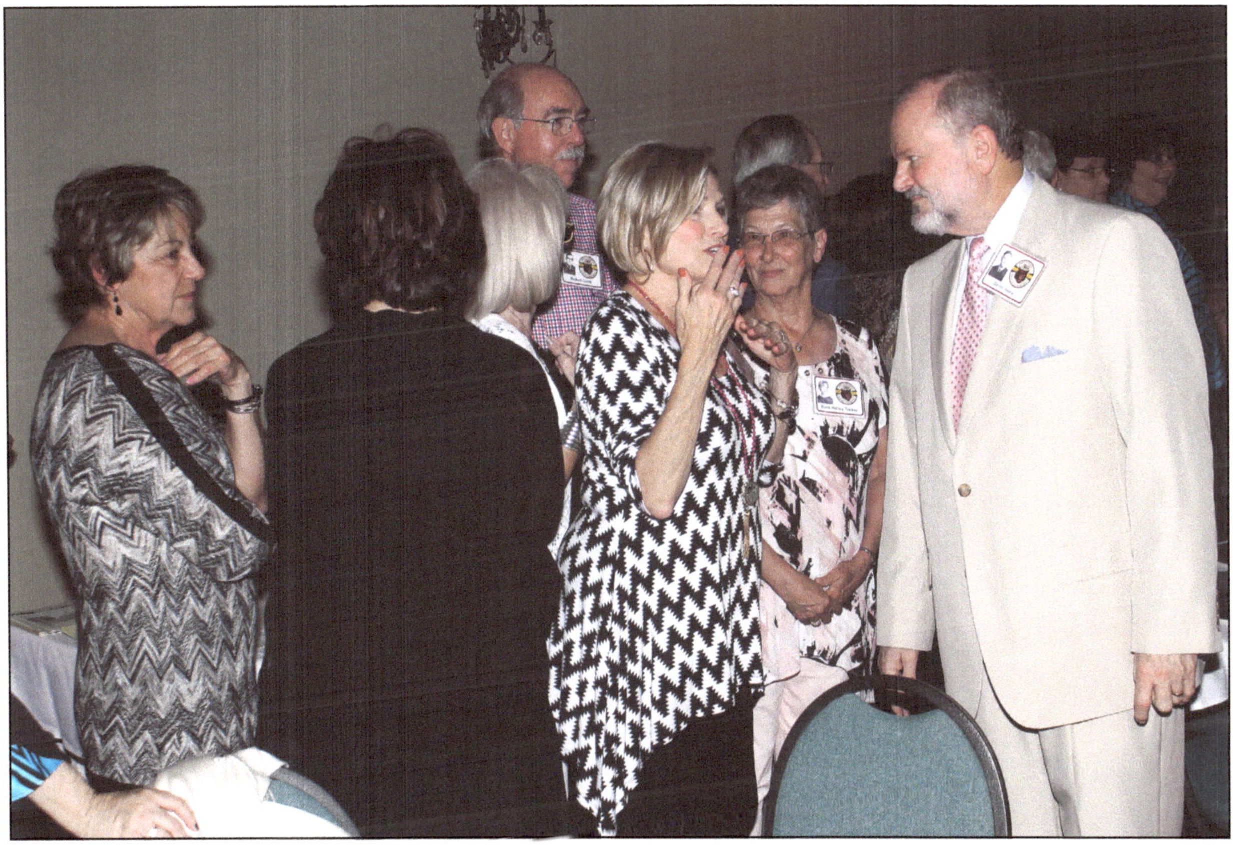

REUNION PHOTOS: OFFICIAL PHOTOS & CANDID SHOTS 51

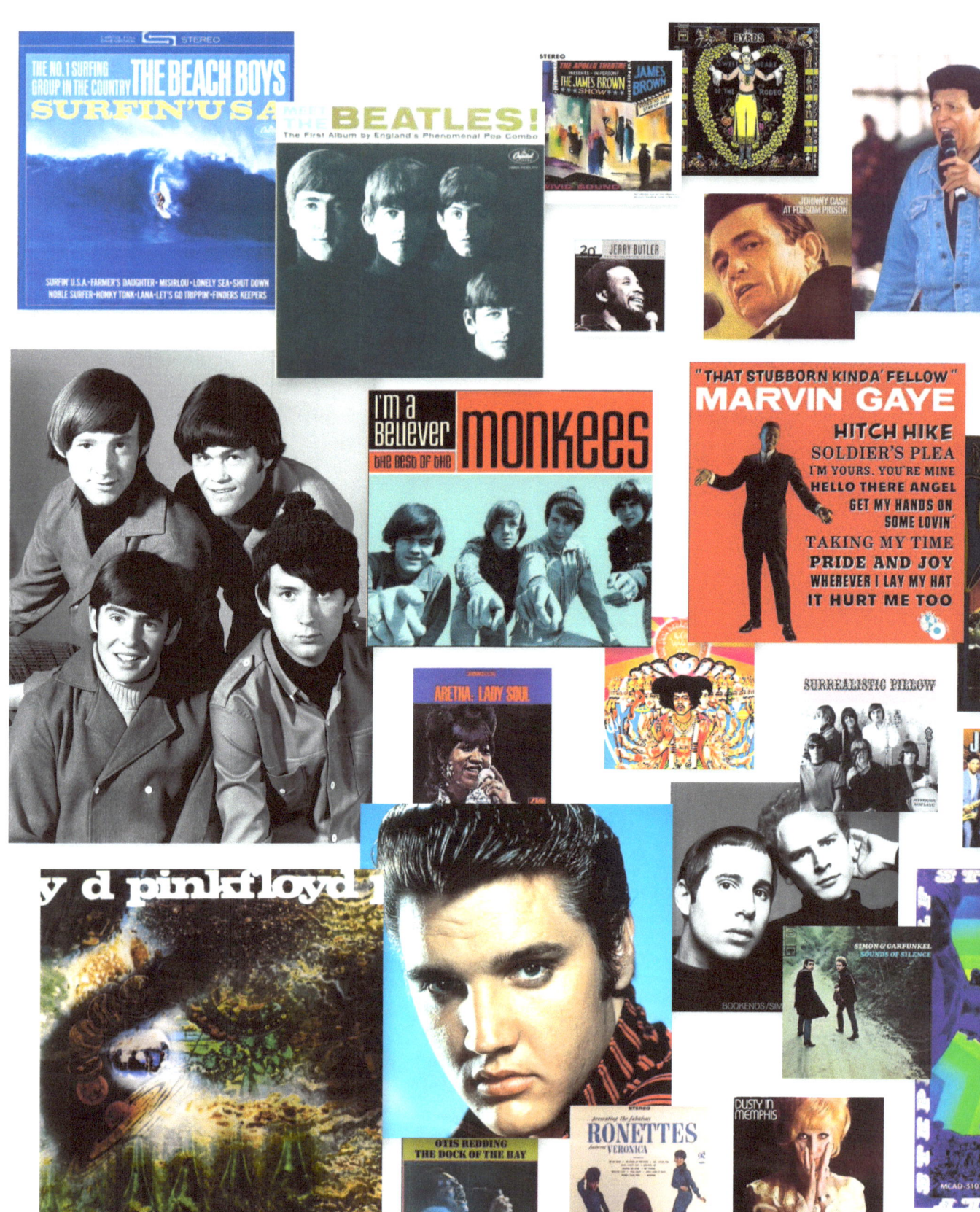

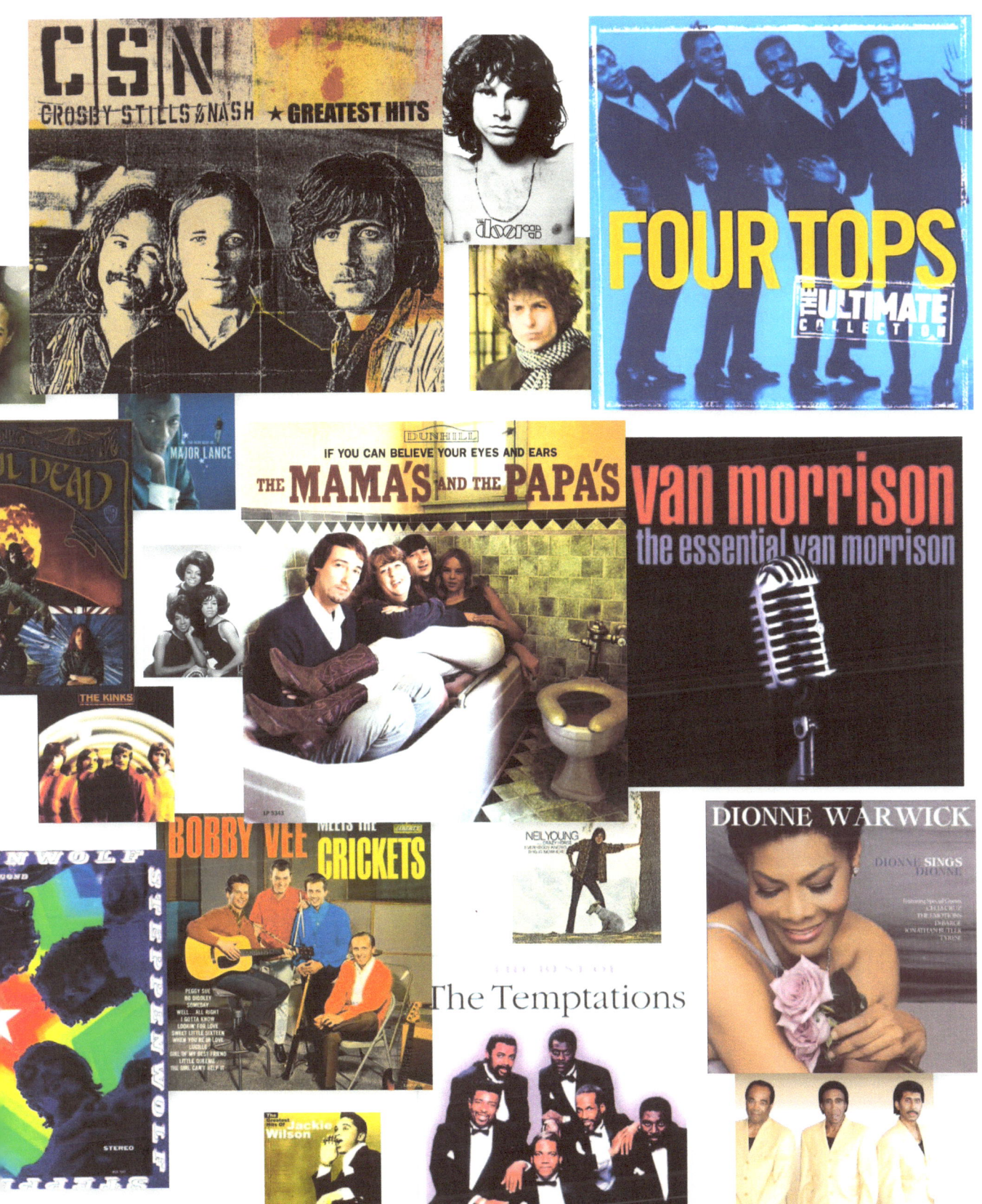

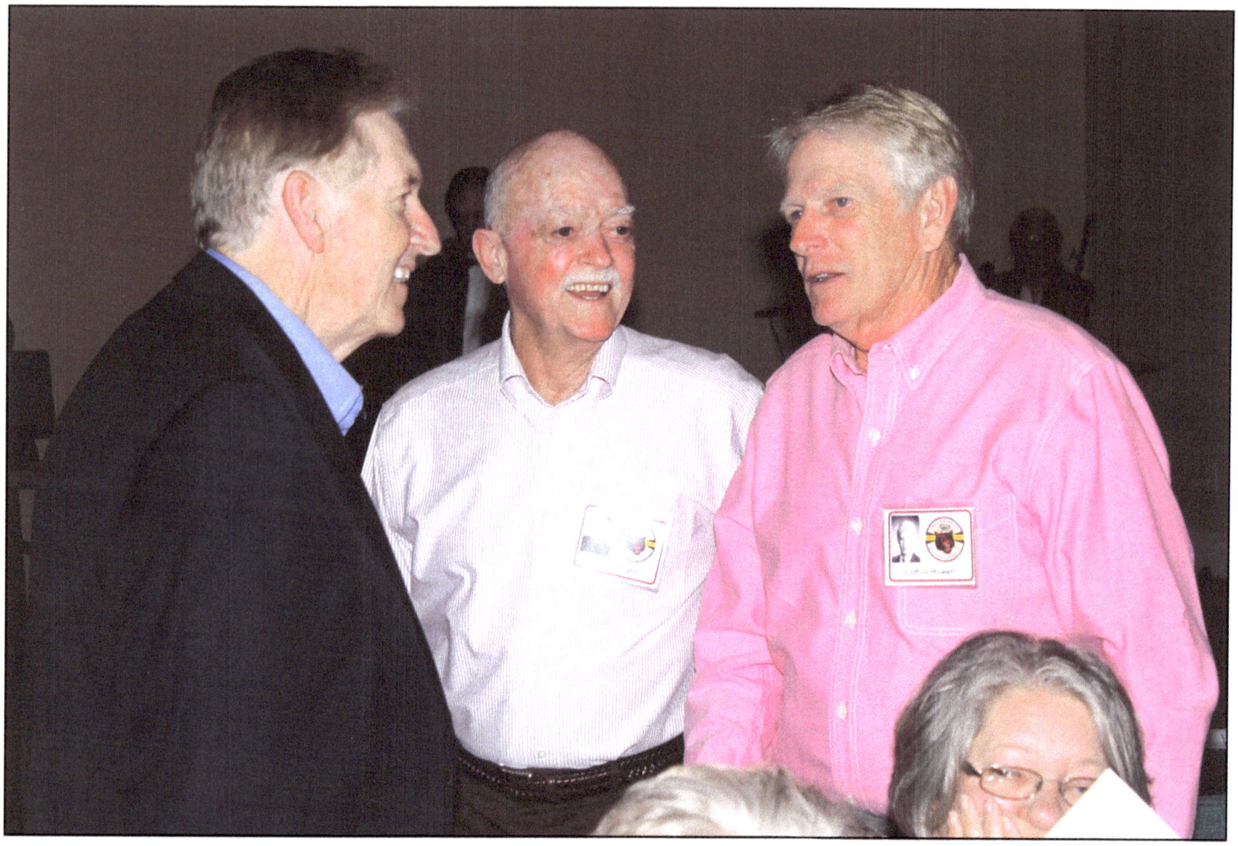

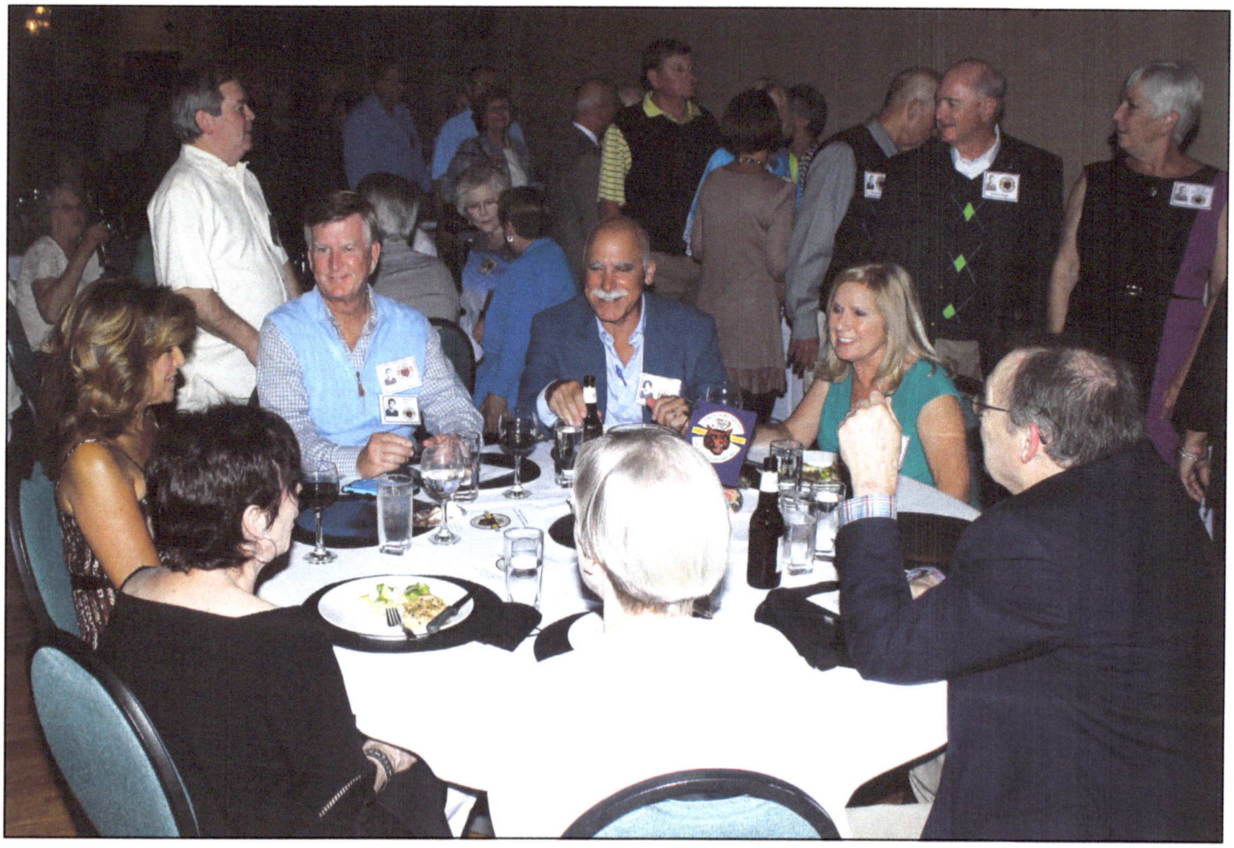

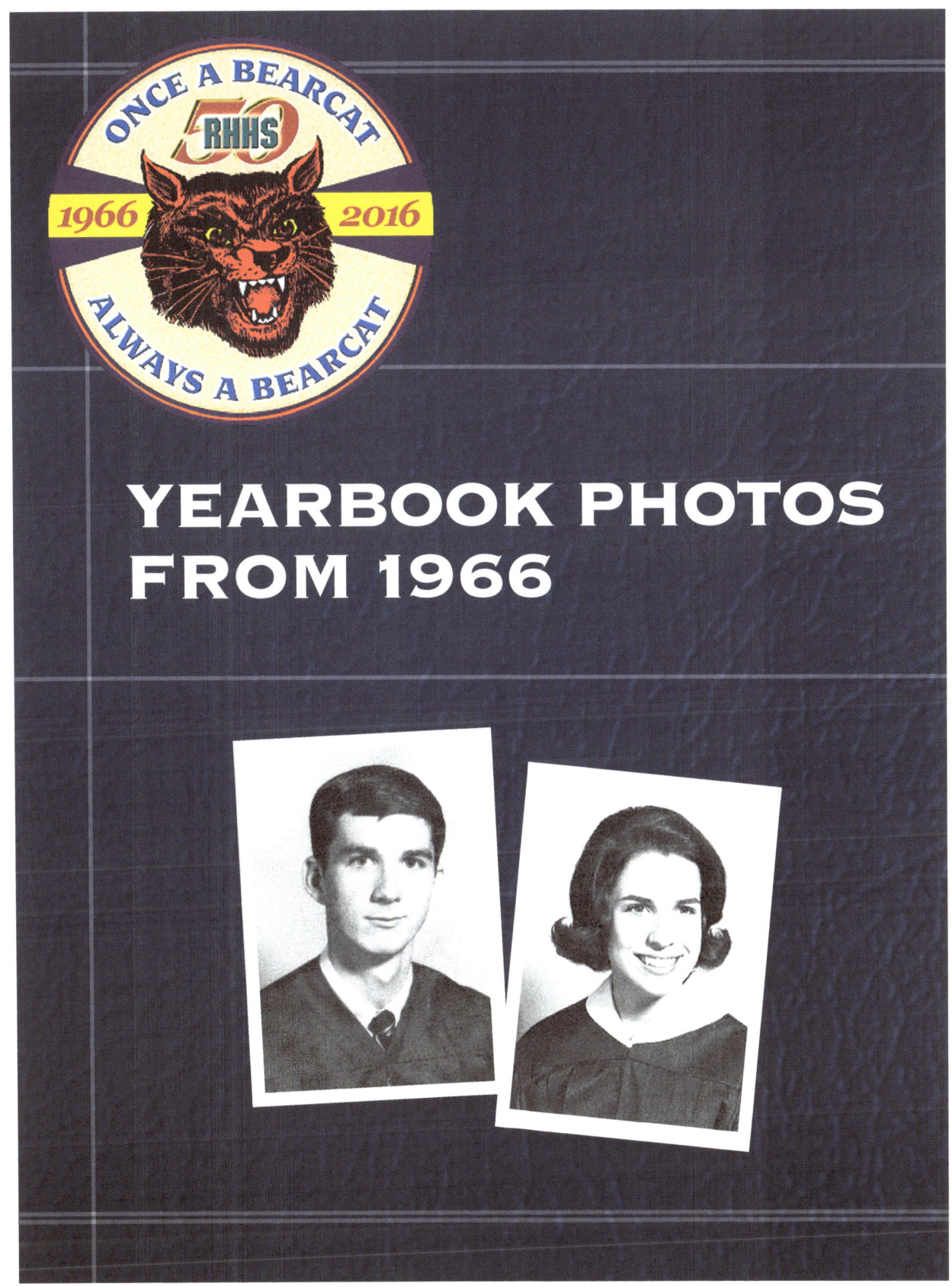

YEARBOOK PHOTOS FROM 1966

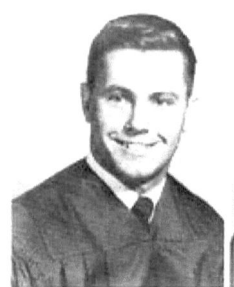 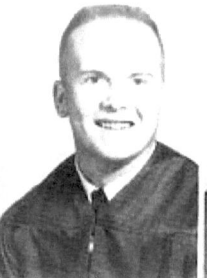 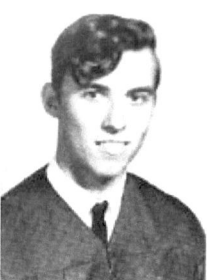 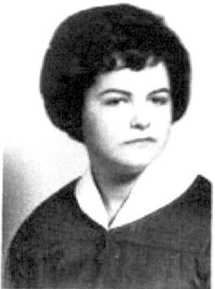 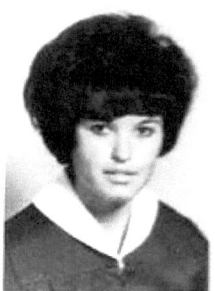

Freddie Adams   Ira Adams   Ronnie Adams   Cathy Adkins   Linda Adkins

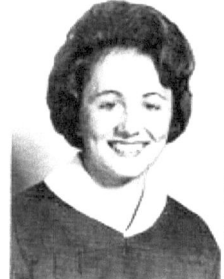 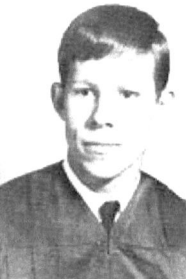 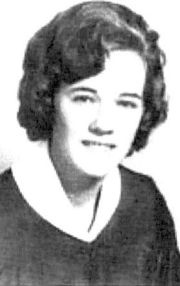 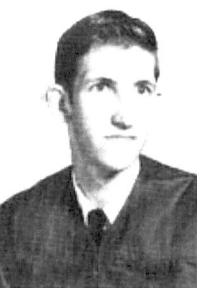 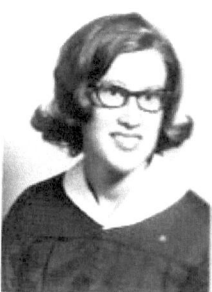

Paula Adkins   Thomas Adkins   Lydia Ainslie   Tommy Aldridge   Dale Alewine

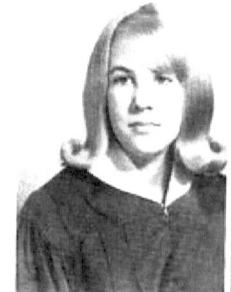 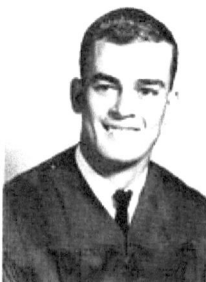 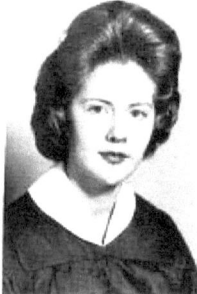 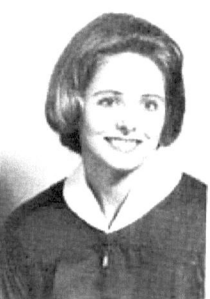 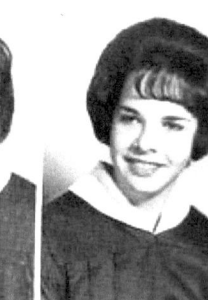

Linda Anderson   Donnie Arant   Shirley Armour   Becky Armstrong   Nancy Arnold

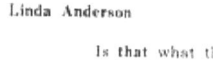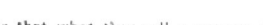
Is that what they call a granny dress?

Riney Ashley   John Atchison

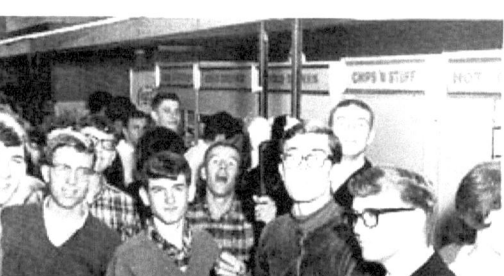

64

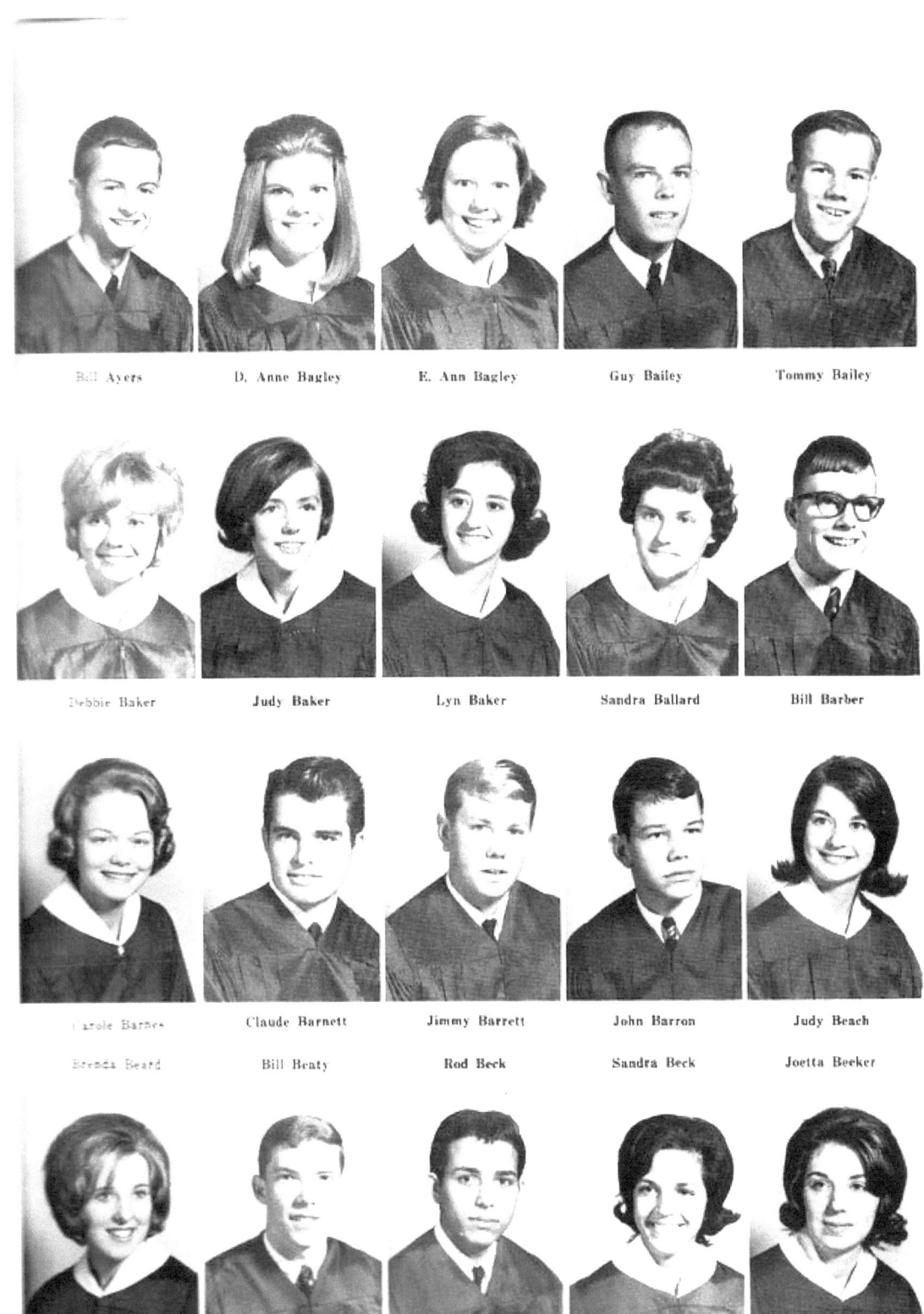

Bill Ayers D. Anne Bagley E. Ann Bagley Guy Bailey Tommy Bailey

Debbie Baker Judy Baker Lyn Baker Sandra Ballard Bill Barber

Carole Barber Claude Barnett Jimmy Barrett John Barron Judy Beach

Brenda Beard Bill Beaty Rod Beck Sandra Beck Joetta Beeker

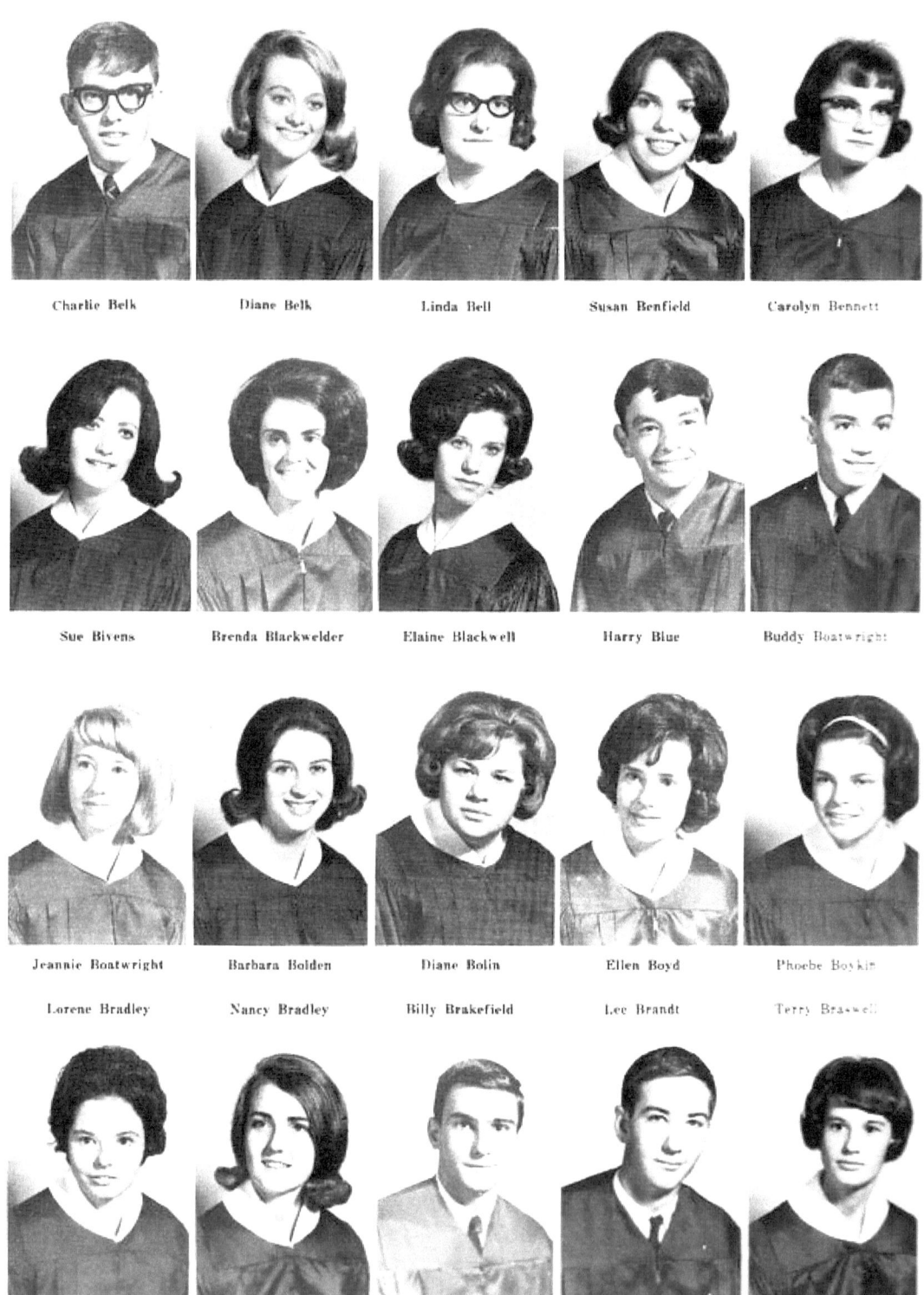

Charlie Belk   Diane Belk   Linda Bell   Susan Benfield   Carolyn Bennett

Sue Bivens   Brenda Blackwelder   Elaine Blackwell   Harry Blue   Buddy Boatwright

Jeannie Boatwright   Barbara Bolden   Diane Bolin   Ellen Boyd   Phoebe Boykin

Lorene Bradley   Nancy Bradley   Billy Brakefield   Lee Brandt   Terry Braswell

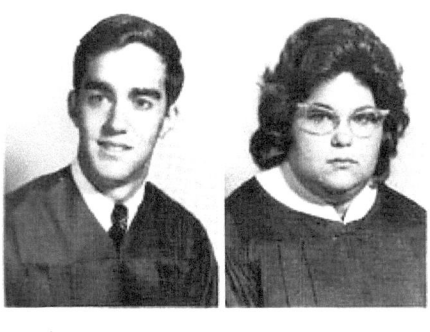

Rufus Bratton   Gail Brewington

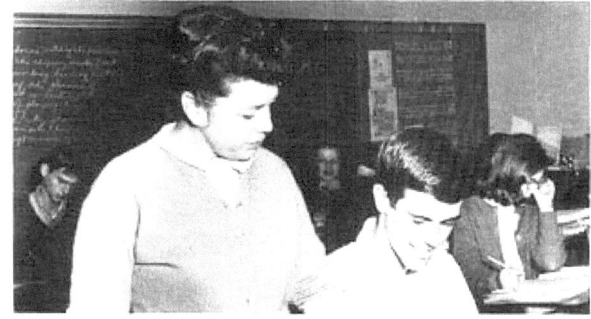

Now, Rocky, this is the last time I'm going to tell you the answer.

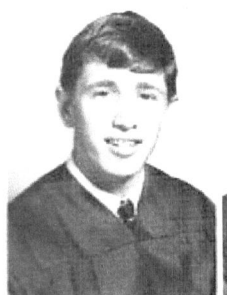 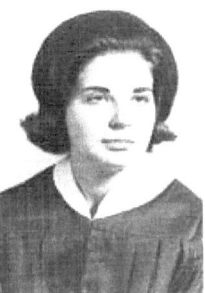 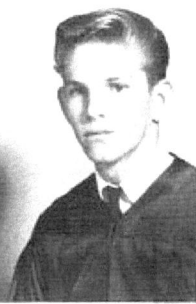 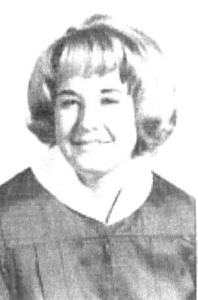 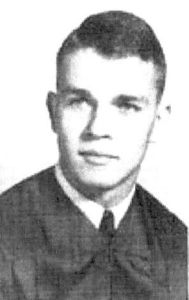

Danny Broadwater   Ellen Brooks   Raiford Brooks   Janie Brown   Robert Brown

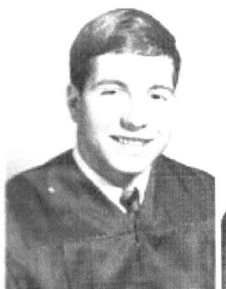 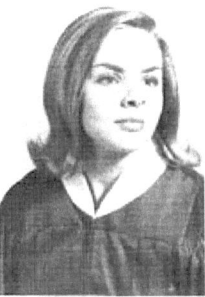 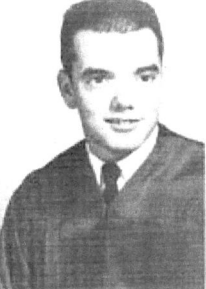 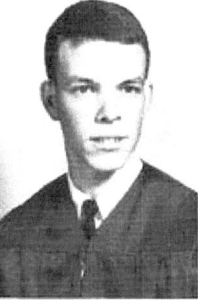 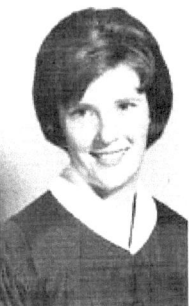

Chris Brumfield   Susanne Buddin   Bobby Burgess   Ed Burwell   Glenda Caldwell

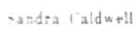 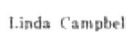 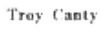 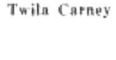 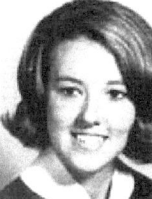

Sandra Caldwell   Linda Campbell   Troy Canty   Twila Carney   Pat Carothers

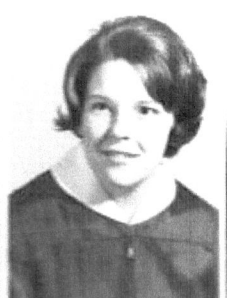 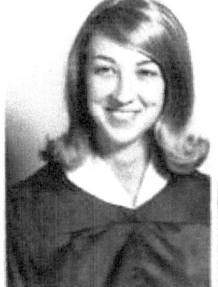 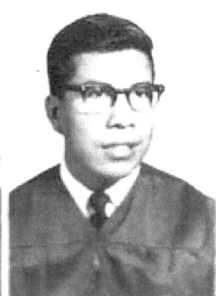 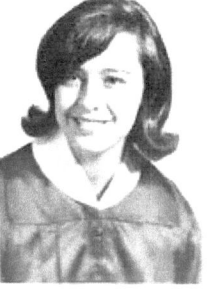

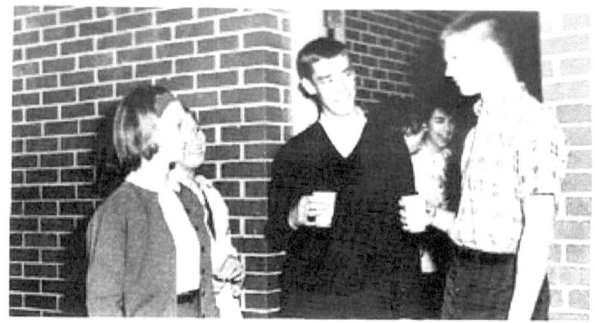
Come on in, the party's just starting.

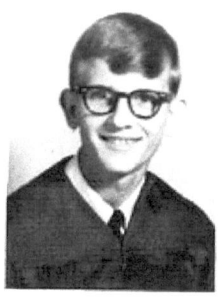
Leon Carpenter

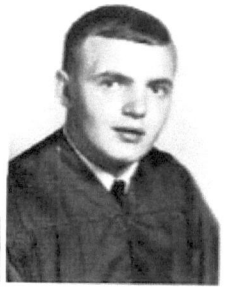
Mike Carpenter

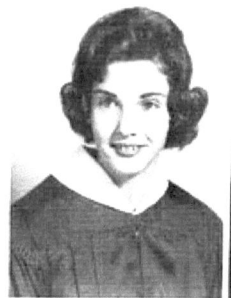
Donna Carroll

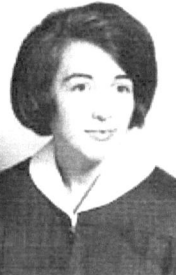
Jenny Carroll

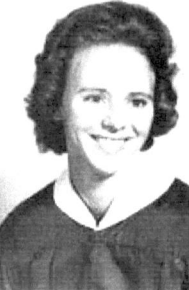
Brenda Carter

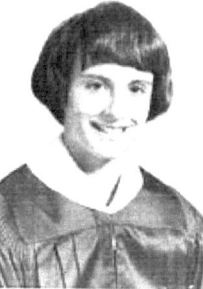
Ding Carter

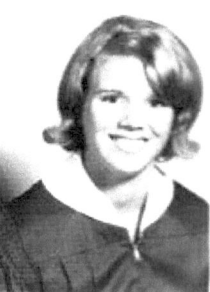
Gayle Carter

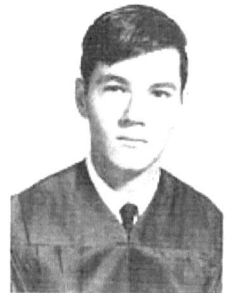
Tommy Carter

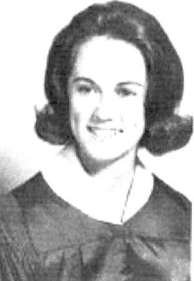
Vicki Carter

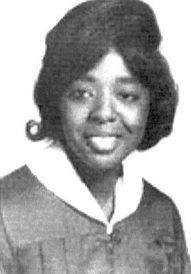
Betty Ruth Cathcart

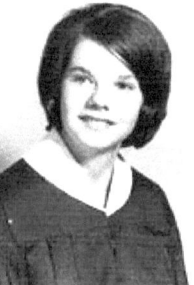
Claire Cauthen

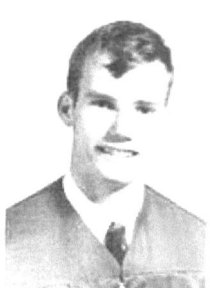
John Cauthen

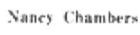
Nancy Chambers

Danny Chapman

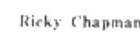
Ricky Chapman

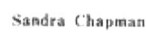
Sandra Chapman

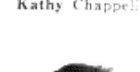
Kathy Chappell

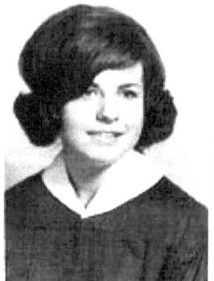
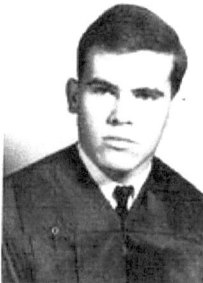
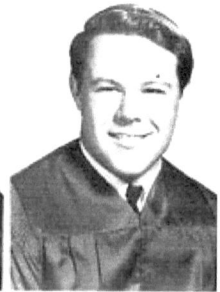
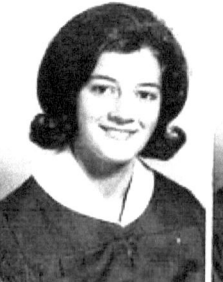
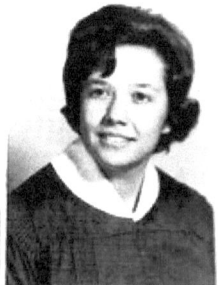

60

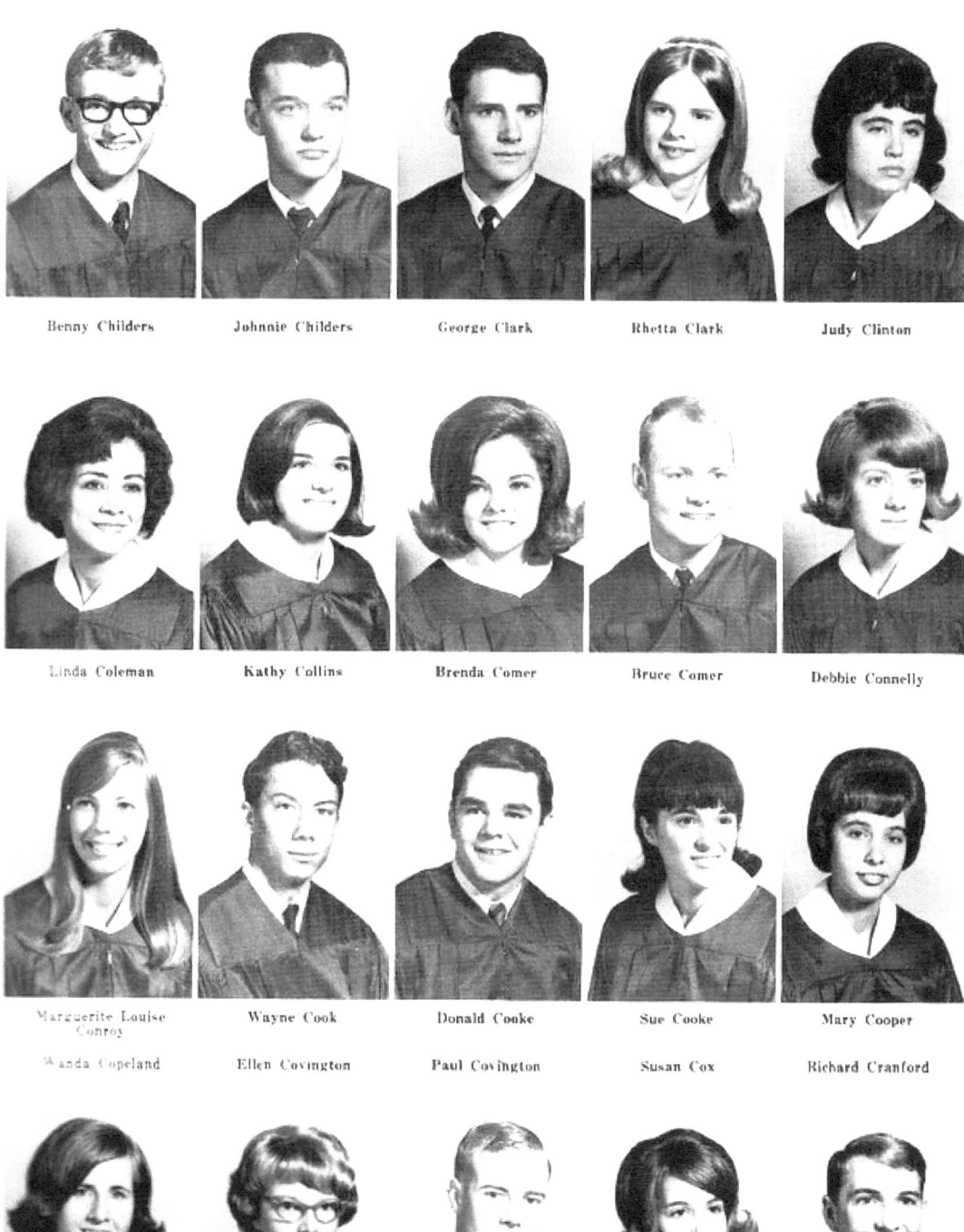

Benny Childers   Johnnie Childers   George Clark   Rhetta Clark   Judy Clinton

Linda Coleman   Kathy Collins   Brenda Comer   Bruce Comer   Debbie Connelly

Marguerite Louise Conroy   Wayne Cook   Donald Cooke   Sue Cooke   Mary Cooper

Wanda Copeland   Ellen Covington   Paul Covington   Susan Cox   Richard Cranford

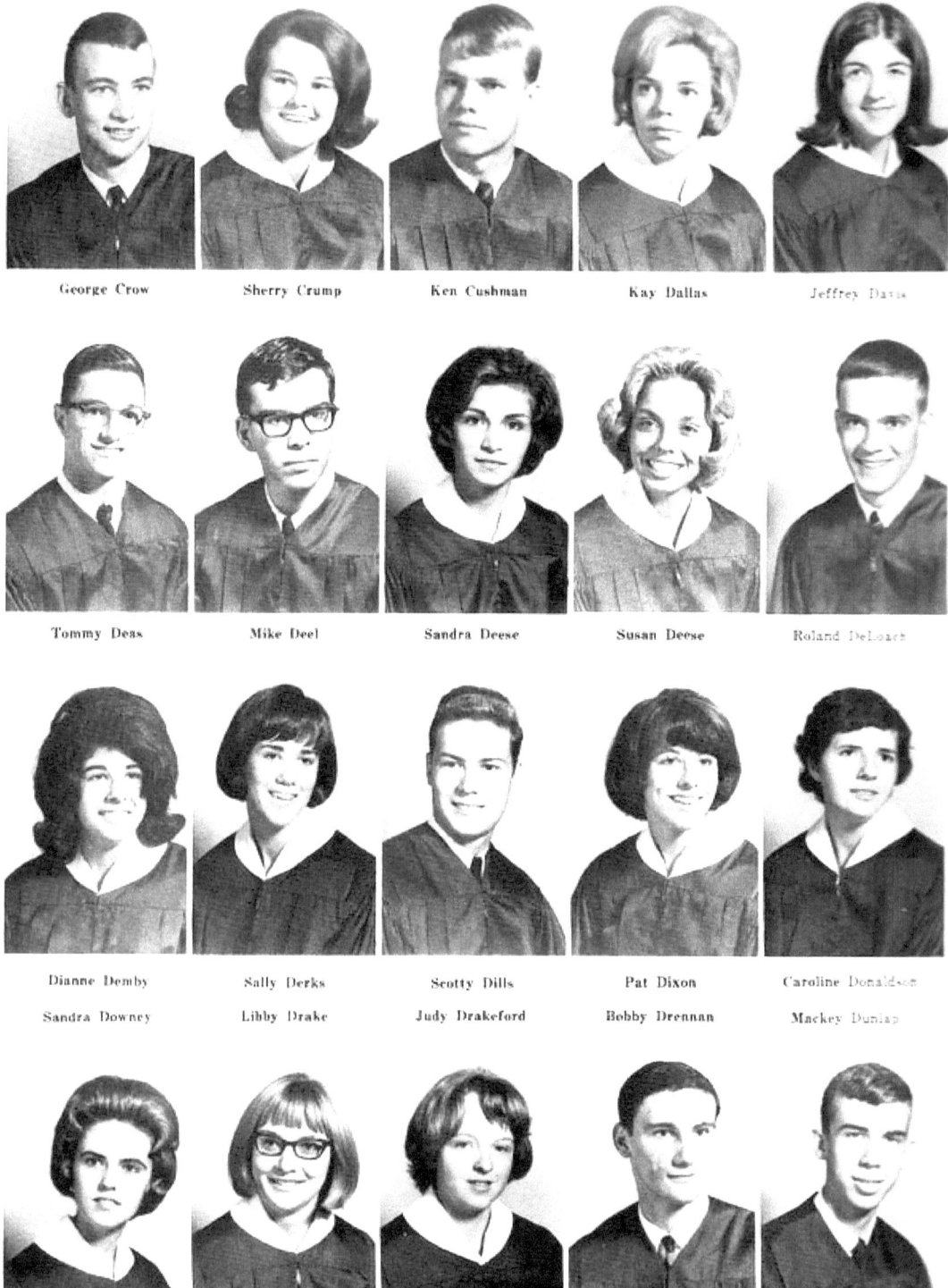

George Crow   Sherry Crump   Ken Cushman   Kay Dallas   Jeffrey Davis

Tommy Deas   Mike Deel   Sandra Deese   Susan Deese   Roland DeLoach

Dianne Demby   Sally Derks   Scotty Dills   Pat Dixon   Caroline Donaldson

Sandra Downey   Libby Drake   Judy Drakeford   Bobby Drennan   Mackey Dunlap

70

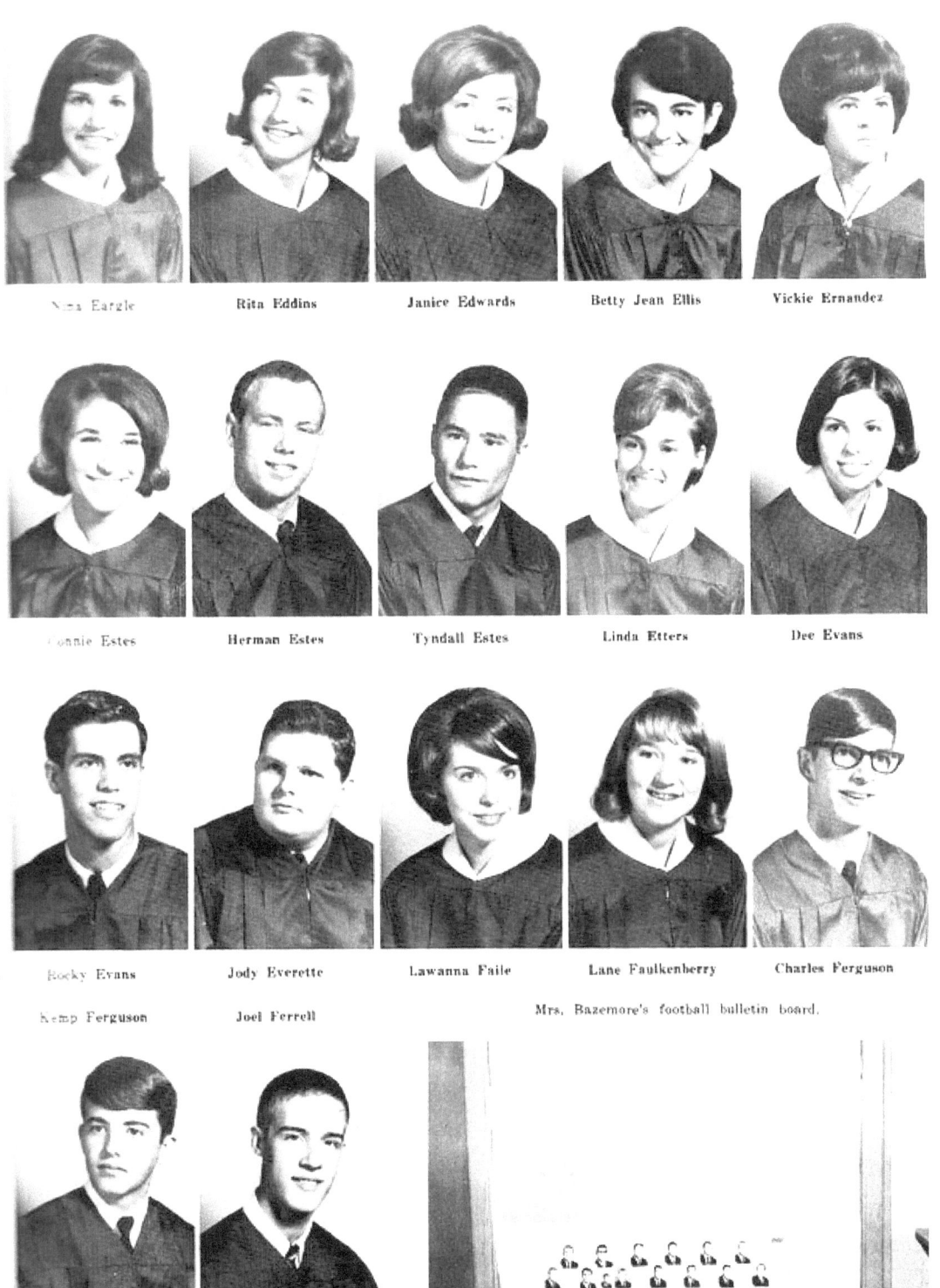

Nina Eargle   Rita Eddins   Janice Edwards   Betty Jean Ellis   Vickie Ernandez

Connie Estes   Herman Estes   Tyndall Estes   Linda Etters   Dee Evans

Rocky Evans   Jody Everette   Lawanna Faile   Lane Faulkenberry   Charles Ferguson

Kemp Ferguson   Joel Ferrell   Mrs. Bazemore's football bulletin board.

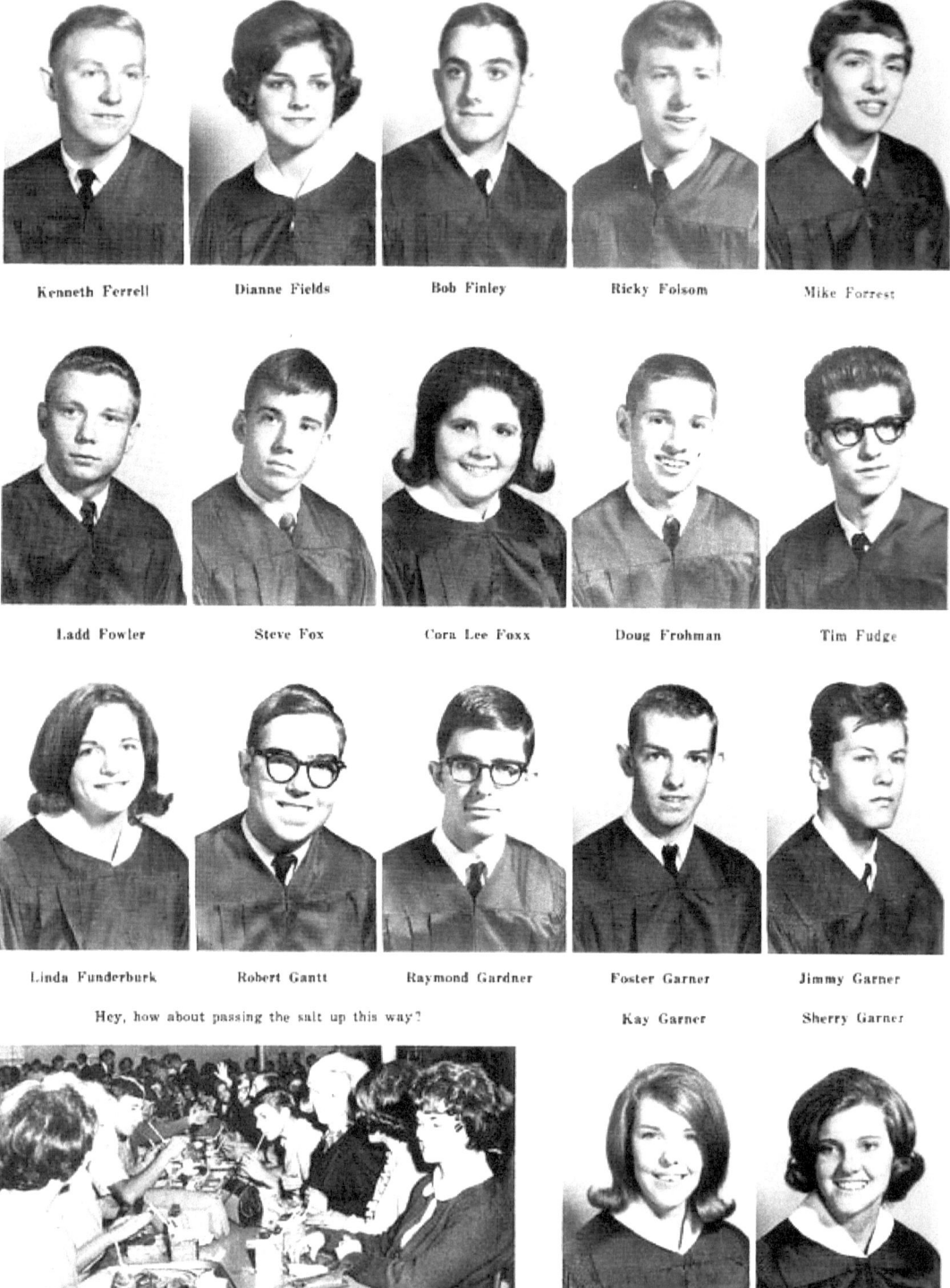

Kenneth Ferrell   Dianne Fields   Bob Finley   Ricky Folsom   Mike Forrest

Ladd Fowler   Steve Fox   Cora Lee Foxx   Doug Frohman   Tim Fudge

Linda Funderburk   Robert Gantt   Raymond Gardner   Foster Garner   Jimmy Garner

Hey, how about passing the salt up this way?

Kay Garner   Sherry Garner

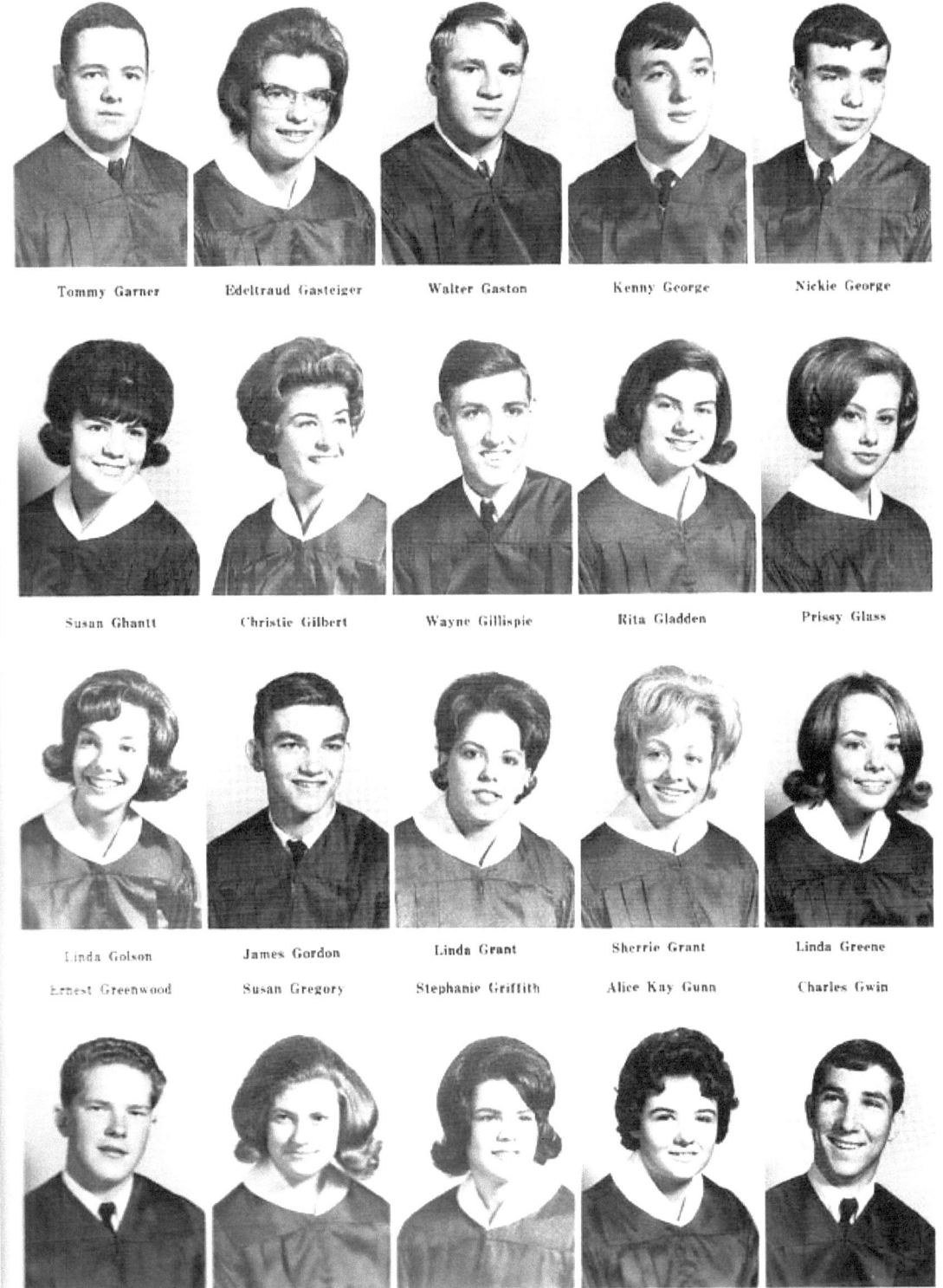

Tommy Garner	Edeltraud Gasteiger	Walter Gaston	Kenny George	Nickie George
Susan Ghantt	Christie Gilbert	Wayne Gillispie	Rita Gladden	Prissy Glass
Linda Golson	James Gordon	Linda Grant	Sherrie Grant	Linda Greene
Ernest Greenwood	Susan Gregory	Stephanie Griffith	Alice Kay Gunn	Charles Gwin

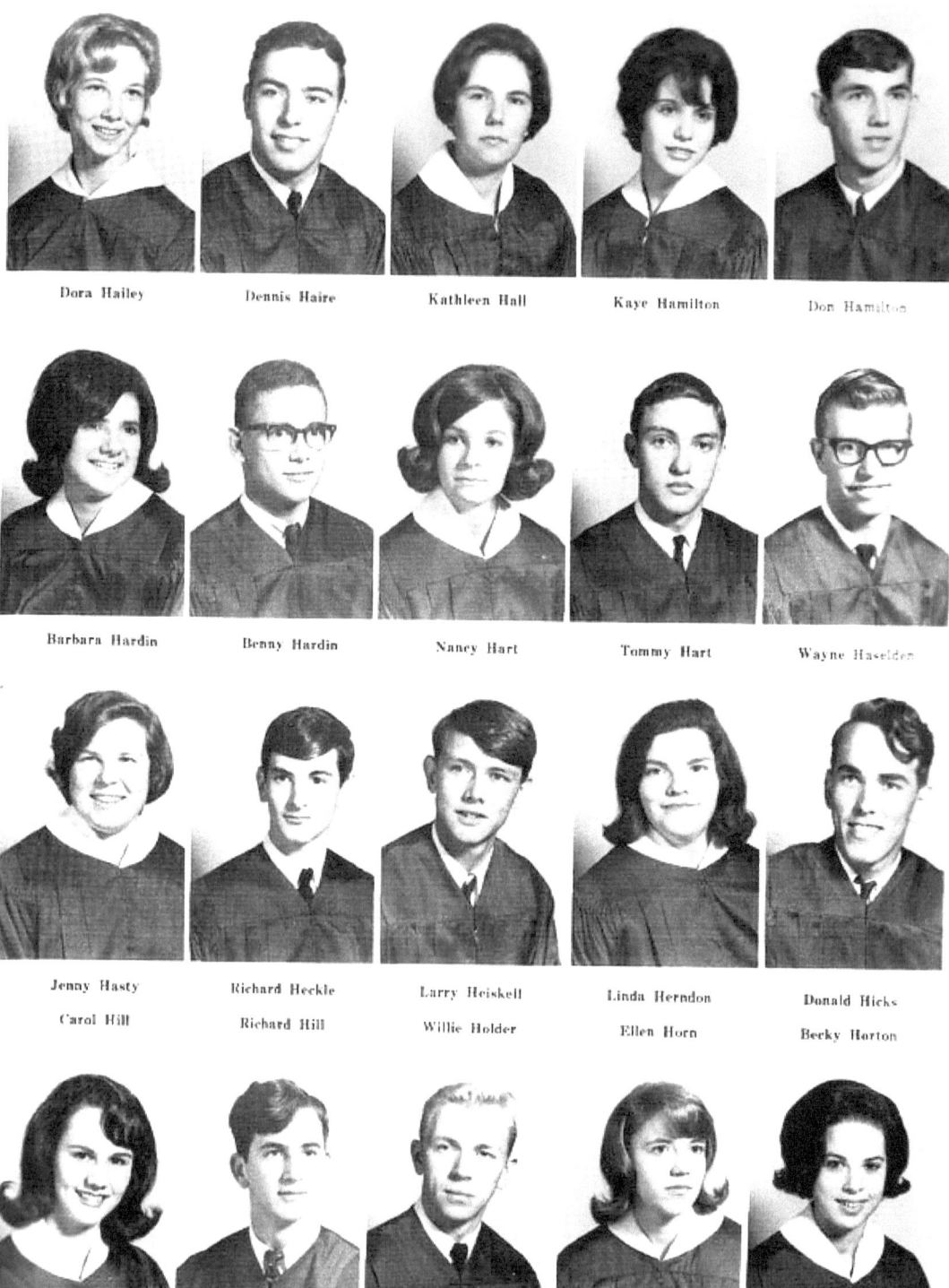

Dora Hailey   Dennis Haire   Kathleen Hall   Kaye Hamilton   Don Hamilton

Barbara Hardin   Benny Hardin   Nancy Hart   Tommy Hart   Wayne Haselden

Jenny Hasty   Richard Heckle   Larry Heiskell   Linda Herndon   Donald Hicks

Carol Hill   Richard Hill   Willie Holder   Ellen Horn   Becky Horton

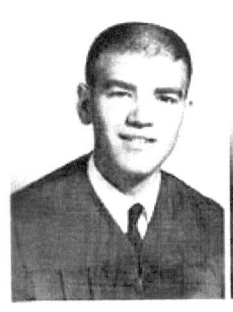
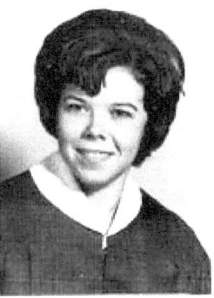
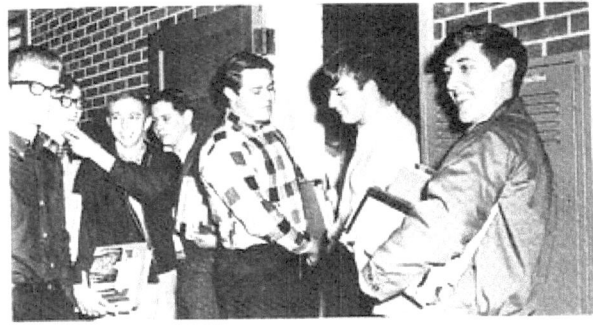

Jerry Howard   Sandra Hudspeth   Don't tell me you got stood up Saturday night, too!

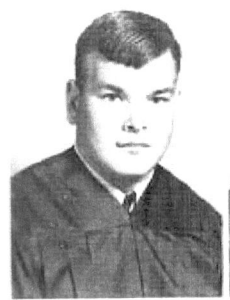
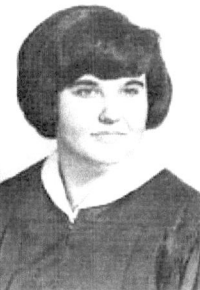
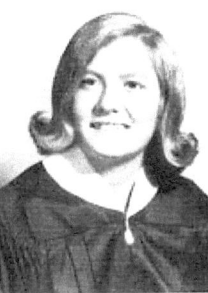
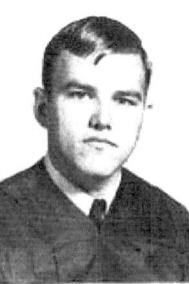
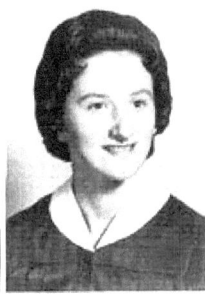

Johnny Hunter   Kaye Hunter   Linda Hunter   Bobby Hunter   Carol Hutchison

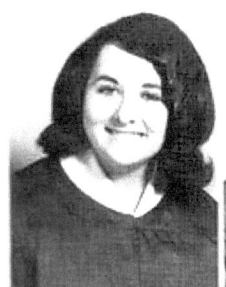
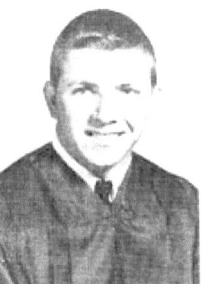
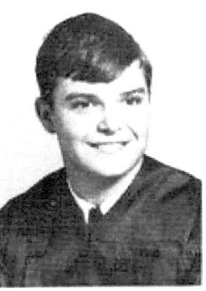
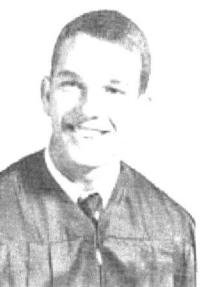
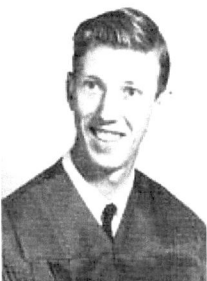

Laurena Hutto   Bobby Hyman   Sidney Ingram   David Inman   Jackie Irvin

Buddy Ivey   Marsha Jackson   Reba Jackson   Bobby Jackson   Wallace Jackson

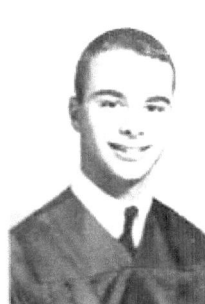
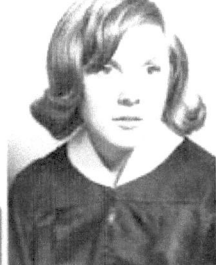
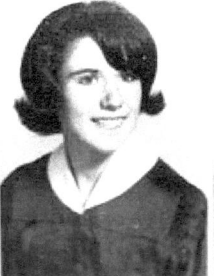
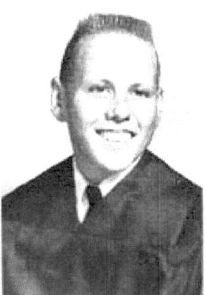
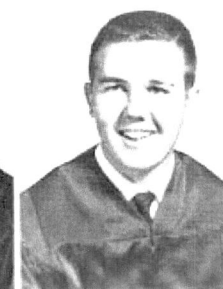

YEARBOOK PHOTOS FROM 1966

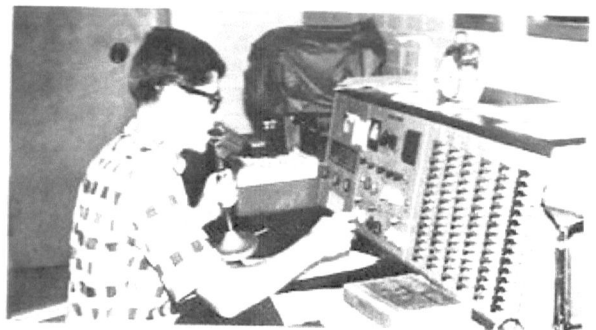

And don't forget about the Scott Martin Show . . .

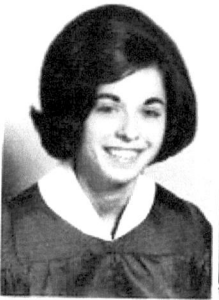

Maxine Jacobs

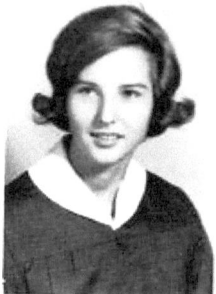

Mickie Jennings

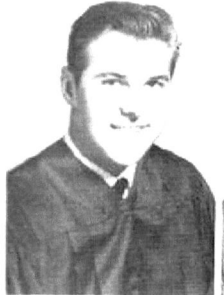

Lyle Jordan

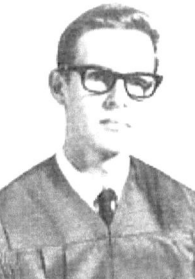

Stan Joyner

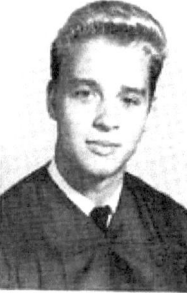

Gary Kennington

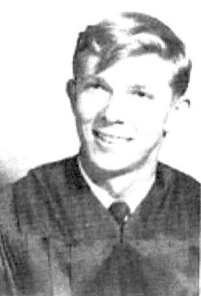

Randy Kessinger

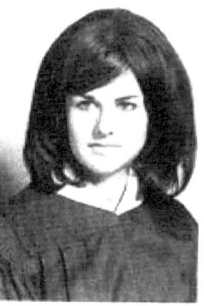

Bobbie Marie Key

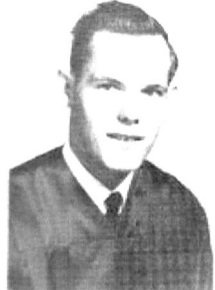

Finley Kimbrell

Gail King

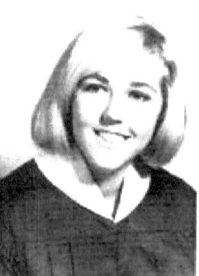

Gloria Kimbrell

Donnie King

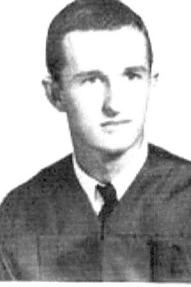

Jackie Kimbrell

Jane Knight

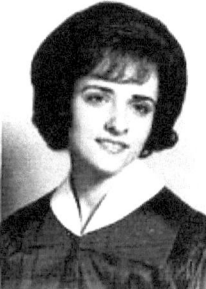

Diane Kimbrell

James Knox

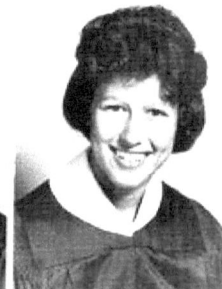

Margaret Kimbrell

Kathleen Knox

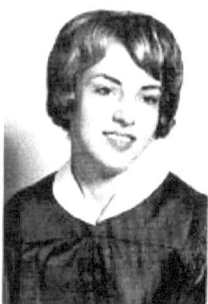

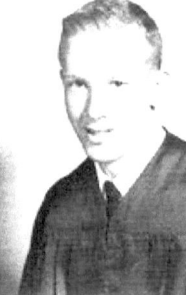

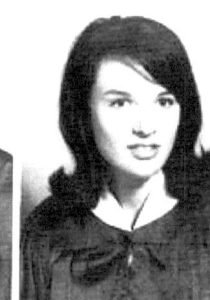

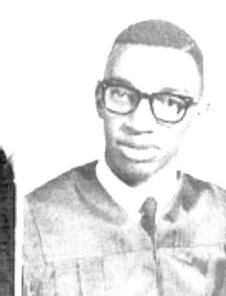

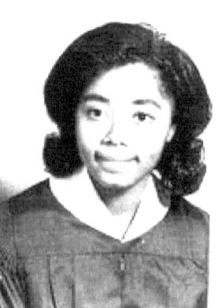

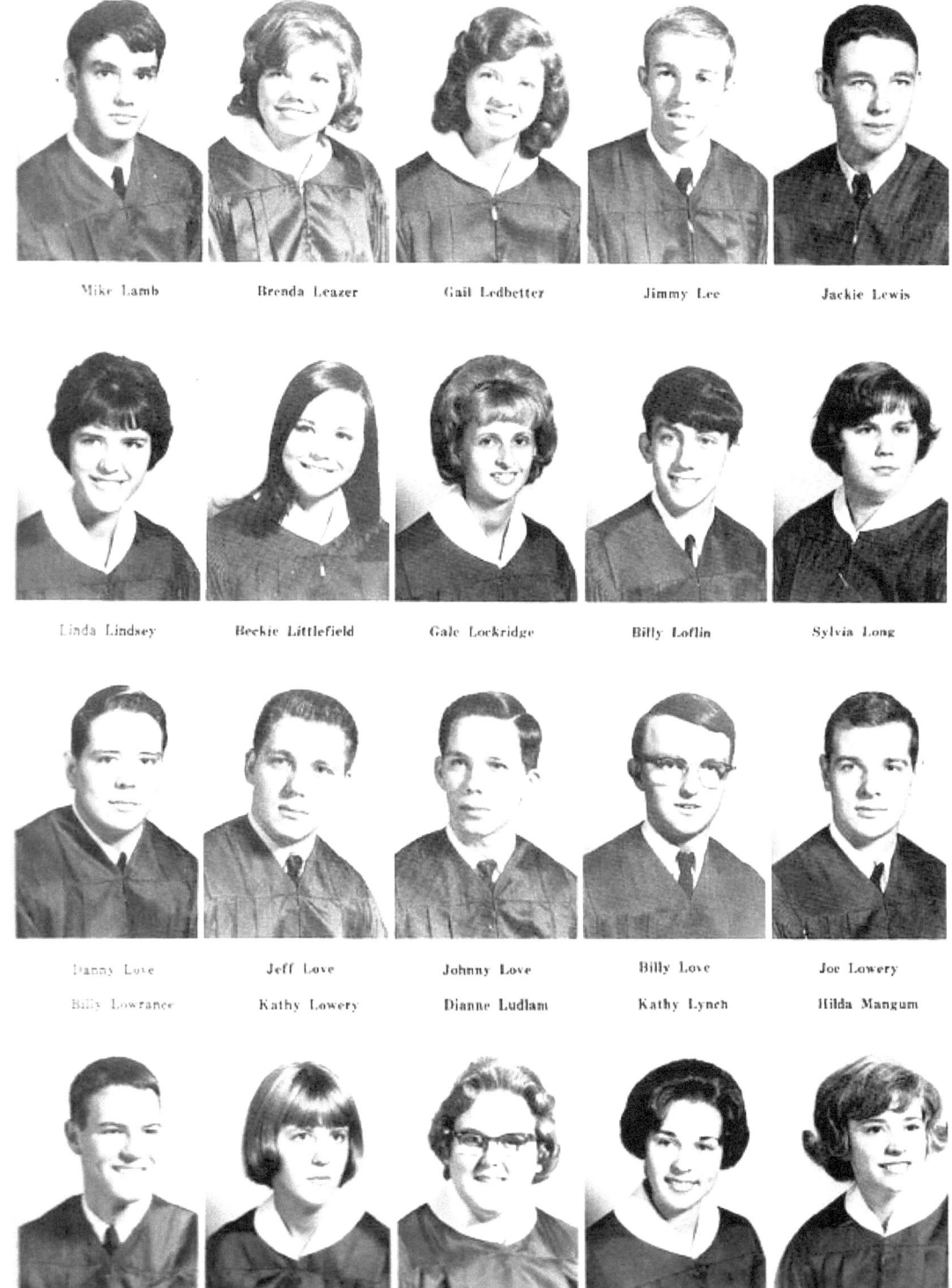

Mike Lamb   Brenda Leazer   Gail Ledbetter   Jimmy Lee   Jackie Lewis

Linda Lindsey   Beckie Littlefield   Gale Lockridge   Billy Loflin   Sylvia Long

Danny Love   Jeff Love   Johnny Love   Billy Love   Joe Lowery

Billy Lowrance   Kathy Lowery   Dianne Ludlam   Kathy Lynch   Hilda Mangum

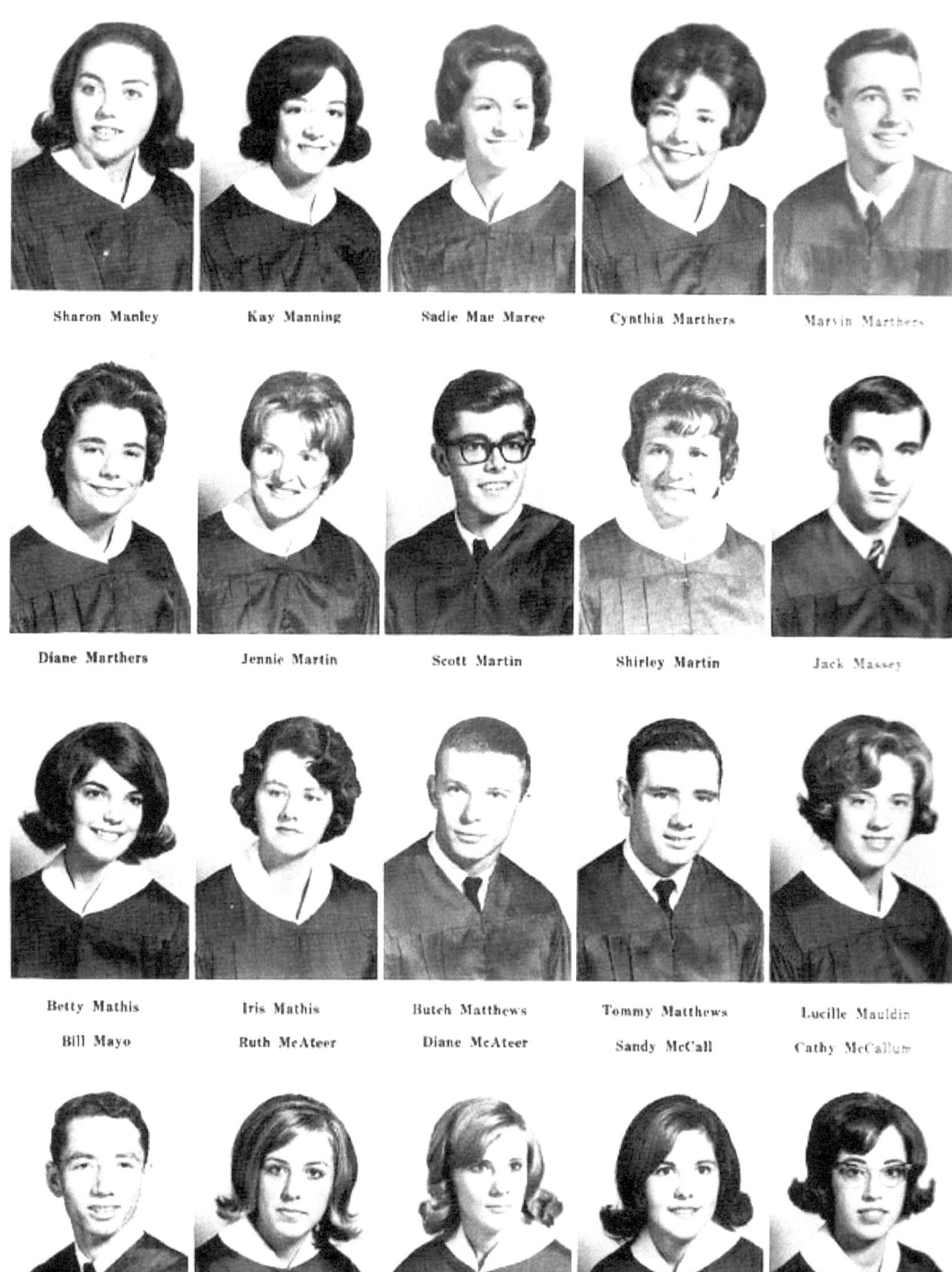

Sharon Manley   Kay Manning   Sadie Mae Maree   Cynthia Marthers   Marvin Marthers

Diane Marthers   Jennie Martin   Scott Martin   Shirley Martin   Jack Massey

Betty Mathis   Iris Mathis   Butch Matthews   Tommy Matthews   Lucille Mauldin

Bill Mayo   Ruth McAteer   Diane McAteer   Sandy McCall   Cathy McCallum

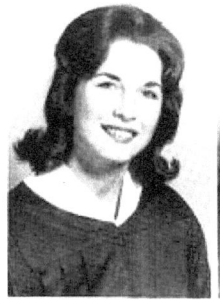 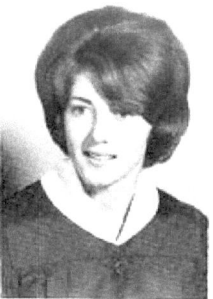 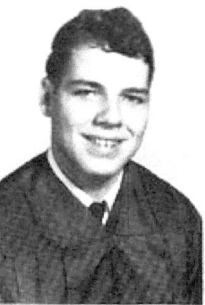 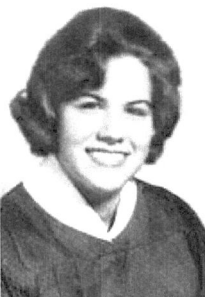 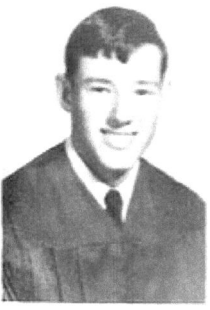

Mary Ann Moody   Elaine Moore   Joe Moore   Phyllis Moore   Bruce Morris

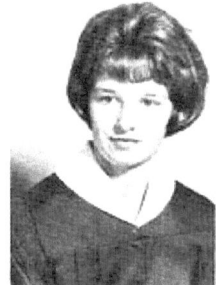 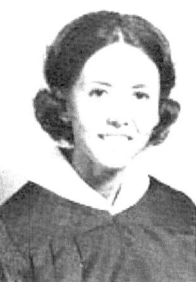 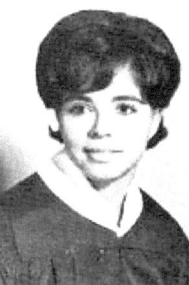 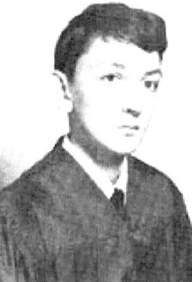 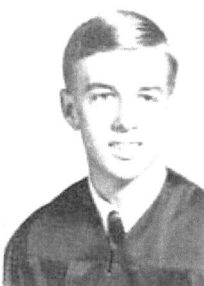

Rosalyn Morton   Norma Mullis   Nancy Munn   John Murphy   Bill Murphy

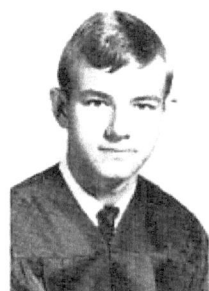 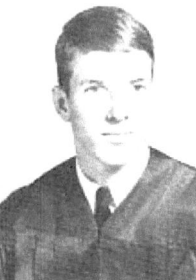 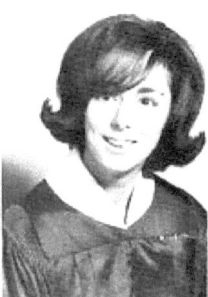 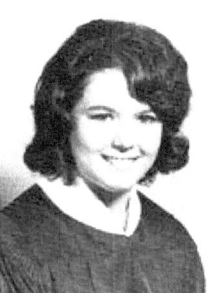 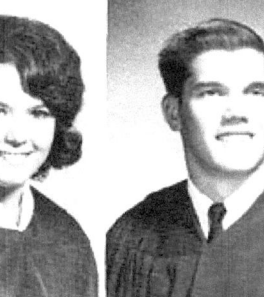

Donnie Mussman   Charles Neely   Sheila Newton   Jerrie Nichols   Jimmy Nies

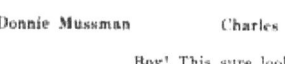

Boy! This sure looks good!

Beverly Nivens   Kenneth Nunnery

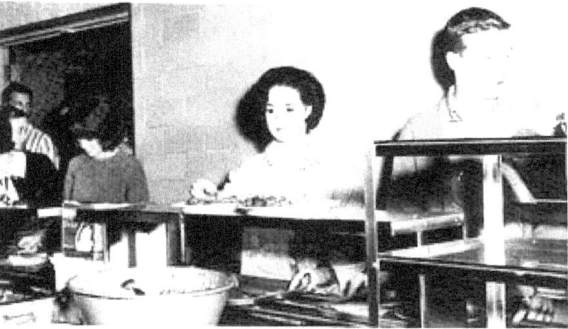

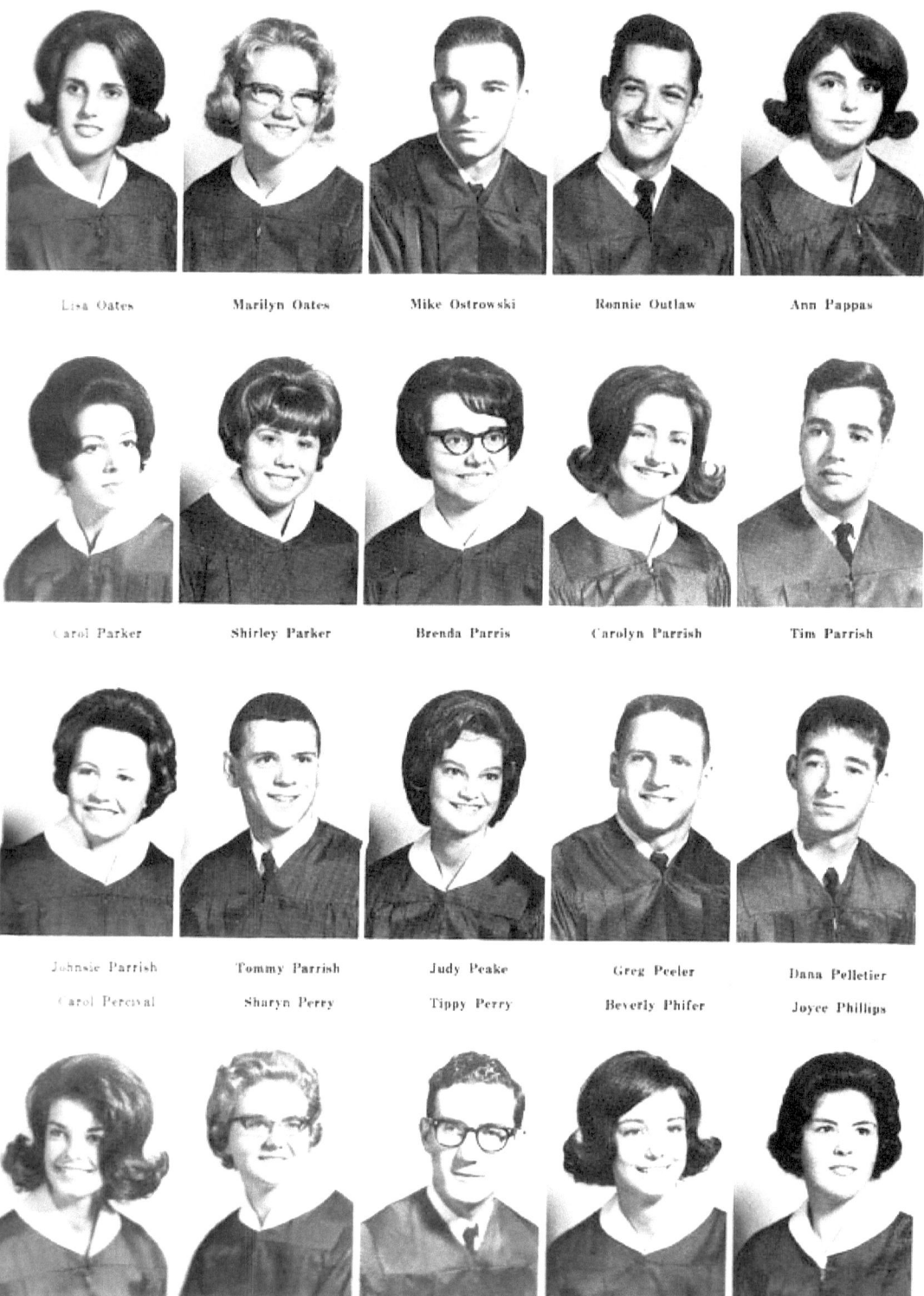

Lisa Oates   Marilyn Oates   Mike Ostrowski   Ronnie Outlaw   Ann Pappas

Carol Parker   Shirley Parker   Brenda Parris   Carolyn Parrish   Tim Parrish

Johnsie Parrish   Tommy Parrish   Judy Peake   Greg Peeler   Dana Pelletier

Carol Percival   Sharyn Perry   Tippy Perry   Beverly Phifer   Joyce Phillips

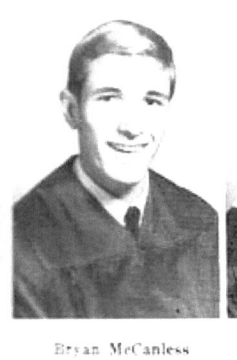 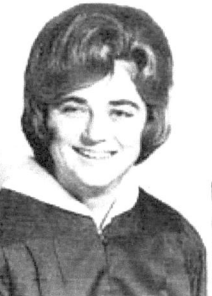 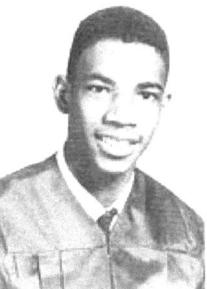 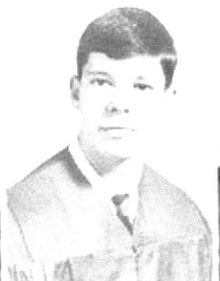 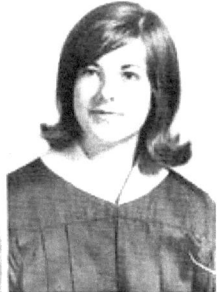

Bryan McCanless   Gayle McClain   Freddie McClurkin   Roland McElveen   Donna McFadden

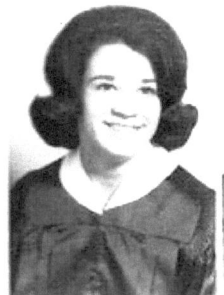 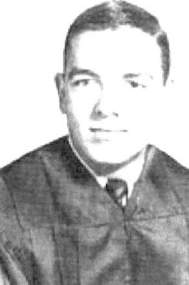 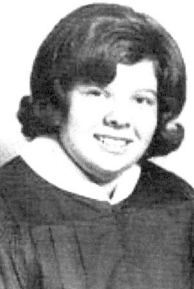 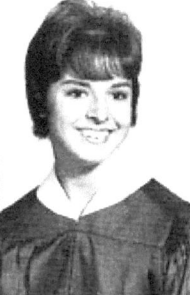 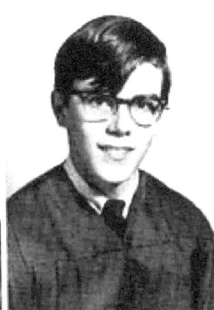

Darlene McGee   Eddie McGuirt   Brenda Means   Dianne Melton   Lawrence Melton

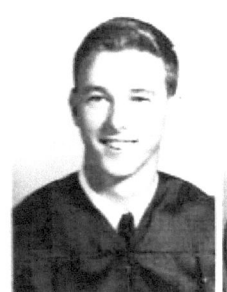 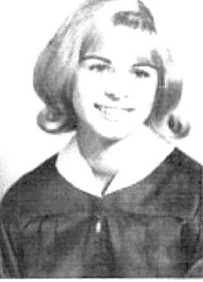 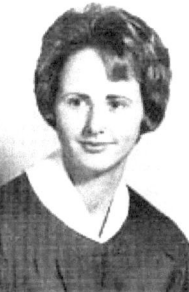 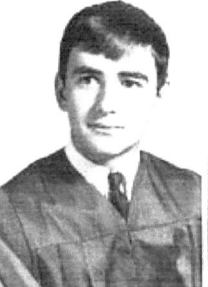 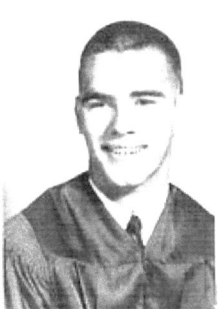

Steve Mickle   Judy Miller   Gail Millstead   Jimmy Mintz   Larry Misskelly

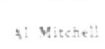 Al Mitchell   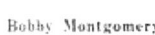 Bobby Montgomery   Man, I'm not believing those new uniforms!

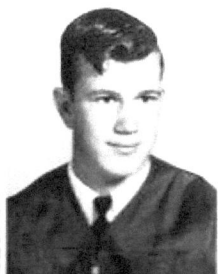 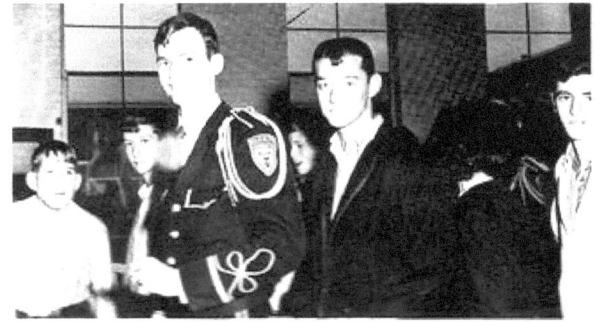

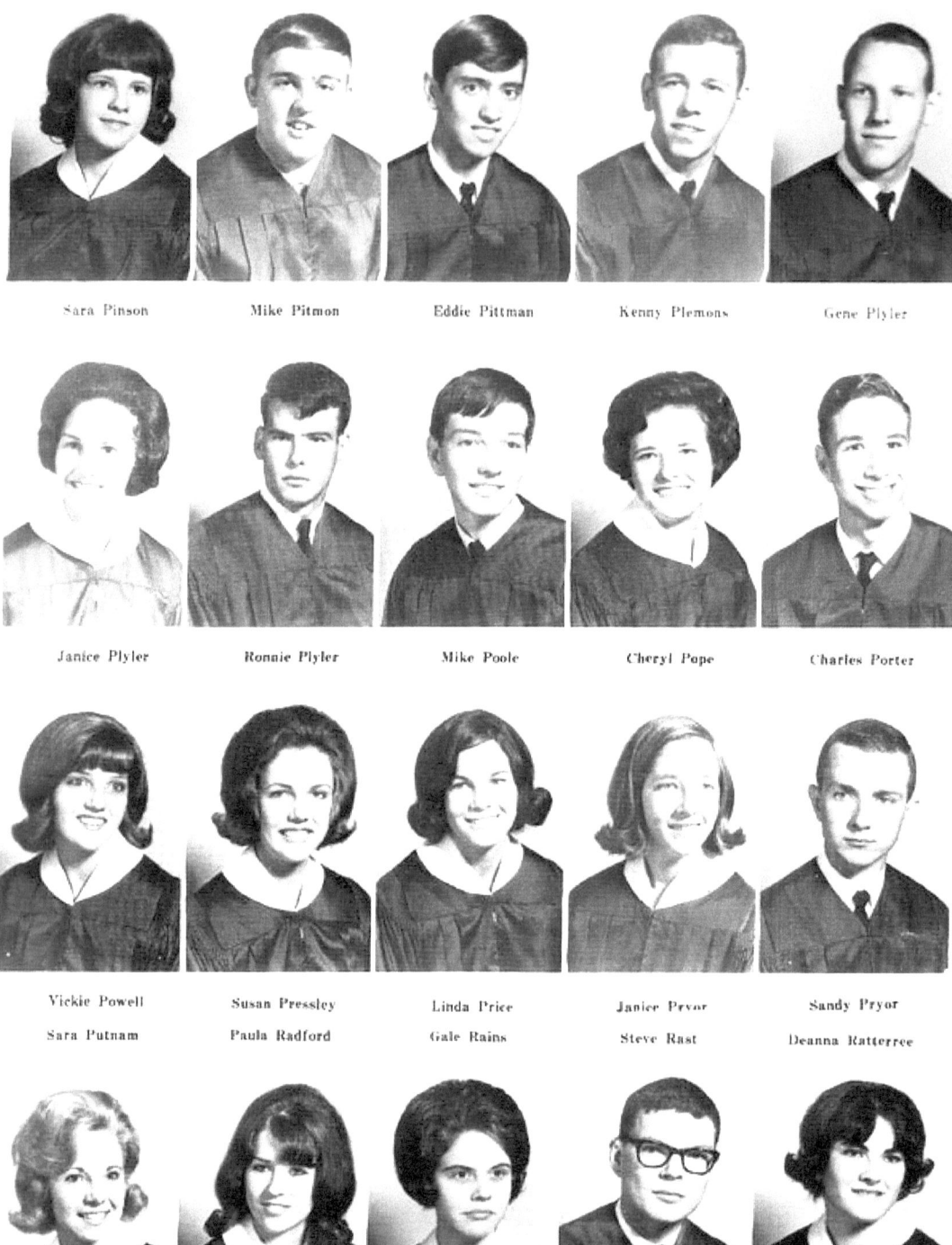

Sara Pinson Mike Pitmon Eddie Pittman Kenny Plemons Gene Plyler

Janice Plyler Ronnie Plyler Mike Poole Cheryl Pope Charles Porter

Vickie Powell Susan Pressley Linda Price Janice Pryor Sandy Pryor

Sara Putnam Paula Radford Gale Rains Steve Rast Deanna Ratterree

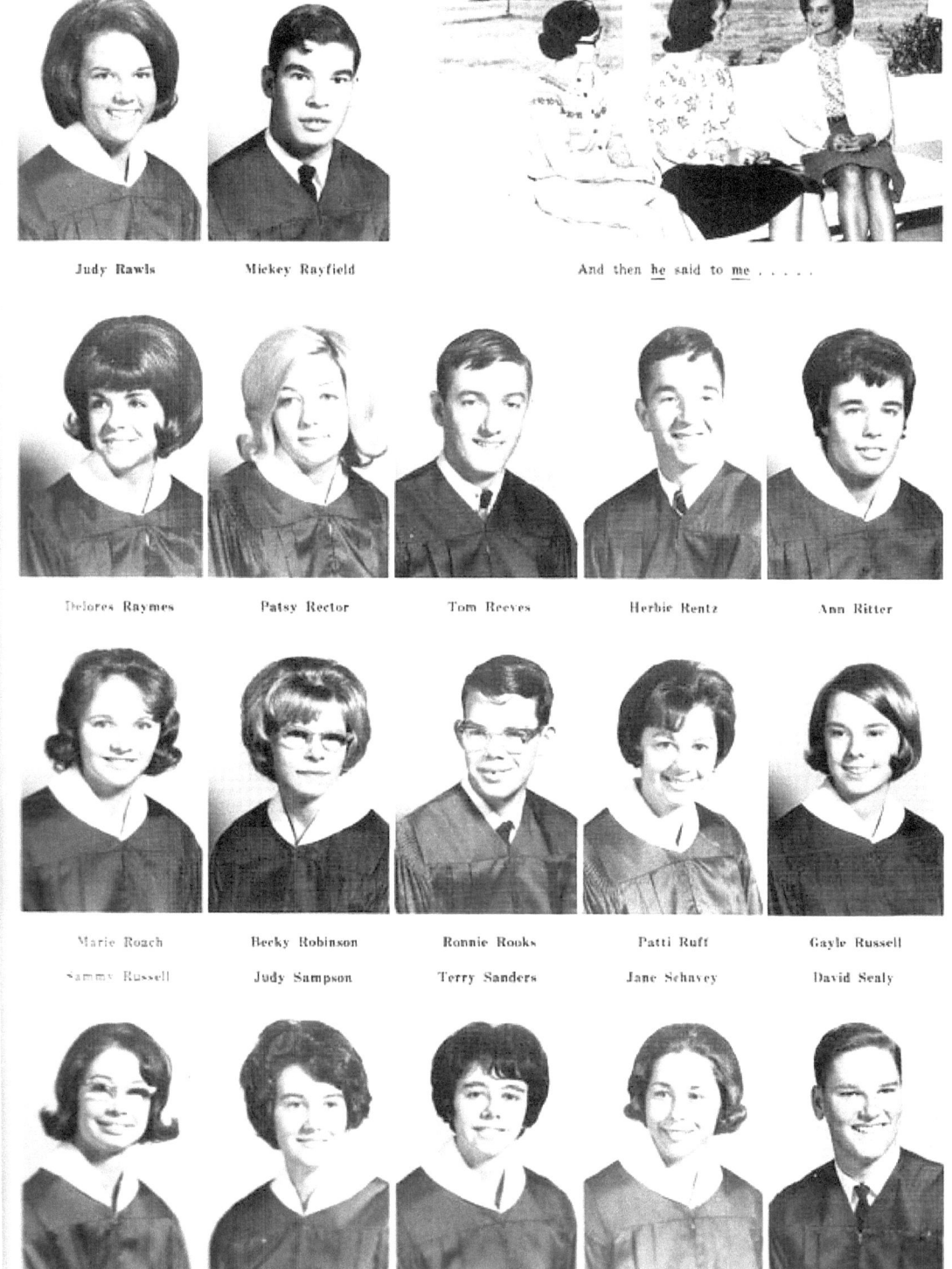

Judy Rawls   Mickey Rayfield   And then he said to me . . . . .

Delores Raymes   Patsy Rector   Tom Reeves   Herbie Rentz   Ann Ritter

Marie Roach   Becky Robinson   Ronnie Rooks   Patti Ruff   Gayle Russell

Sammy Russell   Judy Sampson   Terry Sanders   Jane Schavey   David Sealy

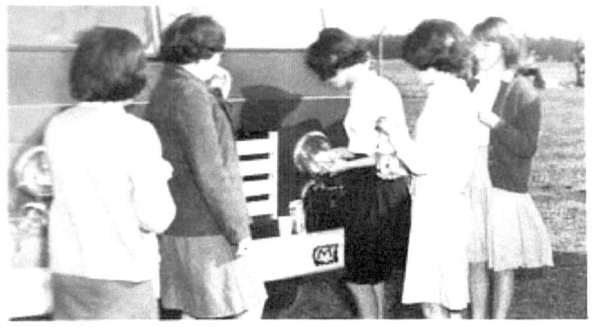
Straight from the truck to you.

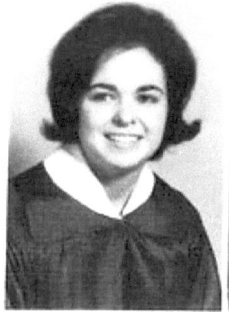
Patsy Seely

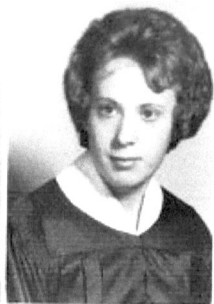
Sandy Sexton

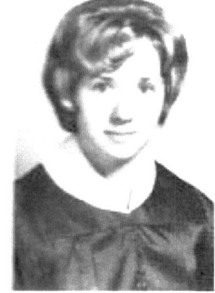
Helen Seymour

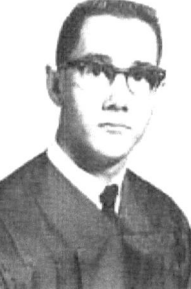
Carl Shaver

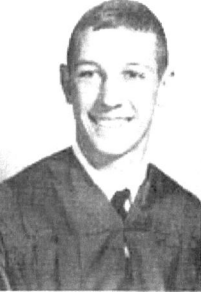
Larry Shaw

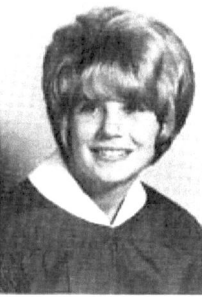
Penny Shaw

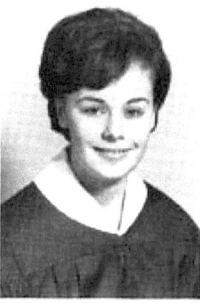
Brenda Simmons

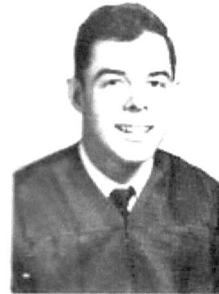
Spenser Simrill

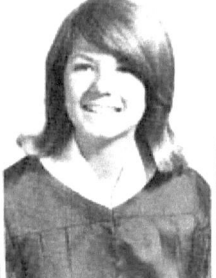
Jane Hall Sims

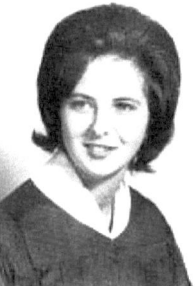
Shirley Sims

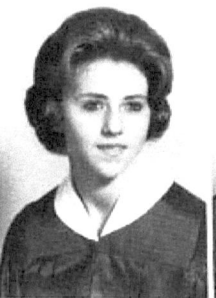
Debbie Sledge

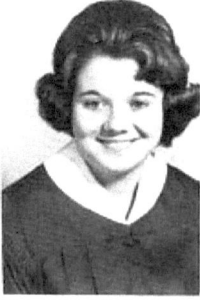
Ann Smith

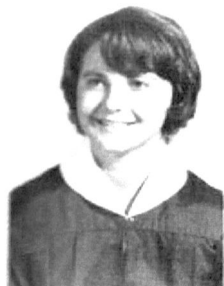
Gail Smith

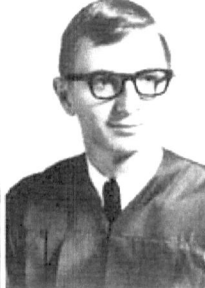
Garrett Smith

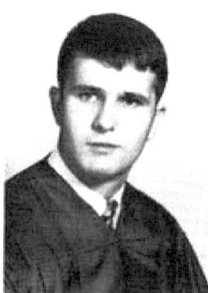
Jakey Smith

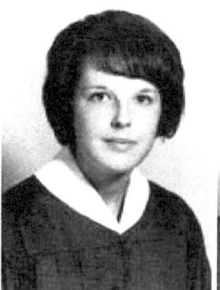
Pat Smith

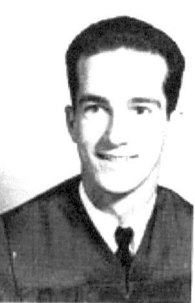
Bobby Snipes

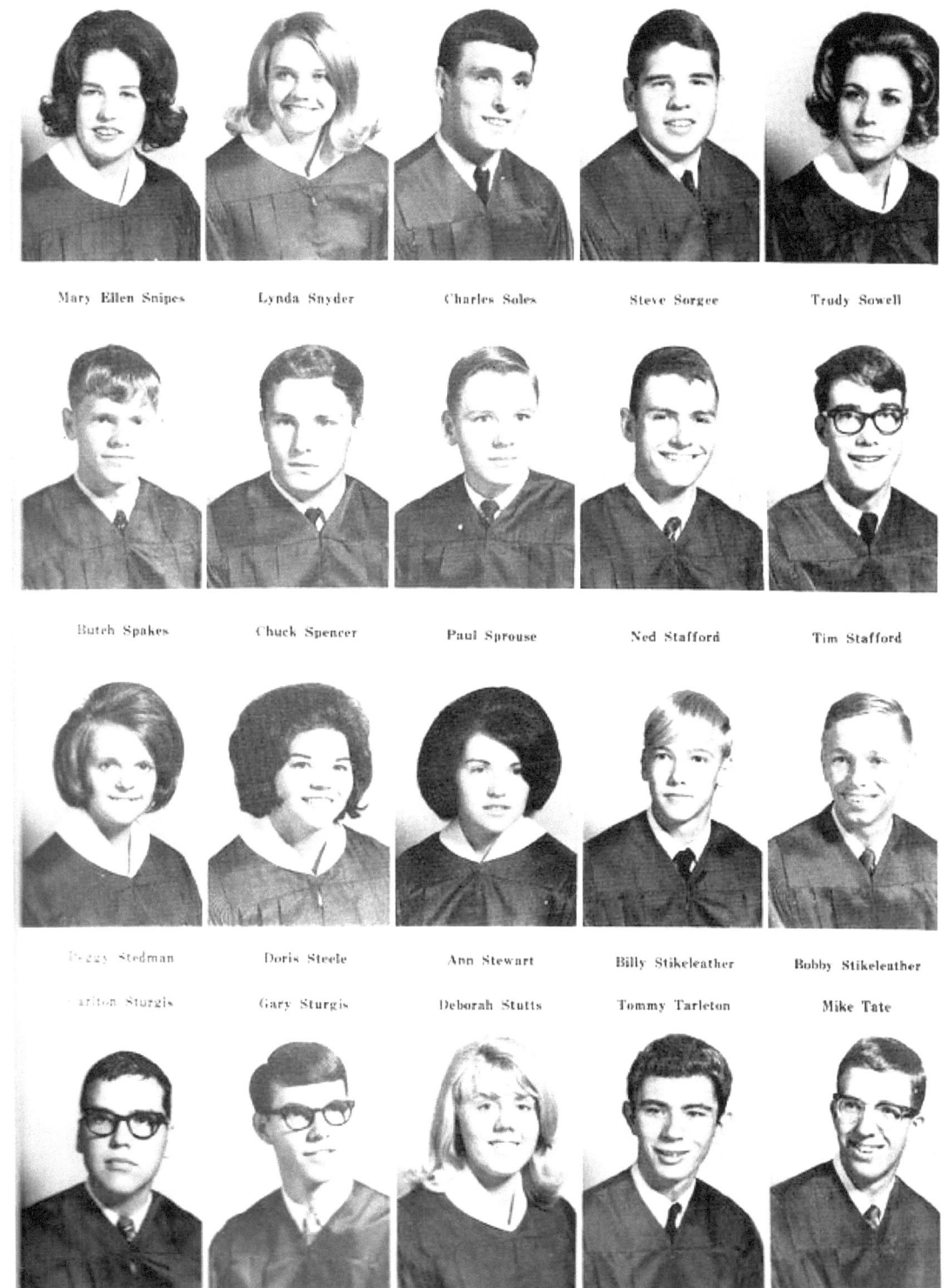

Mary Ellen Snipes   Lynda Snyder   Charles Soles   Steve Sorgee   Trudy Sowell

Butch Spakes   Chuck Spencer   Paul Sprouse   Ned Stafford   Tim Stafford

Peggy Stedman   Doris Steele   Ann Stewart   Billy Stikeleather   Bobby Stikeleather

Carlton Sturgis   Gary Sturgis   Deborah Stutts   Tommy Tarleton   Mike Tate

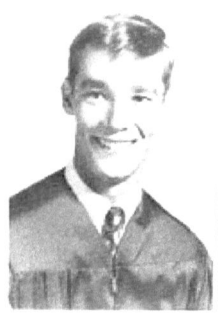 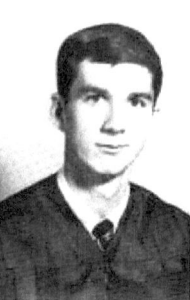 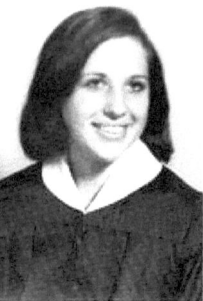 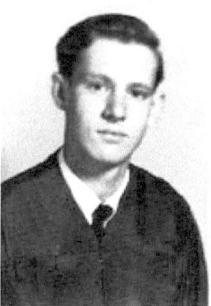 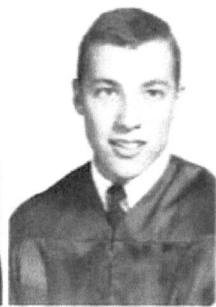

| Furman Asbury Taylor | Tommy Taylor | Linda Tedder | Frankie Thomas | Goody Thomas |

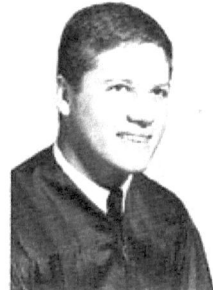 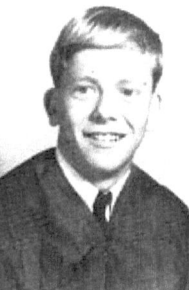 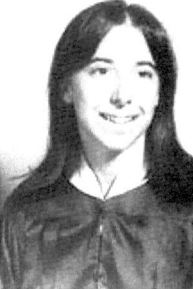 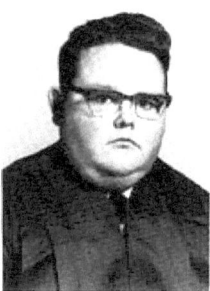 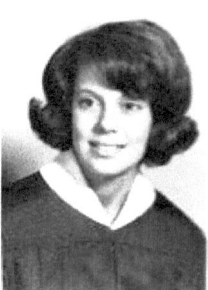

| Steve Thomas | Jerry Thompson | Martha Ticktin | Ted Tinker | Karen Tinsley |

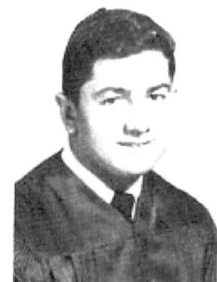 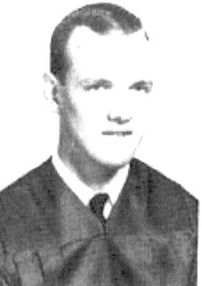 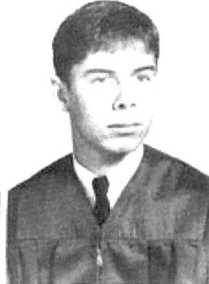 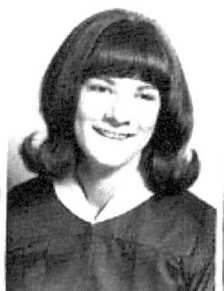 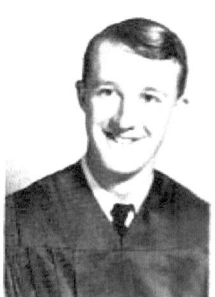

| Neal Tobias | Joe Tucker | Gene Turbeville | Judy Turner | Steve Turney |

| Carol Vails | Jimmy Vick | Wanda Vinson | Jimmy Viola | Saundra Vogel |

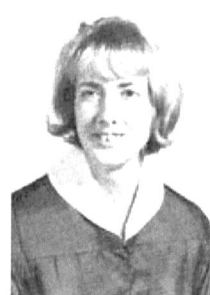 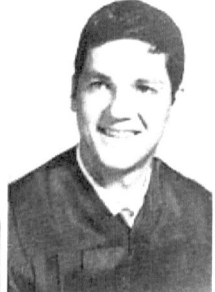 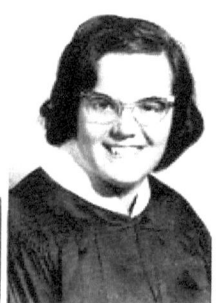 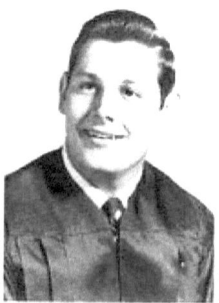 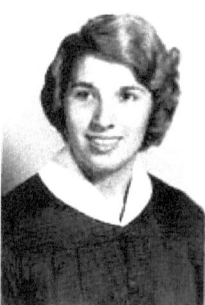

86

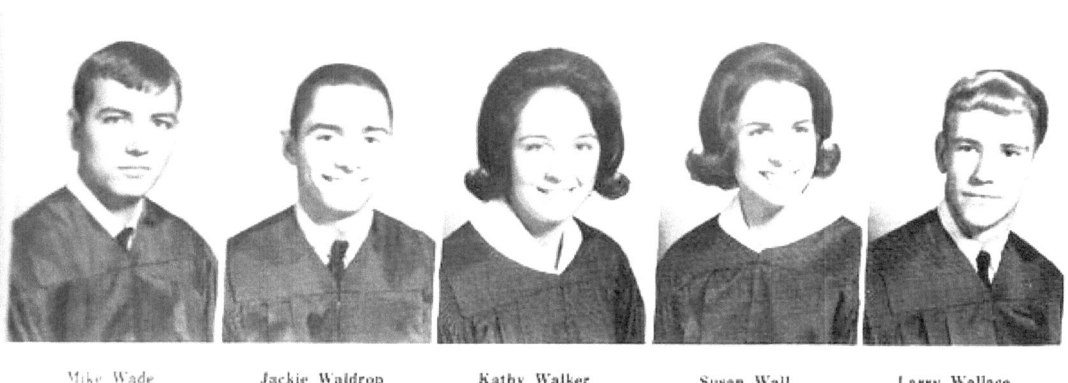

Mike Wade   Jackie Waldrop   Kathy Walker   Susan Wall   Larry Wallace

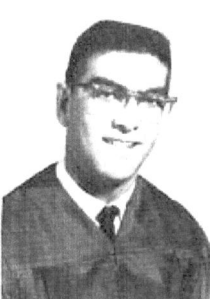 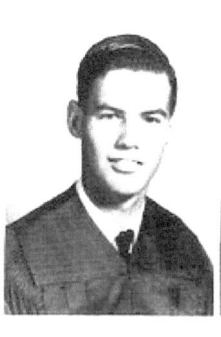 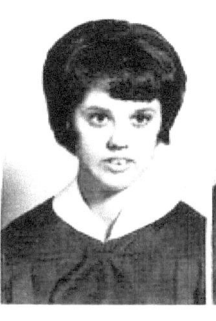 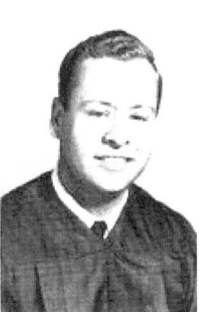

Paul Watson   Dan Webster   Tommy Wells   Pat West   Roy Westerlund

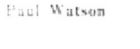

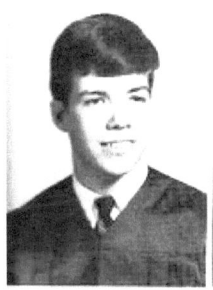 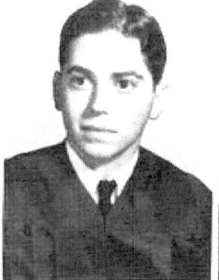 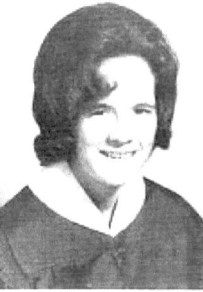 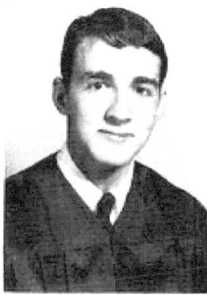 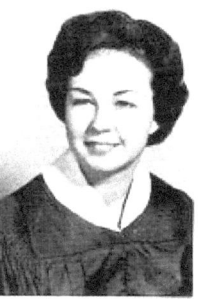

_____ Westmoreland   Lewis Whisonant   Jean White   Robert White   Rosemarie Whitener

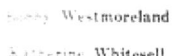

Katherine Whitesell   Rita Whitesides   We never had it so easy,

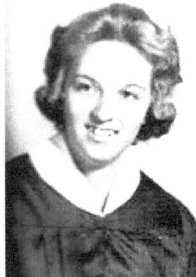 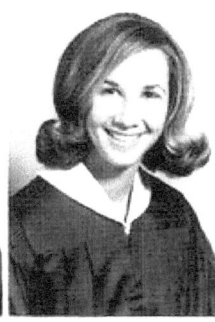 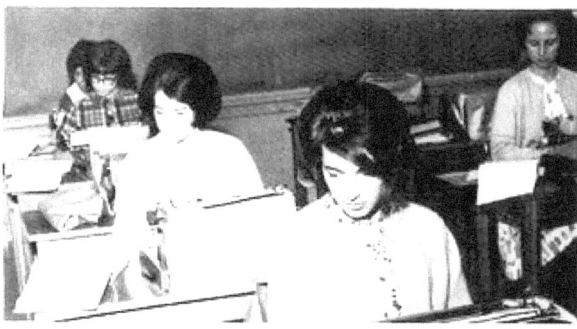

87

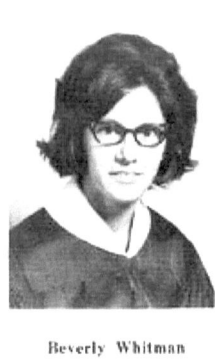 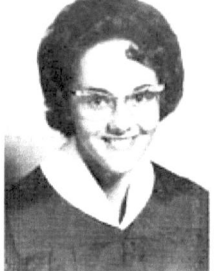 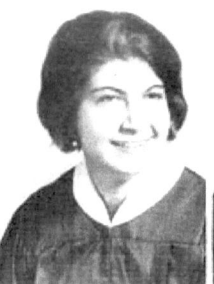 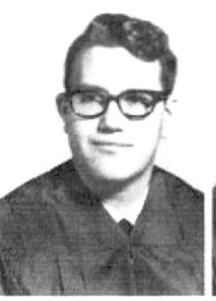 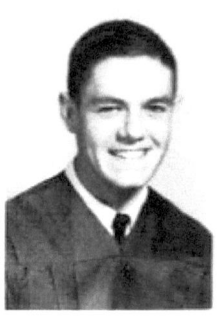

Beverly Whitman   Brenda Williams   Ellen Williams   Herbert Williams   Jerry Williams

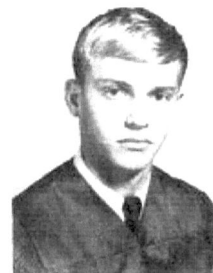 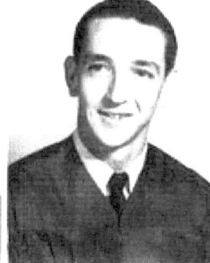 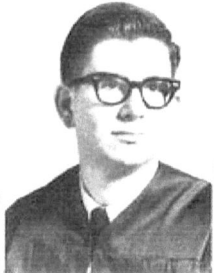 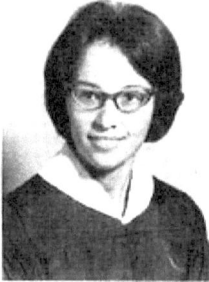 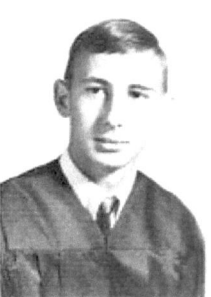

Ricky Williams   Steve Williams   Terry Williams   Patricia Williford   Charles Wilson

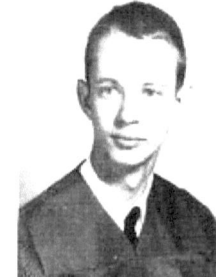 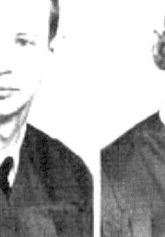 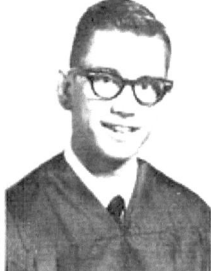 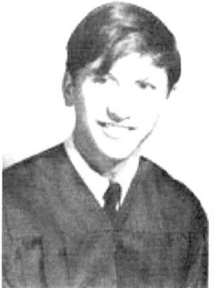 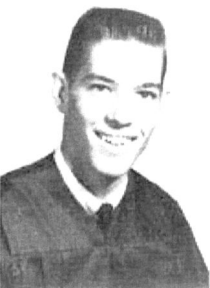 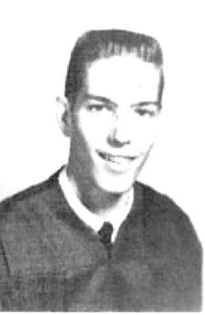

Curt Wilson   David Wilson   Jimmy Winchester   Jerry Wingate   Terry Wingate

Are these our secretaries of tomorrow?   Ricky Wisher   Jean Wolfe

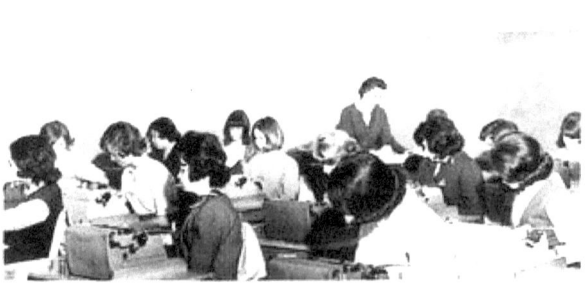 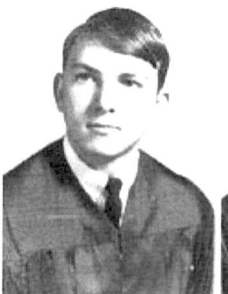 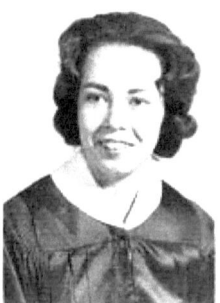

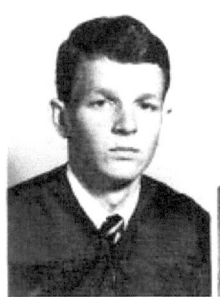
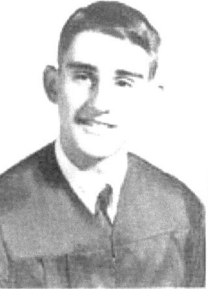
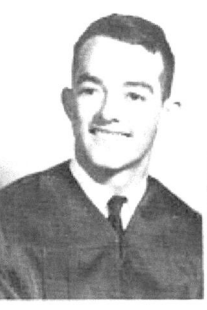
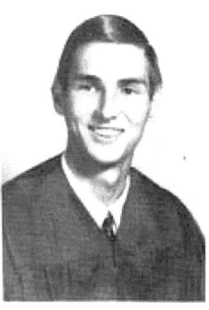
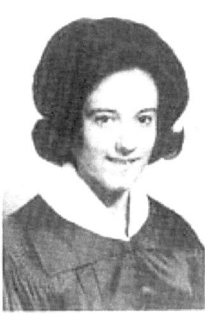

| Mike Woodall | Steve Wrenn | Ernie Wright | Tommy Wright | Marsha Yandle |

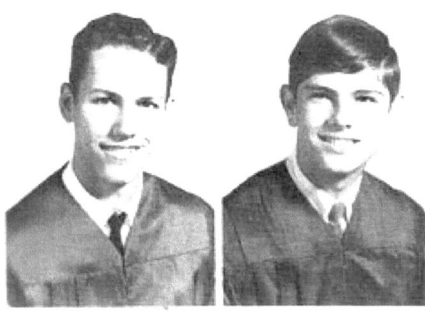

Kenneth Yates   Max Youngblood

NOT PICTURED:

Frank Robert Alford, Harriett Merle Bell, Sidney P. Bray, Ronnie D. Broome, Jerry E. Brown, Glenn R. Buchanan, Herbert Clay Carruth, Hubert L. Collins, Phillip D. Comer, Carl W. Drakford, Gerald W. Faries, John T. Gaston, Frank W. Harp, Homer V. Harris, Terrie S Hinson, William R. Hoke, James D. Kirkland, Darrell McDaniel, Roland J. Morris, Don Reece Oliver, John R. Ostrowski, David G. Rogers, Michael D. Snyder, Jeffrey L. Stanley, James R. Stephenson, Dudley C. Sturgis, Robert A. Sutton, Richard L. Threatt, Danny Lee Tipton, Randy L. Warren, Grady W. Watkins, John W. Williams, Albert E. Workman.

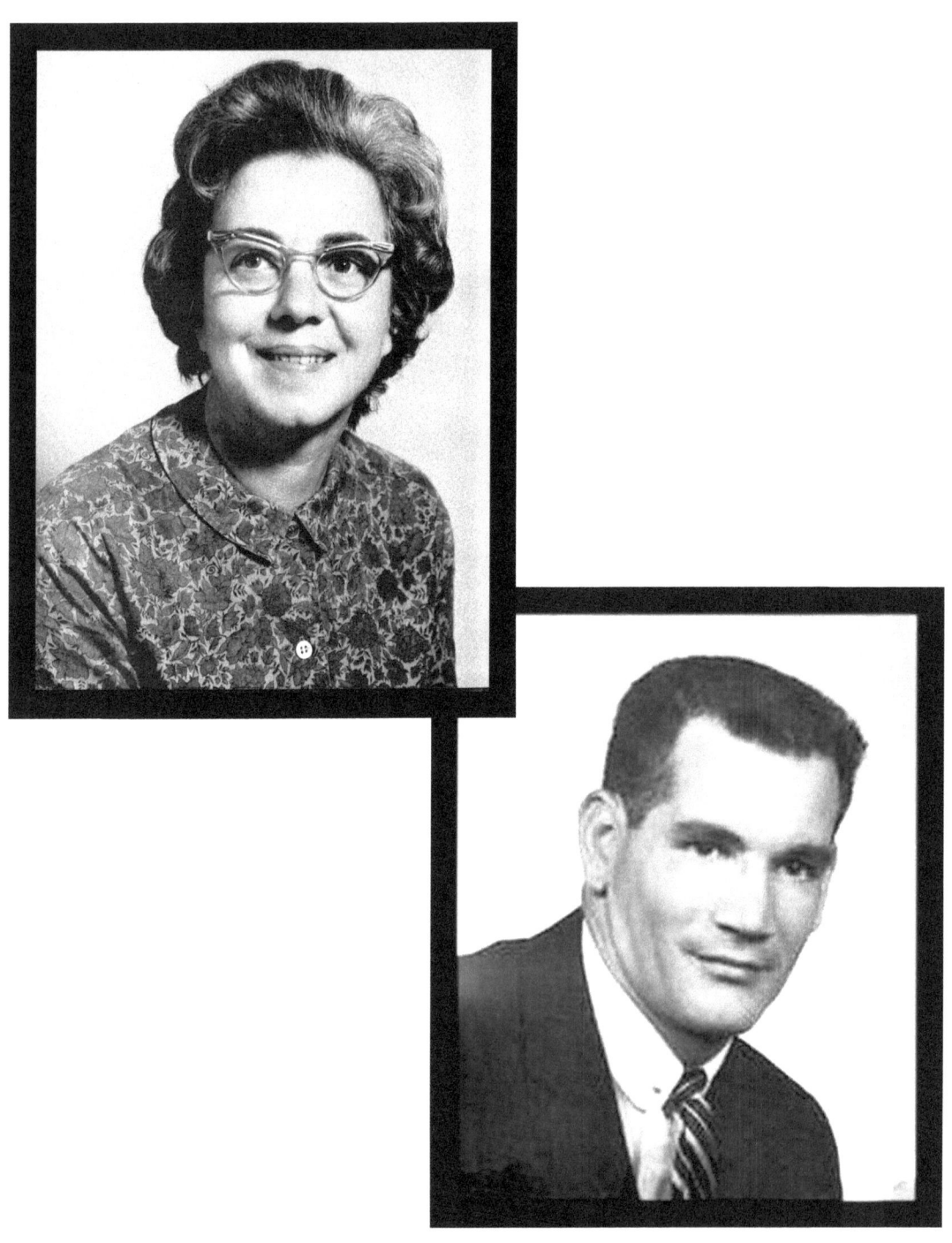

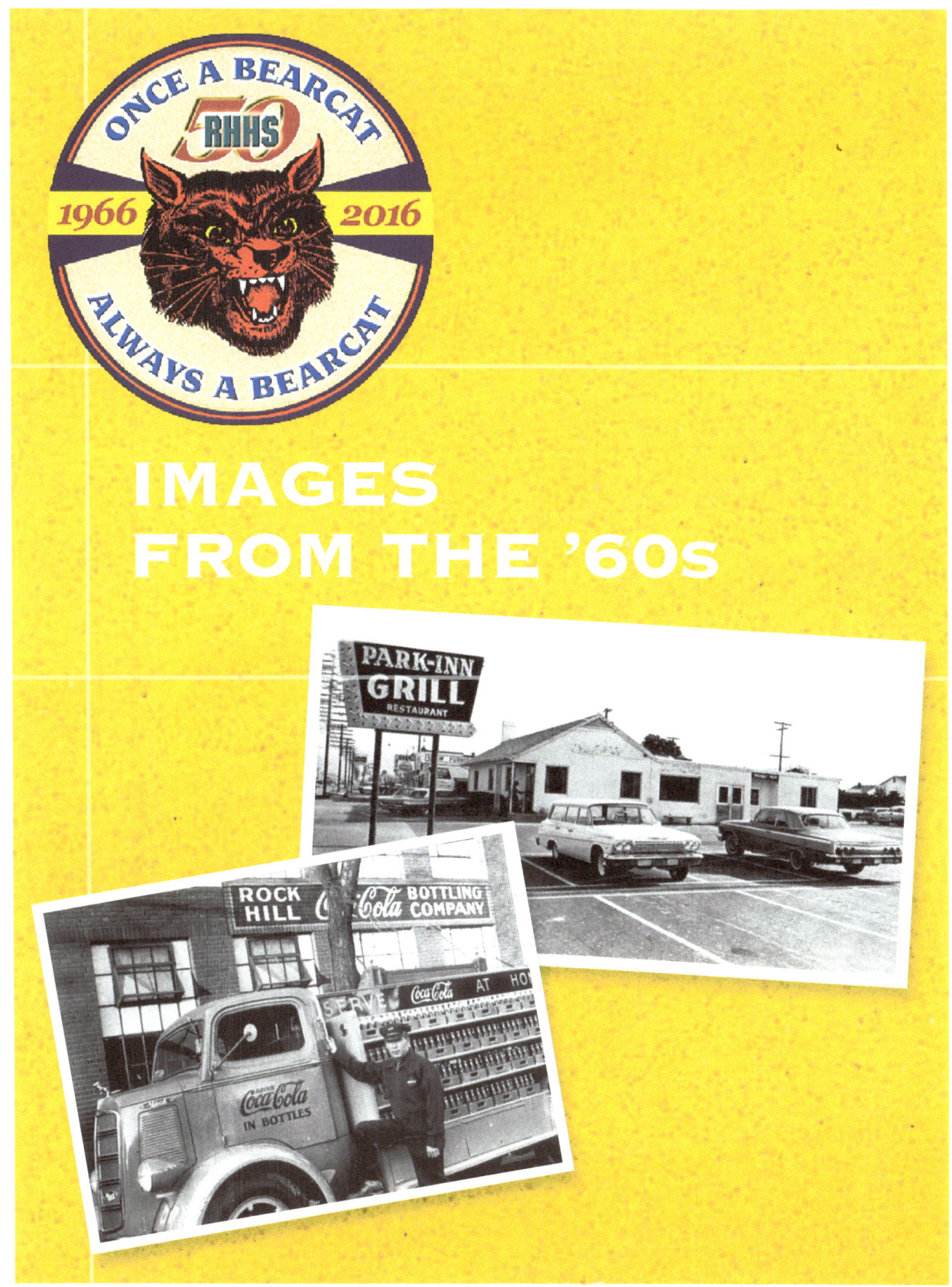

ONCE A BEARCAT
RHHS 50
1966 2016
ALWAYS A BEARCAT

IMAGES FROM THE '60s

PARK-INN GRILL RESTAURANT

ROCK HILL Coca-Cola BOTTLING COMPANY

Coca-Cola AT HOME

SERVE

Coca-Cola IN BOTTLES

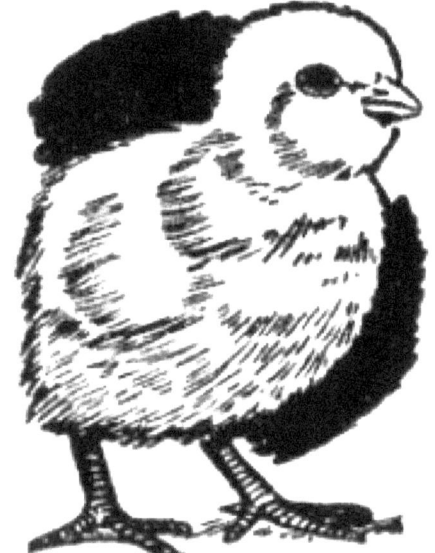
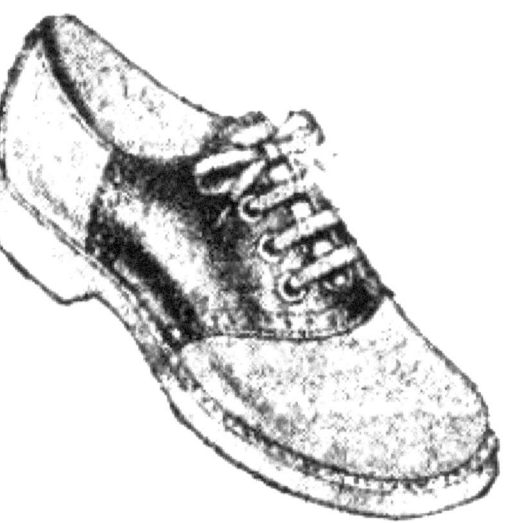

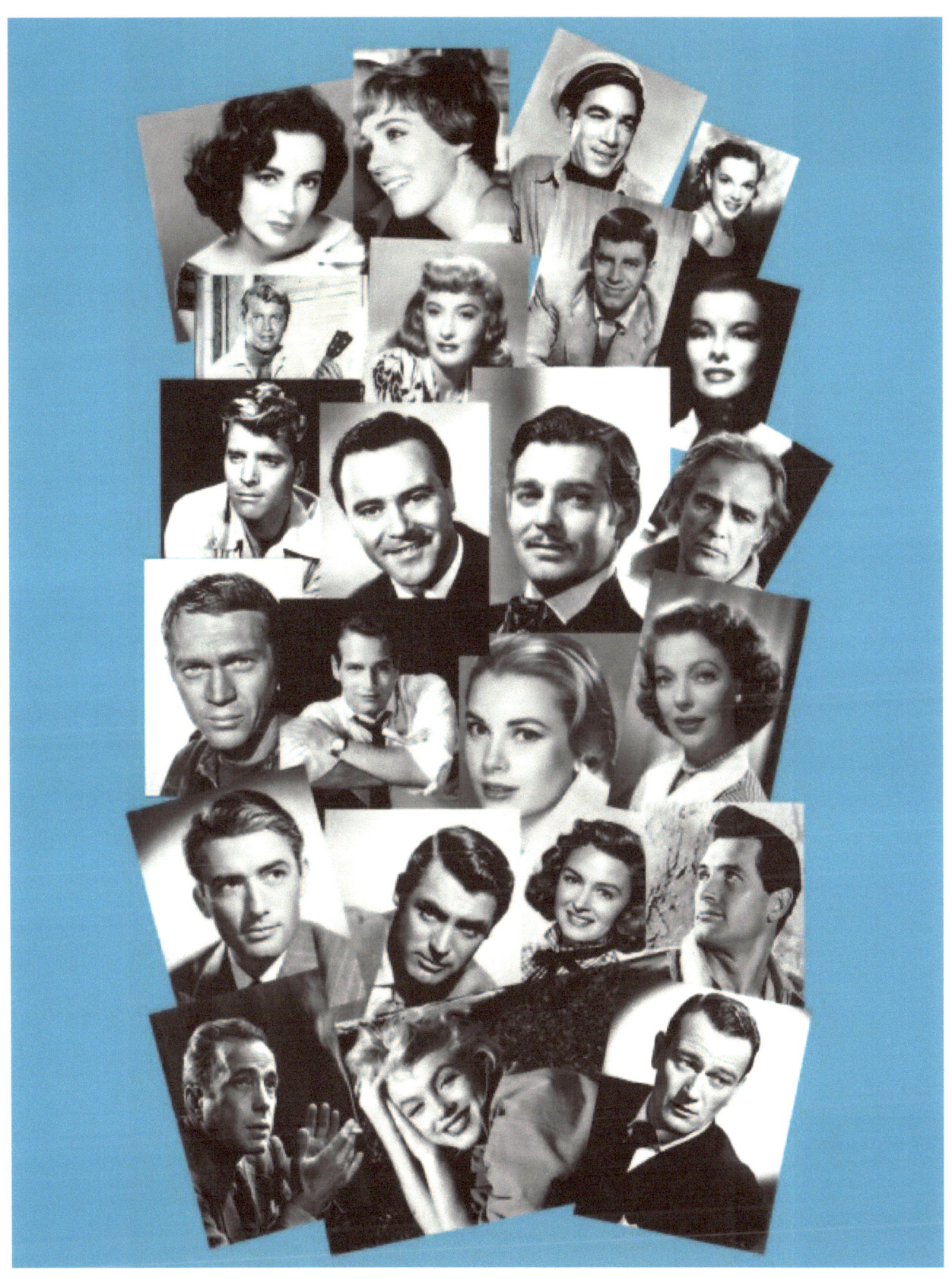

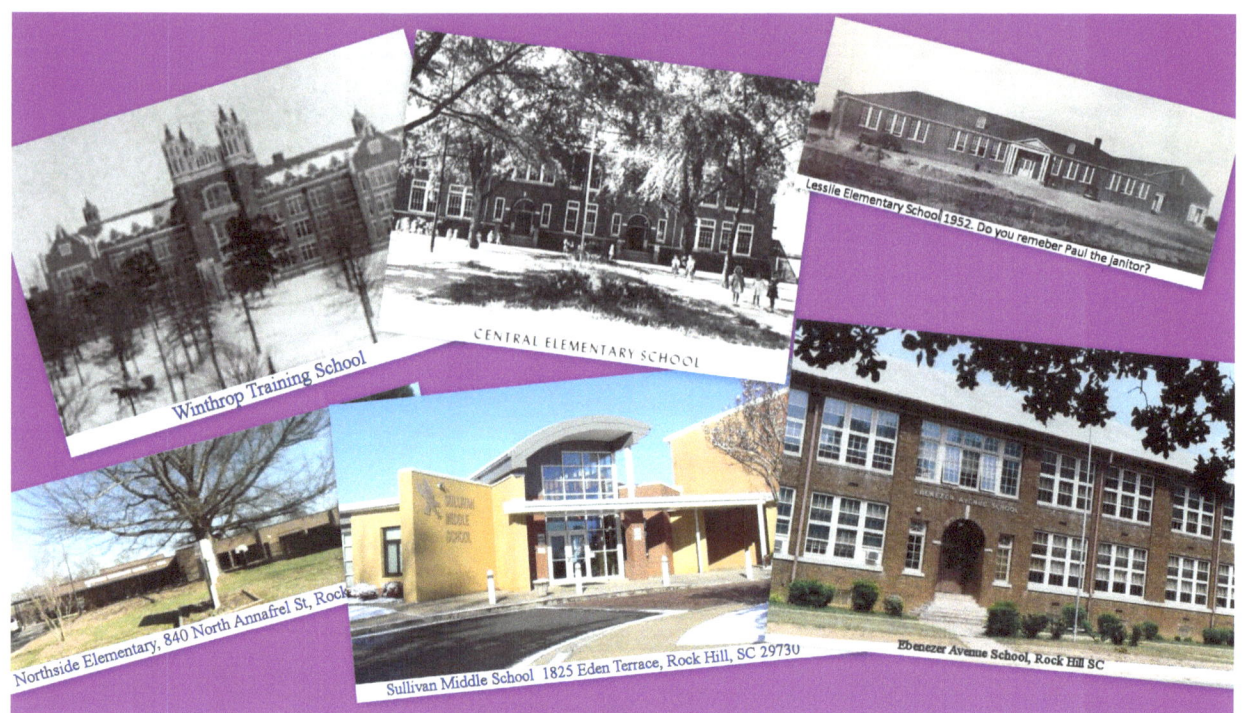

Lessiie Elementary School 1952. Do you remeber Paul the janitor?

CENTRAL ELEMENTARY SCHOOL

Winthrop Training School

Northside Elementary, 840 North Annafrel St, Rock

Sullivan Middle School 1825 Eden Terrace, Rock Hill, SC 29730

Ebenezer Avenue School, Rock Hill SC

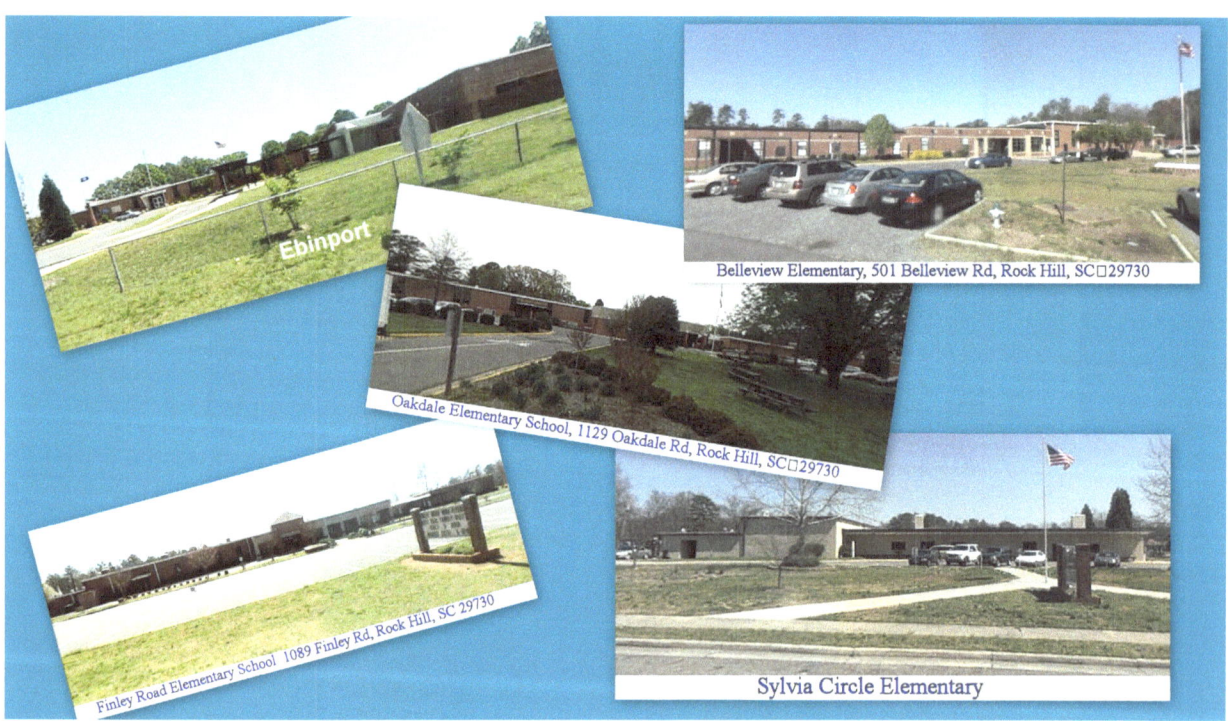

Ebinport

Belleview Elementary, 501 Belleview Rd, Rock Hill, SC 29730

Oakdale Elementary School, 1129 Oakdale Rd, Rock Hill, SC 29730

Finley Road Elementary School 1089 Finley Rd, Rock Hill, SC 29730

Sylvia Circle Elementary

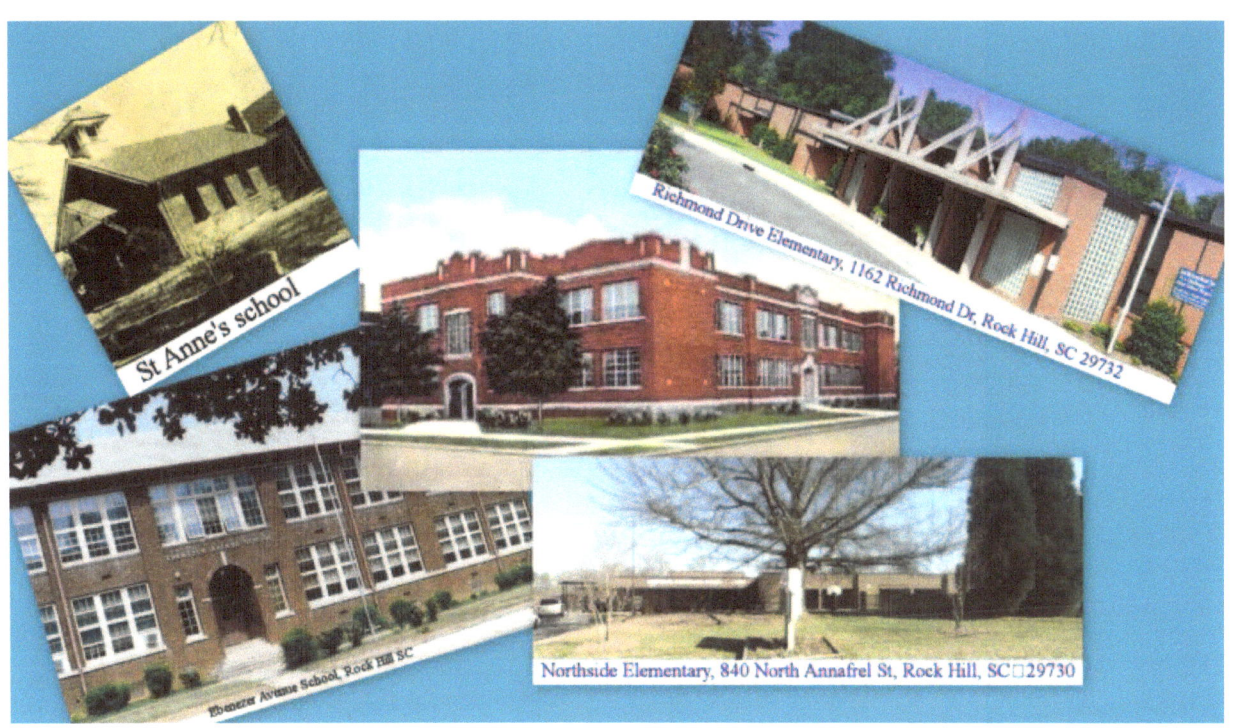

St Anne's school

Richmond Drive Elementary, 1162 Richmond Dr, Rock Hill, SC 29732

Ebenezer Avenue School, Rock Hill SC

Northside Elementary, 840 North Annafrel St, Rock Hill, SC☐29730

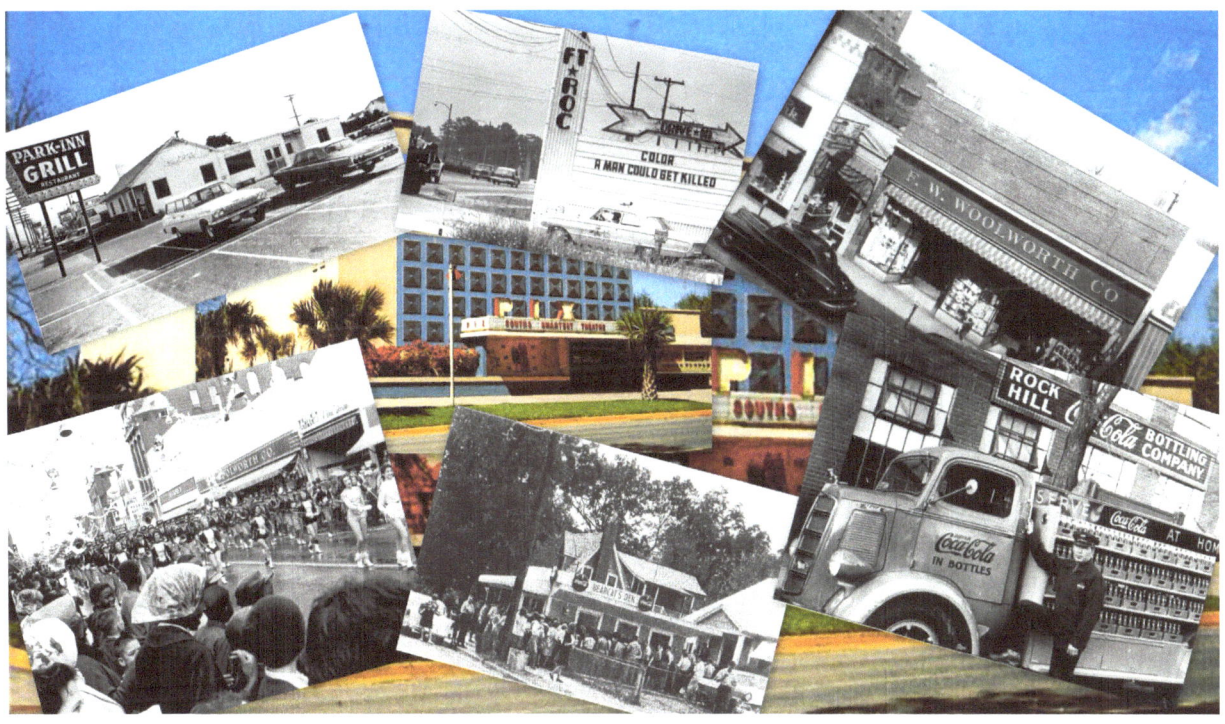

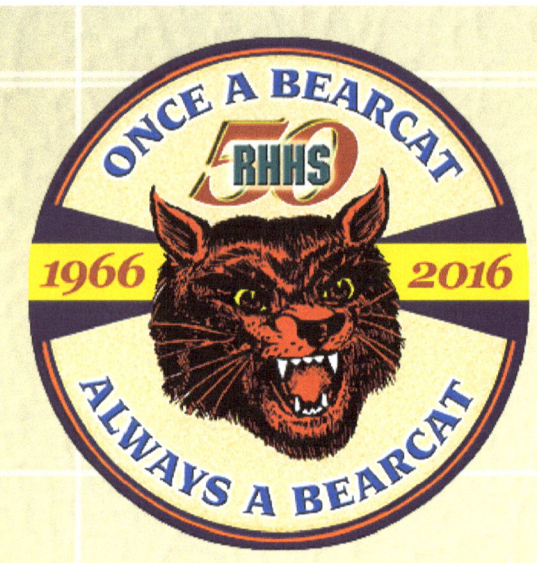

GARNET & BLACK
ARTICLES, QUOTES FROM FELLOW CLASSMATES AND ADS

GARNET & BLACK

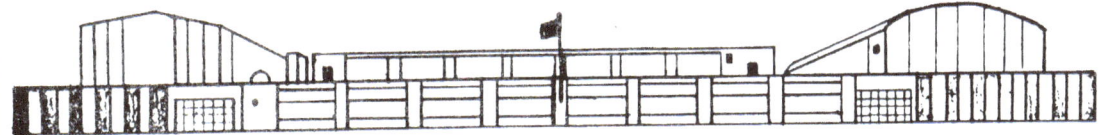

THE GARNET AND BLACK

Published monthly by the students of Rock Hill High School, Rock Hill, South Carolina. Advertising rates: $1.00 per column inch. Subscription rates: $1.00 per year.

EDITORIAL STAFF

Editor-in-Chief	Steve Sorgee
News Editor	Beth Roddey
Editorial Editor	Steve Sorgee
Feature Editor	Nina Eargle
Sports Editor	Becky Baker
Associate Sports Editor	George Crow
Photographer	Chucky Burgess
Artist	Nancy Reese
Editorial Advisor	Mrs. Judith Bazemore
Typists	Barbara Bolden, Deanna Ratterree, Linda Campbell, Darlene McGee, Minerva Wylie, Diana Andrew

REPORTERS: Janice Mattox, Rachel McGinnis, Helen Campbell, Samm Hook, Nell McDow, Dale Carroll, Martha Wells, Tommy Taylor, Bobbie Marie Key, Jimmie Viola, Ellen Boyd, Brien Ward, Steve Ellison.

BUSINESS STAFF

Business Manager	Nancy Bradley
Assistant	Jane Yongue
Circulation and Exchange Editor	Lawanna Faile
Assistant	Wendy Abernathy
Distribution Editor	Sheila Newton
Assistant	Wendy Abernathy
Assistant	Mary Williford
Business Advisor	Miss Elizabeth Stowe
Other Assistants	Diana Andrews, Brenda Lane, Elaine Yandle, Marie Barrett, Donna Ross, Mary Ann Beckham, Deborah Alewine, Chan London, Truly Bracken, Steve Baker, Betty Mathis, Harriet Leslie, Becky Harper, Adrian Shelley, Minerva Wylie, Linda Newton, Judy Williams, Sandra Belue, Jean Faile, Jimmy Lynn, Rosalyn Morton.

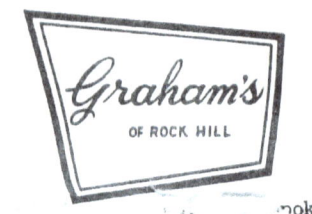
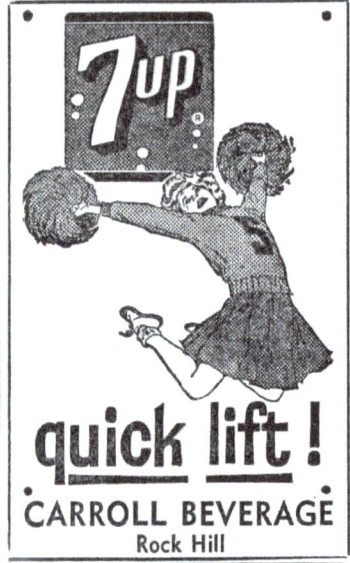
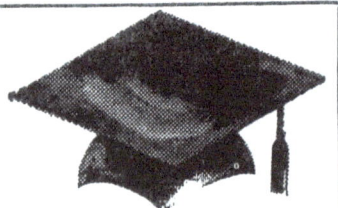
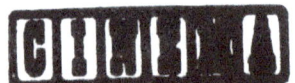

The Screen Scene

One of the most controversial subjects of today is that of the television and the entertainment it has to offer. Though many of us claim to be too busy for the big eye, most of us make the screen scene daily, whether we like to admit it or not. In fact, today the most common mode of entertainment is the television. It also carries the news quite well, but for now we will concern ourselves with the entertainment it brings.

It seems one of the most popular types of programs today is the same old story brought up to date, the bad guy vs. the good guy. In a poll (the results of which are shown) taken among students of RHHS., the favorites were the secret agent programs, of which there are several, both serious and spoofs. (If such a difference can be determined)

For the music lovers, there is quite a variety of shows, from Hullaballo to the Arthur Smith Show to The Andy Williams Show. Such a variety covers just about every type of music to be desired.

After the networks released their new shows in January, a controversy arose over several of these second season goodies. NEWSWEEK stated of ABC's new shows, "With the sole exception of **Batman**, the second season premiere was dud." Holy backfire! In newspapers and magazines everywhere, **Batman** has been attracting criticism like Robin attracts bad lines. However according to the poll, the show is very popular, ranking third. It has been called camp, which means that it is so terrible that it is wonderful. But in the eyes of those for whom it was contrived, the grammar schoolers, it isn't camp at all, but wonderful. Those who can't stand Batman should realize that it wasn't designed for them to enjoy anyway. The ones that watch it realizing this fact enjoy it as a novelty. It's all in how you look at it.

Results of the T.V. Poll
1. Man from Uncle
2. I Spy
3. Batman
4. The Fugitive
5. Peyton Place
6. Secret Agent
7. The Baron
8. Get Smart
9. Andy Williams
10. Bonanza

Twirp Time Rolls Around

On Friday ,March 25, the Tri-Hi-Y Club will hold their annual Twirp Dance. The T W I R P comes from the sentence—The woman is required to pay. The dance will be held at the Celanese Union Hall. "Around the World" is the theme.

If you are a boy and haven't been invited, you had better get to work because TWIRP week is the girl's week.

Club Close-Up

FFA

The Rock Hill Chapter of the Future Farmers of America visited Clemson University October 30. Nineteen chapter members toured the campus, visited the dormitories and Agriculture Department, and then saw Clemson down Wake Forest 26 to 13.

THESPIANS

Officers of the National Thespian Society are President, Herbie Rentz, Vice-president, Max Youngblood, Secretary, Butch Spakes, and Treasurer, Gary Sturgis.

The Thespians have been invited to attend several plays in other towns. They are sponsored by Mrs. Abernathy.

F.B.L.A.

The Future Business Leaders of America members attended a cookout on October 28, 1965 at the home of their sponsor, Miss Kneece. Officers for 1965-66 are President, Cora Lee Foxx; Vice-president, Pat Williford; Secretary, Mickey Jennings; Treasurer, Aleda Ashley; and Reporter, Nancy Jo Arnold.

SENIOR DRAMATICS

At a recent Senior Dramatics meeting new officers, President Susan Deese, Vice-president Carolyn Parrish, Secretary Karen Tinsley, Treasurer Steve Sorgee, and Reporter Carol Percival, were elected. Club membership is open to Juniors and Seniors. Senior Dramatics is sponsored by Mrs. Good.

Have You Seen This Man?

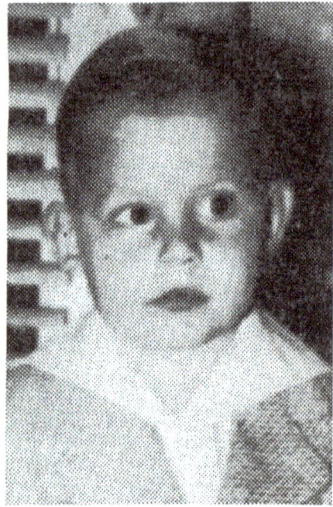

Do you know who this is??? We admit the person has changed since this picture was taken, but it is someone you all should know.

Come on students, get your thinking caps on and see how well you do. If you are unable to solve the mystery, we promise to tell all in the next issue of the paper.

Good luck!

Fads We'd Like To See

What would you like to see or what do you think will be the next fad in Rock Hill?

Muggsie Sparks—short skirts
Margret Dunlap — football shirts for sleepie time

Wanda Perry—shorts and long sweaters

Paul Neal—pants with two different colored legs

Susan Gordon—braces and glasses

Mary Ritter—V-neck sweaters without blouses

Steve Elison—Double-breasted blazers or corduroy blue jeans

Susan Horne — Sneakers with holes in them

Samn Hooke—berets

Beth Parks—pierced noses

Clay Carruth — The Algonquin Indians are going to make a come back and drive the white eyes from their land.

John Fantry—burning your draft cards

Cindy Percival—Mohawks for for girls

John Parkinson—everyone wear jackets like monks

RHHS Pet Peeves

Isn't there a little something somewhere that you dislike. Most fellow students get peevish at:

Jimmy Viola—Taking a bath then drying off with a wet towel.

Sammy Broughton—Everything's perfect, nothing peeves me.

Twila Carney—Boys' shirt-collars unbuttoned in back.

Harry Blue—Literature.

Penny Shaw—My desk in homeroom and History.

Dennis Haire—Making speeches.

Sue Cooke—Wrecks!

Phyllis Moore—Pet Peeve Poll Takers!

Itsy Bits

Congratulations to Mrs. Laura Cannon. Mrs. Cannon has received a National Science Foundation Scholarship to study biology this summer at Wake Forest College in Winston Salem, North Carolina.

. . .

Things will really be going in Rock Hill this weekend because of the Come See Me Festivities. Senior girls will serve as hostesses at Glencairn Gardens. Special guests visiting Rock Hill this weekend include Senator Strom Thurmond, Senator and Mrs. Donald Russell, Congress-Governor and Mrs. McNair, and Former Governor Fritz Hollings.

. . .

Seniors who have a **93** average in any subject can exempt their exams in that subject second semester. The class of 1966 is the first graduating class to have this privilege.

. . .

Mrs. Paul Whitney, who spoke to the student body April 1, has devoted her life to counseling youth and helping them with their problems. She is glad to help with any problems you may have. Her mailing address is Fulton Hotel, St. Paul Minnesota.

. . .

Margaret Bradford and Kathy Powell will be active as two of the fourteen members of the Tri-Hi-Y Council of the Carolinas. The members of the council were elected for their qualifications in leadership and Christian character.

. . .

The G.A.A. girls of R.H.H.S. defeated the girls of Dreher High School at G.A.A. Playday 1966.

Lend An Ear To Eargle

TODAY'S TOPIC: What's Happening's

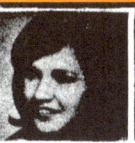

This is the last issue before the last issue and could possibly be compared to the calm before the storm. I would like to dedicate this issue to spring and its loveliness. Also, I would like to dedicate it to the feeling spring gives a person and the joy it spreads.

I guess the warm weather has really heated Clay Carruth up. He was seen out at Hardee's with his knees exposed. I heard there were quite a few remarks made —something about bird legs. Jimmy Viola got locked up in the refrigerator compartment at Do-ziers one night not too long ago —probably couldn't stand such warm weather. He told me to say something about a vacation Cathy and Dora had but I didn't know what it was all about, so I decided not to. Richard Cranford and Cathy Walker went to the Twirp dance, but seemed to have enjoyed the trip to Hardee's more. Bobby and I didn't go to the dance, but we were entertained by those who did. They kept leaving the dance and landing at Hardees.

What's this I hear Herbie says each day leaving class?; something like, "Touchie, Away!" I think we should all take up a collection for Janice Edwards— to make it possible for her to get a pair of glasses. Janice wore one shoe of one kind on her right foot, and on her left, a shoe of another kind. None would do that unless they were blind, or stu_____!

Is Bill Beaty really going to dance in the May Day program?

School will soon be out and summer is coming on. Enjoy one of the most beautiful seasons of the year. Remember, one more issue, and your secrets are safe. But there is **still that last** issue!

Dear Seniors,

Take heart! The big day is approaching faster than we realize. Yes, graduation is getting closer every second. Our big battle is almost won. The number of obstacles blocking our way, such as term papers and exams, is getting smaller with each English composition and trig problem. Those college and job offers are becoming very attractive as we struggle to meet a deadline on term papers and science projects.

If we can only resist falling into the clutches of "spring fever", our last few months will pass quickly and we can loaf with a great feeling of self-satisfaction on June 1. Much of our school work is almost over now and we can still look forward to Junior-Senior, the '66 BEARCAT maybe exam exemptions, and— most important of all—our graduation! So let's try to bear the next two and a half months and look beyond our homework and tests to see our diplomas.

Linda Golson

Beautification Drive Underway

A beautification drive, which was launched by the Student Council, is now underway. The drive's purpose is to buy shrubbery and flowers for the courts. Each class is asked to participate by raising money. When all homerooms have turned in their money, it will be combined and used to buy shrubbery and flowers.

Mrs. Westmoreland's homeroom was the first to start the ball rolling. The drive chairman in her homeroom was Nancy Williams. A goal of twenty-five dollars was set. Each student contributed, and the goal was reached. Mr. Godbold was presented with the money.

Seniors To Present <u>Once</u> <u>In A Lifetime</u>

On December 3 at 8:00 P.M. in the RHHS auditorium the Senior Class will present as their annual play **Once in a Lifetime**. This satire, which concerns the movie industry in the 1920's when the "talkies" replaced the silent pictures, was written by George Kaufman and Moss Hart.

The play concerns three out-of-jobs vaudeville actors, May (Nina Eargle), George (Spencer Simrill), and Jerry (Richard Cranford), and their adventures in Hollywood.

The cast is made up of fifty-six talented seniors. Eighty members make up the technical crews. A list of the cast and crew is posted in the library.

The appearance of the Twelve Schlepkin Brothers, talented actors who have accepted an invitation to appear in the play, is an extra attraction. Members of cast don't even know who these visitors are.

Lend An Ear To Eargle

TODAY'S TOPIC: ABOUT LOVE

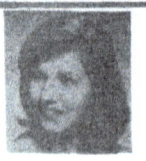

The last edition of the **Garnet and Black** was just prior to exams. It was a time of struggle, but as I said in my last column, "By the time you receive the next issue, it will all be over." It's over now but we have new things to occupy our minds; term papers, and all the joys that go with them. A lot of things have been happening recently to various people at high school.

Many girls received at Christmas time one of the most important gifts of their lives, an engagement ring. Having received a ring myself, I can appreciate the speical thrill that it gives, and I know the girls won't mind if I print their names. Among those who have joined the "engaged ones" are Rose Jordan, Trudy Sowell, Diane Melton, Lynda Snyder, Brenda Carter, and Janice Plyler. Gail Letbetter and Jane Schavey are old hands at this business, as they have been engaged for several months.

Ellen Brooks is now going steady with Alton Robbins, a graduate of Rock Hill High. I'd like to mention that David Wilson is very much in love. You can look at him and tell. It seems that Spencer Simrill has finally stabilized his love life and Susan is glad. Penny Shaw is still living a notorious life during study period and Vicki Ernandez is still looking for her true love. Jimmy Viola and Linda are spreading out into broader horizons due to a third party. Connie Estes has attended some rather interesting get togethers lately and found it necessary to wear track shoes. Larry and Tic are still around, somewhere. Nancy Hart's family has had some interesting new developments. Donna is going steady with a boy from York. Larry and Suzanne found more time for each other during the holidays.

NOTE: Miss Gill was seen throwing snow balls during the unscheduled vacation.

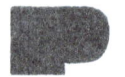
Miss Jackson . . . "That will be quite enough."

Miss Hardin . . . . "Salvete, amici."

Mr. Burleson . . . "That Jimmy Viola has more gears than a Mack truck."

Mrs. Good . . . "Yes, Virginia, there is a Santa Claus."

Miss Stowe . . . "Just fifty cents a bar."

Mrs. Westmoreland . . . "No talking on the way to assembly."

Mrs. Connelly . . . "Prenez du pieces papier et un crayon."

Mrs. Linder . . . "Now, where were I?"

Miss Gettys . . . "Take nothing for granted."

What do you admire most in a date?

Marie Barrett—"honesty"

Scott Martin—"good personality; she must be charming to date me"

Sue Wilson—"the way the boy treats me"

Bill Barber—"the girl!!"

Keith Elliot—"a nice framework"

Perry Ann Hope—"punctuality"

Martha Moore—"nothing"

Elaine Whitton—"the way he looks"

Kay Thomas—"the drive-in"

Billy Clarkson— "Whether she loves me or not"

Evelyn Aycock—"somebody with brown hair, brown eyes, 5 feet seven, and in Mrs. Broome's homeroom."

There Are Going To Be Some Changes Made

Moving into the new high school building will begin as soon as possible after school is out. Every room's equipment both at RHHS and at Sullivan, Jr. High must be ready to move so that transferring will be exact. The new RHHS will have approximately 1685 students ranging from the 10th through the 12th grades. There will be about 625 sophomores, 555 juniors, and 505 seniors. At least six new teachers will be required to help accommodate the large number of students.

Class schedules and lunch hours will probably remain the same, possibly with a third lunch hour. All club activities, sports, and regular curricular events will continue. Simply, RHHS will be the same, only in a newer building.

The present RHHS building will become the W. C. Sullivan Jr. High School with grades seven through nine. The Jr. High activities will be along the same grade level as they are now. Many people wonder how bus schedules will be planned. No immediate information as to details can be given; however, all bus runs will simply be as they are now —routine.

Mr. Godbold believes that the move will help the RHHS physical education program and will provide more space both for curricular and extra-curricular activities. He hopes that everyone will take his part to carry on the same, old traditions, maintain the same warm sense of loyalty, and do his best for RHHS as before.

Lend An Ear To Eargle

TODAY'S TOPIC: Our Boys and the Draft

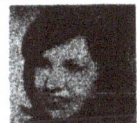

"Eat, drink, and be sorry; for tomorrow you may be drafted!" These are words of wisdom spoken from the lips of a wise old senior, Bill Barber. After pondering upon this idea for awhile, I suddenly realized that I have nothing to worry about because I'm a Girl! But then I realized what a messed up world it would be if Gary Sturgis was drafted or Butch Spakes or Bubba Estes —or a number of Rock Hill High boys, Men. Gary would start each day off with a solo in the shower, putting all the boys in a fighting mood (beating him up for singing.) Butch would start each day with a sermon in the barracks. As for Bubba; he'd spend all day trying to get started so that he wouldn't bother anybody. And what about Bill himself? He'd sit around thinking of wise old sayings and never win the war. Ladd Fowler and Rufus Bratton would refuse to wear ill-fitting uniforms and get thrown in the brig for insubordination. Scott Martin would feel too compassionate toward the enemy to do us any good— and Spencer would waste all his time writing letters to Susan. Max Youngblood would kill the first guy that tried to give him a G.I. haircut and Bill Lowrance would have a lot to laugh about.

Tyndall Estes would want to fight the war single handed and Clay Carruth would try to laugh his way out of it. Rocky Evans would knock the enemy's teeth out and Mike Woodall would bite them on the hand. Lee Brandt would use a golf club as his defense mechanism. Stan Joyner would run them with a bus, and Steve Sorgee would write editorials in an attempt to end the fighting. Jimmy Viola would dance his way clear of the fire.

Consequence Of Lingering

She had warned me the night before, and I was fully aware of the consequence. Staying in my blissful state would only put more pressure on me during the last minute on the ordeal, but I lingered. I struggled within myself. It was difficult, but I was almost there. Suddenly in the midst of my agony, I heard shouts; someone was calling me. I ran as fast as I could. My heart was pumping with fear; every muscle of my starving body ached. But it was too late. Feeling beaten and dejected, I turned back. The bus had left me.

Kitchen Beauty Popularity Plus

The kitchen provides the economical girl with many inexpensive beauty preparations. For instance, the high school girl who cannot afford expensive cleansing grains can apply an oatmeal and water paste to her face, let dry, and remove with warm water. This produces the same results at a lower price. Vinegar applied to the final rinse water of your shampoo will add lovely highlights. A beaten eggwhite is beneficial to those enlarged pores. An egg shampoo is often above a teenager's beauty budget, but three egg yolks is not and it works equally well. Many blonds will tell you that lemon juice is a mild bleach which works beautifully on hair, but have you ever thought to use it on elbows and heels to lighten the skin? Oily scalped people, dissolve a tablespoon of salt in water and use in your rinse water. Cuts down that excessive oiliness that makes every other day hairwashing necessary. Mineral oil and olive oil are great substitutes for hair conditioners. They are applied just as any hot oil treatment. Heavy make-up can be removed with regular cooking oil. But the most important beauty aid of all is eating the proper types of food.

WE'RE GONNA MISS YA !!

Since this is the last paper which the Senior Class '66 will read, I decided to see if I could put myself in the place of some of the Seniors as they walked across the threshole of opportunity. I believe what I would be thinking is completely different than what they will be thinking. At any rate, if I was Dora Haily, I'd be wondering if when I got on the other side, if I could smoke a ciragette without getting into trouble. Twila Carny would probably be wondering if Ed would be waiting on the other side to send her flying, and Linda Tedder would be hoping that Melvin was over there too, waiting to tell her he was finally satisfied. Knowing Terry Sanders as I do, she would probably be praying that her Dad would give her her sunlamp back, so she could get nice and hot and develop a nice tan. I have no fears that Chuck Spencer will be hoping that his diploma has been bronzed, and Kathy Collins will probably be counting the minutes until she can let out a Rebel Yell at Mr. Burleson. Most likely, Susan Wall will be imagining herself on the stage of Atlantic City Hall receiving a dozen roses and the title of Miss America, insttead of being on the stage in Rock Hill and receiving her diploma.

I guess when I walk across that stage along with the rest of my Senior friends this year, I will feel a lot different. I believe the Senior Class of 1966, in all seriousness, is the best class what am. I am also very sure every one of the Seniors will make dear ole Rock Hill High very proud to have had them.

Jimmy Viola

What Is Service Life?

What is life in the Army? I imagine most men today are thinking about this. Sooner or later just about every young man who is reading this article will face some type of service.

You usually rise early in the mornings around four-thirty. After you get up and before breakfast, you have about 45 minuites of physcial training (P.T.). This usually consists of running about two miles.

You are also trained to use bayonets, rifles, and your hands for defense.

The basic training program consists mostly of a course that prepares the soldier to be able to defend himself in actual combat.

But most of all the army teaches individuals to think as a group, live as a group, and to work as a group.

Most young men upon entering the service think of themselves, but this is broken up by the army.

The basic strive for the training cadre is to teach discipline and to teach the group to pay attention. In other words they say, "Keep your mouth shut and your eyes open."

Most of the time when a person goes into the service with a chip on his shoulder it doesn't last long. He finds out that he had better straighten up or he's headed for trouble.

Sometimes you don't get a long too well with the other guy, but most of the time it's like a happy family.

After a soldier graduates from Basic Training he takes mos. training or A.I.T. training A.I.T. training stands for Advanced Individual, or sometimes Advanced Infantry Training .

When you reach your training area you find you have a lot more privileges. After five o'clock you are usually free until eleven when they have bed check.

But life is still lonely. Some guys are several thousand miles from home while others only a few hundred.

Some of the guys you are with want attention because they are lonely. One in particular kept saying he boxed in "golden gloves" and was a champ, until a guy about half his size knocked him flat. He shut up then.

The guy that slept in the bunk on my left was a grammar school dropout while the guy on my right was a biochemist.

But life is difficult without being close to your family and home. When life gets depressing, and you're broke and hungry you can always get food and money from your parents when you live with them.

But if you're on a pass for the weekend; you don't have any money and you're a couple thousand miles from your family you have nowhere to turn.

I think that if some of the young people of this school and of this country live on their own for a month they would appreciate their parents more. I think they would do more for their parents and try to make their parents be proud of them.

Manners of 1920

Manners have changed during the last 45 years. Here are some examples of this.

1) If you are well brought up, girls, you will not loiter on the street to talk to one another, much less to boys.

2) When you enter your classroom, as well as leave it, glance towards your teacher and if she is looking, bow pleasantly.

3) Avoid raising your hand when you wish to ask or answer a question. Instead, rise quietly, face your teacher, and wait for her to recognize you as though you were at a club meeting.

4) When dancing, face your partner at a distance of at least six to eight inches. Remember bobbing and wriggling are bad. Let the spring come from the ankles and the knees. Imitate the grace of the swallow.

Dear Seniors,

Take heart! The big day is approaching faster than we realize. Yes, graduation is getting closer every second . Our big battle is almost won. The number of obstacles blocking our way, such as term papers and exams, is getting smaller with each English composition and trig problem. Those college and job offers are becoming very attractive as we struggle to meet a deadline on term papers and science projects.

If we can only resist falling into the clutches of "spring fever", our last few months will pass quickly and we can loaf with a great feeling of self-satisfaction on June 1. Much of our school work is almost over now and we can still look forward to Junior-Senior, the '66 BEARCAT maybe exam exemptions, and—most important of all—our graduation! So let's try to bear the next two and a half months and look beyond our homework and tests to see our diplomas.

Linda Golson

TEEN TIPS

Boys, when asking a girl for a date, don't put her on the spot by asking, "What would you like to do? Since the gal has no way of knowing what financial shape you're in, why not make three or four suggestions and let her take her pick.

Try it! You have nothing to lose, and nine times out of ten, you'll both wind up having a very good time.

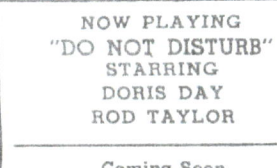
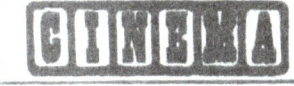

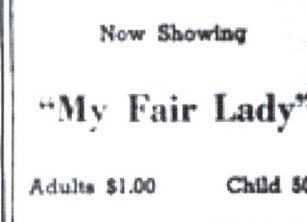
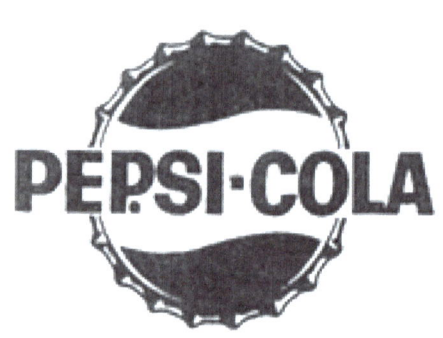

"We sing to thee our Alma Mater
From hearts that glow with pride sincere.
Thy memory ever lingers with us
Though we be scattered far and near.
What ere we win of fame or fortune
For high school days we oft will sigh.
We'll cherish still our Alma Mater
Our dear old Rock Hill High."

SPONSORS

We are grateful for your interest in Rock Hill High School and the **Bearcat.**

CHANEY GLASS CO., INC.

BLACKWELL'S CLOTH SHOP

HOME FURNITURE STORE

ROCK'S LAUNDRY

McCLAIN OIL COMPANY

ROCK HILL COLD STORAGE

HOLLIS CLEANERS

T. E. JONES AND SONS

CENTRAL NEWS STAND

TILLMAN'S MUSIC

DAVIS MARKET, INC.

WALKER ELECTRIC CO.

JONES BARBER SHOP

W. T. GRANT CO.

DIXIE CHEMICAL AND
  SUPPLY CO.

GREENE FUNERAL HOME
  AND FLOWER SHOP

WYLIE CONSTRUCTION CO.

MARION DAVIS

YORK COUNTY NATURAL
  GAS AUTHORITY

CELANESE FIBERS CO.

BURGER CHEF

COURTNEY ELECTRICAL
  SUPPLY COMPANY

WINN DIXIE

YONCE MOTORS

REYNOLDS FOOD STORE

PEOPLE'S BARBER SHOP

REID BROTHERS ELECTRIC CO.

ANDERSON MOTORS

NEW CAR DEALERS ASSOCIATION
  BURNS CHEVROLET, INC.

WILLIAMS MOTOR CO.

GOOD MOTOR CO.

HARVEY MOTORS

JUSTUS PONTIAC

WELCH MOTORS

HEARN MOTORS

C. J. PATTON MOTORS

WEST MAIN HARDWARE AND
  SUPPLY CO.

SHAW FURNITURE COMPANY

BAKER'S SHOE SERVICE

C & S NATIONAL BANK

TOLLISON-NEAL DRUG CO.

ROCK HILL PRESS

ROCK HILL SEAFOOD

BUCK'S RESTAURANT

WILKERSON OIL COMPANY

MAXWELL BROTHERS FURNITURE

BEA'S BOOK STORE

EFIRD'S DEPARTMENT STORE

HALLMAN BATTERY AND IGNITION

MERLE NORMAN COSMETIC STUDIO

DON YONCE—INSURANCE—
  REAL ESTATE

OAK RIDGE GROCERY

ROCK HILL PRINTING AND
  FINISHING CO.

BROOKS JEWELERS

MARSHALL OIL COMPANY

ROCK HILL COCA-COLA
  BOTTLING COMPANY

SHRIMP BOAT

WHITE PRINTING COMPANY

1956: Early boomers are ten years old; late boomers are eight years away from birth. Meanwhile President Eisenhower wins re-election, but Nikita Khrushchev says, "History is on our side. We will bury you!"

1957: The Russians launch Sputnik I and Sputnik II; President Eisenhower uses troops to enforce desegregation in Arkansas.

1958: The U.S. launches the Explorer I satellite; the first Pizza Hut opens.

1959: Barbie is "born"; Buddy Holly dies; Castro takes over in Cuba.

1960: The soviets shoot down a U.S. spy plane; John Kennedy is elected president; and Chubby Checker introduces the Twist.

1961: The Russians and then the U.S. put a man into space; the Berlin wall goes up.

1962: K-Mart and Wal-Mart open; Russian warheads in Cuba bring the world to the edge of war.

1963: President Kennedy is assassinated; Dr. Martin Luther King declares, "I have a dream."

1964: President Johnson declares a "war on poverty." But he also plans the huge escalation of a much larger war to be fought half-way around the world. The Beatles "invade" the U.S.

1965: Civil disturbances over race and the Vietnam war play in increasingly larger roles in American society. President Johnson unveils his plans for the "Great Society."

1966: The Supreme Court issues its "Miranda" ruling; U.S. troop strength in southeast Asia reaches 400,000.

1967: The first heart transplant operation is performed; race riots kill dozens in Detroit. "Rolling Stone" magazine rolls off the presses.

1968: Dr. Martin Luther King and Bobby Kennedy are assassinated; President Johnson declines to run for re-election; Richard Nixon wins the presidency.

1969: The U.S. lands a man on the moon; teens celebrate at Woodstock, then demonstrate in Washington.

1970: Campus demonstrations close down several colleges; four die at Kent State University. The Beatles break up.

1971: The "Pentagon Papers" are published; President Nixon freezes wages and prices. The Supreme Court affirms the legality of bussing to achieve racial desegregation.

1972: President Nixon shocks the world by visiting communist China. Nixon wins re-election in a landslide; but the break-in at the Watergate complex seals his fate.

1973: A ceasefire ends U.S. ground troop involvement in Vietnam. The military draft ends; the Supreme Court legalizes abortion; the noose around the president's neck tightens.

1974: Richard Nixon resigns; President Ford declares, "Our long, national nightmare is over." The youngest of the boomers are nearly teenagers; the oldest are nearly middle aged.

1975: "The Greatest" retains his title in "The Thrilla' in Manila"; Saigon falls and the U.S. bails out of Vietnam; but "Jaws" scares the living daylights out of us.

IN HONOR OF THOSE CLASSMATES* WHO HAVE SERVED OUR COUNTRY.

Rickie Joe Ballard
Jim Barrett
Charlie Belk
Harry Blue
Rufus Bratton
Dennis Brewer
Chris Brumfield
Ed Burwell
Clay Carruth
Johnny Cherry
George Clark
Paul Covington
Richard Cranford
George Crow
Tommy Deas
Ricky Folsom
Robert Gantt
Tommy Garner
Wayne Gillespie
Tommy Hart
Wayne Haselden
Don Hicks
Cotton Howell
Bob Hyman
Buddy Ivey
Bobby Jackson
Michael Lamb
Jimmy Lee
Billy Loflin
Joseph Lowery
Billy Lowrance
Marvin Marthers
Scott Martin
Bill Mayo
Freddie McClurkin

Eddie McGuirt
Al Mitchell
Joe Moore
Bruce Morris
Roland Morris
W.H. Morris
Bill Murphy
John Murphy
Ronnie Outlaw
Eddie Pittman
Herbie Rentz
Thomas Sanders
David Sealy
Garrett Smith
Butch Spakes
Chuck Spenser
Paul Sprouse
Billy Stikeleather
Bob Stikeleather
Carlton Sturgis
Tommy Tarlton
Mike Tate
Tom Taylor
Neal Tobias
Gene Turbeville
Steve Turney
Jimmy Vick
Grady Watkins
Roy Westerlund
Lewis Whisonant
Curt Wilson
Jimmy Winchester
Kenneth Yates

*These classmates are known to us as of this printing. There may be others.

What were your favorites?

Favorite Classmates?

Favorite Teachers?

Favorite Songs?

Favorite Movie Stars/Actors?

Favorite Movies and TV Shows?

Other Recollections: